For
the
Public
Good

LOLEEN BERDAHL, JONATHAN MALLOY, AND LISA YOUNG

For the Public Good

Reimagining
Arts Graduate
Programs
in Canadian
Universities

UNIVERSITY
of **ALBERTA**
PRESS

Published by

University of Alberta Press
1-16 Rutherford Library South
11204 89 Avenue NW
Edmonton, Alberta, Canada T6G 2J4
amiskwaciwâskahikan | Treaty 6 |
Métis Territory
ualbertapress.ca | uapress@ualberta.ca

Copyright © 2024 Loleen Berdahl,
Jonathan Malloy, and Lisa Young

**Library and Archives Canada
Cataloguing in Publication**

Title: For the public good : reimagining
   arts graduate programs in Canadian
   universities / Loleen Berdahl,
   Jonathan Malloy, Lisa Young.
Names: Berdahl, Loleen, 1970- author. |
   Malloy, Jonathan, 1970- author. |
   Young, Lisa (Jennifer Lisa), author.
Description: Includes bibliographical
   references and index.
Identifiers: Canadiana (print)
   20230541720 | Canadiana (ebook)
   20230541755 | ISBN 9781772127423
   (softcover) | ISBN 9781772127645
   (EPUB) | ISBN 9781772127652 (PDF)
Subjects: LCSH: Arts—Study and teaching
   (Graduate)—Canada. | LCSH: Arts in
   education—Canada. | LCSH: Graduate
   students—Canada. | LCSH: Common
   good.
Classification: LCC NX313.A1 B47 2024 |
   DDC 700.71/1—dc23

First edition, first printing, 2024.
First printed and bound in Canada by
Houghton Boston Printers, Saskatoon,
Saskatchewan.
Copyediting and proofreading by
Angela Pietrobon.
Indexing by Tanvi Mohile.

All rights reserved. No part of this
publication may be reproduced, stored in
a retrieval system, or transmitted in any
form or by any means (electronic, mechan-
ical, photocopying, recording, generative
artificial intelligence [AI] training, or
otherwise) without prior written consent.
Contact University of Alberta Press for
further details.

University of Alberta Press supports
copyright. Copyright fuels creativity,
encourages diverse voices, promotes free
speech, and creates a vibrant culture.
Thank you for buying an authorized
edition of this book and for complying
with the copyright laws by not reproduc-
ing, scanning, or distributing any part
of it in any form without permission.
You are supporting writers and allowing
University of Alberta Press to continue
to publish books for every reader.

This book has been published with the
help of a grant from the Federation for the
Humanities and Social Sciences, through
the Awards to Scholarly Publications
Program, using funds provided by the
Social Sciences and Humanities Research
Council of Canada.

University of Alberta Press gratefully
acknowledges the support received for its
publishing program from the Government
of Canada, the Canada Council for the
Arts, and the Government of Alberta
through the Alberta Media Fund.

Contents

vii	Acknowledgements
1	1 | Canada's Public Good Problem
23	2 | Three Imperatives to Advance Canada's Public Good
41	3 | Canada's Arts Graduate Education Problem
75	4 | How We Got Here, and Why We Feel Stranded
107	5 | Canada's Arts Graduate Credentials: Realities and Possibilities
139	6 | The EDITS Vision
175	7 | Reimagining Arts Graduate Education Through EDITS
193	8 | Imagining Excellent Arts Graduate Programs
221	9 | Implementing the Vision
249	10 | Moving Forward
255	Appendix 1: EDITS Rubric
261	Appendix 2: EDITS Program Rubric, "Excellent" Column Focus
267	Appendix 3: EDITS for Supervisors
275	References
289	Index

Acknowledgements

In writing this book, we hope to spark a new conversation about graduate education. But it is also the product of many previous conversations. We have benefited a great deal from the input of students, faculty colleagues, and others on the challenges and the opportunities for arts graduate education in Canada.

In our administrative leadership roles at three different universities in three different provinces, we have had the privilege (and sometimes the frustration) of seeing the nuts and bolts of graduate education up close, and have worked alongside many people who also want to make it the best that it can be—for students, and ultimately for the public good. We have also interacted with colleagues across Canada through the Canadian Association of Graduate Studies, the Federation for the Humanities and Social Sciences, disciplinary associations, and other bodies also dedicated to making graduate education better. We have learned from others, and in turn we hope that this book provides the path to make these intentions a reality.

In writing the book, we incurred some more specific debts. Thanks to Suzanne Curtin, Shannon Dea, Samantha Hossack, Lisa Hughes, Wendy James, Jeff Keshen, Rebecca Major, Alex Marland, Gabriel Miller, Fahim Quadir, Ethel Tungohan, and Matthew Lebo for comments on the concept or early drafts of the manuscript. We also thank the anonymous reviewers for their helpful feedback. Of course, the arguments presented in this book and any errors remain ours alone.

We also offer deep gratitude to Bianca Jamal for her careful and detailed assistance with manuscript preparation.

Loleen and Jonathan are grateful to the Social Science and Humanities Research Council of Canada for providing an Insight Grant (file number: 435-2018-0019) to support our research on graduate education and career outcomes. We are also grateful to the Canadian Association for Graduate Studies and CREIVAT at Université Laval for giving us access to the 2019 Canadian Graduate and Professional Student Survey dataset.

Thank you to our families for their continuing support of our writing efforts: Troy Berdahl, Katie Berdahl, and Zoë Berdahl; Ruth Malloy, Alida Malloy, and Emma Malloy; Mike Griffin, David Griffin, and Josh Griffin.

Finally, we express our sincerest appreciation to our University of Alberta Press editor, Mat Buntin, who believed in this book project from the start. All academic writers should have the pleasure of working with a supportive editor and we are grateful for the experience.

This is a book directed primarily at faculty, university leaders, and other stakeholders and organizations interested in arts graduate education in Canada. But the ultimate focus is students, and how we can transform arts graduate education to better serve their well-being and future, as well as Canada's. It is thus to students that we dedicate *For the Public Good*.

Canada's Public Good Problem

We live in challenging times. Climate change, pandemics, and international conflict intrude on the peace and prosperity that Canada has enjoyed since the Second World War. Canadians are confronting and coming to terms with the ugly reality and legacies of the country's colonial founding while struggling to form one of the most racially diverse political communities in human history. Social cohesion seems to be dissolving, with increasing political polarization and a growing gap between rich and poor.

At the same time, many feel our postsecondary education system is underperforming. Students question the value of their degrees. Employment prospects for graduates vary significantly across different fields and industries. Faculty and staff themselves feel pressured to do more with less amid a myriad of conflicting expectations. Governments question whether investments in postsecondary institutions are the best use of tax dollars. And while these issues can be found across the board in nearly all academic disciplines, they are more prevalent in discussions of university arts education.

These two sets of problems have the potential to be part of each other's solutions.

Part of the answer to society's challenges is through progress in science and technology. Our lives are enriched by technological innovations and the fruits of scientific inquiry. Science seems to offer the answers to many of our challenges. Scientists develop batteries that can store the power the sun generates; they invent vaccines to save us from novel viruses; they advance technology that allows us to connect in ways that could not have been imagined just a generation or two ago.

But science and technology cannot independently save us from ourselves—a reality that comes as a great disappointment to those of us who came of age watching *Star Trek*. Solar batteries will become commonplace sooner if there is a tax regime that makes solar power competitive with natural gas. Vaccines are helpful only if they are widely accepted and not undermined by distrust and disinformation. Technology requires content and moderation to protect us from one another.

To survive and prosper in these challenging times, Canada needs a sophisticated understanding of the world around us and the tools to manage human affairs and the perils and pitfalls of intervention. We need expertise in communications, interpretation of data, and governance of technology. We need advanced practitioners trained to understand humanity and human systems, and we need them to be ready to mobilize their expertise to address these challenges. The human spirit has unlimited potential. But humans are complex, and we need to understand people in order to make a better world. While some of the world's most pressing challenges are scientific or technological in nature, many are not. This is why we need the advanced training in and knowledge of the arts. And this is where the greatest gap between potential and current reality occurs.

Our most fundamental societal challenges are related to clashes in values and cultures, and to the legacies of the past that shape how we view the future. While some people cling to "alternative facts" and refuse to accept evidence that does not fit their prejudices, there are also genuine differences in how we filter and understand information. Reasonable people can look at the same set of facts and come to very different interpretations. These can be rooted in personality, lived experience, group membership, or a range of other factors.

Often these human factors override consensus. While we wrote this book, we celebrated one of the most remarkable scientific achievements of our lifetimes: "The development of several highly efficacious vaccines against a previously unknown viral pathogen...in less than 1 year from the identification of the virus [which] is unprecedented in the history of vaccinology" (Fauci 2021, 109). But then we watched a surprising number of our fellow citizens resist the COVID-19 vaccines that seemed to offer a route out of the pandemic (Benham et al. 2021).

There are many other examples of scientific progress being overwhelmed by human factors. Even as we contemplated our own mortality in the face of COVID-19, it became ever more clear that humanity faces an existential crisis of unprecedented proportions. The science behind climate change is irrefutable, yet many either deny the scientific reality or choose to ignore it as the planet steadily warms.

The lesson is clear: modern problems are complex and involve understanding and managing humans. Scientific knowledge and technological innovation are still essential. But it is ever more clear that *all* our modern problems require careful design solutions and user acceptance—that is, an understanding of humanity and human systems. As Shah observes, "In diverse cases, social factors—cultural norms, educational understanding, kin and social networks, power dynamics, or simply the layout of a building—must be accounted for before policy can succeed" (2020, 285).

The challenges of the twenty-first century—many of which are hangover challenges from the twentieth, nineteenth, and even earlier centuries—are increasingly recognized as being "wicked problems." This term was coined by Rittel and Webber in 1973 when they observed that "As distinguished from problems in the natural sciences, which are definable and separable and may have solutions that are findable, the problems of governmental planning—and especially those of social or policy planning—are ill-defined; and they rely upon elusive political judgment for resolution. (Not 'solution.' Social problems are never solved. At best they are only re-solved—over and over again.)" (160).

Since that landmark article was published, there has been a steadily accelerating uptake of the concept, to the point that it has been dismissed as "faddish" (Head 2022). By definition, wicked problems are those that lack definitive solutions and have poorly defined boundaries (Head 2022). They are intractable, in part because they are complex. When the Australian Public Service Commission issued *Tackling Wicked Problems: A Public Policy Perspective*, it noted that the people tackling or managing these problems require "thinking that is capable of grasping the big picture" and "collaborative and innovative approaches" (2007, iii).

The common feature of all wicked problems is people. Humans do not always behave predictably, either as individuals or collectively. Their preferences and behaviours shift; they adapt differently to different contexts; there is often a discrepancy between words and actions. Often, they cannot even articulate why they believe or do certain things. While most human behaviour is rational, there can be many different ways to calculate rationality. And some behaviour is altruistic, impulsive, or otherwise beyond self-interested rational calculations.

Humanity and human relations are also growing ever more complex, especially with the growth of information and communication technologies that allow instantaneous global networks and connections. While this has led to waves of utopian predictions that technology will lead to universal human progress and understanding, the reality has of course been more mixed. Technology has led to greater global awareness and appreciation of other cultures and value systems. But it can also lead to new clashes and tensions. Social media in particular has both allowed greater human connections but also enabled more narrowness than ever, as algorithms and lists explicitly cater to our individual beliefs and values rather than expanding them. And life, in general, has accelerated because of technology. We can connect and share information faster than ever. But this means we also need greater reflection and nuance to help us digest and use information.

Tackling these issues effectively, in the real world rather than theoretically or in the abstract, will require people with the ability to work with *human* complexity. Many of the skills required to solve wicked problems lie in the "home domain" of the arts disciplines: critical thinking, design thinking, systems thinking, creativity, an ability to navigate ambiguity and to integrate different ways of knowing and disciplinary approaches, and a capacity to move between the concrete and the abstract.

Where will we find these people? This brings us back to the second issue. The good news is that we have a ready stream of people interested in these very topics. In Canada's universities, thousands of smart, thoughtful young people driven by these very concerns are devoting years of their lives to graduate study in the arts disciplines. Governments are investing heavily in their education. Unfortunately, students in and graduates of these programs often report struggling to make the transition to the workforce, and to connect their advanced research skills and subject-matter competencies to the real world (Council of Canadian Academies 2021).

Again, these two sets of problems have the potential to be part of each other's solutions. In *For the Public Good: Reimagining Arts Graduate Programs in Canadian Universities*, we argue that arts graduate education is uniquely positioned to deliver many of the public good needs of twenty-first-century Canada. We invite you, our readers, to enter a world of possibility with us to imagine a bold new role for arts graduate training in Canada that addresses these challenges.

These possibilities are exciting to us, and with this book, we aspire to inspire and excite you with them as well. This book is a manifesto to elevate the role of the arts, and arts graduate training in particular. We fearlessly seek to foster a movement among Canadian arts faculty members, academic leaders, students, and alumni to elevate arts graduate training to a position of prominence in the Canadian economy and society.

We believe, simply put, that Canada's arts graduate education programs have the potential to make significant and valuable contributions to Canada's economies and societies to an even greater extent than they do today. Liberal arts education, which we will simply call arts education, includes a range of social science and humanities disciplines, as well as interdisciplinary studies that combine such disciplines. (We recognize the classical definition of "liberal arts" often includes mathematics and natural science as well; to avoid confusion, we use the single word "arts.") At all levels of education, the arts promote the study of humans: our values, thinking, and behaviour, in the past, present, and future.

Graduate education in all disciplines, including science, technology, engineering, and mathematics (widely known as the category STEM), builds on undergraduates' base of knowledge to promote more sophisticated and independent thinking and inquiry. Graduate study in the arts trains students to think deeply about humanity and human systems and to develop their research and analysis skills to advance understanding of humanity and human systems. We believe that deliberately connecting arts graduate education to Canada's training and knowledge needs around humanity and human systems will benefit both Canada and the arts. In *For the Public Good: Reimagining Arts Graduate Programs in Canadian Universities*, we present a vision for arts graduate training that explicitly and thoughtfully ties arts graduate education to the Canadian public good.

Achieving this vision will take some work. While some arts graduate programs already align with the Canadian public good, in most cases programs are only partway there. Thus, we are not arguing that arts graduate education in its current form provides the best solution to Canada's current and future problems. In fact, we believe the current state needs some serious work. What we are arguing is that this unique form of education and training is best positioned—with some thoughtful reimagination—to be that solution. In the chapters that follow, we suggest a path forward to make this a reality.

Nothing in our arguments should be understood as belittling or devaluing current MA or PhD degrees or their holders. We recognize the good quality of graduate education in the arts disciplines in Canada, and we acknowledge the many ways in which this education and those who have benefited from it contribute to knowledge and society. We do believe, however, that degree programs can and should be reformed to improve students' experiences of them and to support their transition from graduate education to employment.

Defining the "Public Good" and "Arts Graduate Education"

Any good conversation requires that people are talking about the same thing, so we want to be very clear about what "public good" and "arts graduate education" do and do not include, at least for our purposes in this book.

What Do We Mean by "Public Good"?

We began by discussing the contemporary challenges facing Canada and other societies. We did so because we feel the need to keep our eyes focused on the prize—the overarching motivating "why" that drives us to seek change in arts graduate programs rather than accepting the status quo. After all, change requires work. Change requires managing conflicting ideas, overcoming institutional inertia, and expending energy that could be directed elsewhere. Doing the work of change—both starting it and seeing it through to completion—requires a compelling reason for the change. It requires a "why." And the "why" for reimagining arts graduate programs is Canada's public good.

Mention of "public good" immediately perks up the ears of anyone who has taken an introductory economics course. The discipline of economics defines "goods" (note the plural) as things that provide value (utility) to those who consume them. Further, economics draws a clear distinction between private and public goods (again note the plural). Private goods in the economics definition are goods that are excludable (some people are excluded from access) and rivalrous (one person's consumption of the good means there is less for others). Commonly used examples of private goods include food and clothing. Public goods in the economics definition are goods that are non-excludable (no one is excluded from access) and non-rivalrous (one person's consumption of the good does not limit another's). Commonly used examples of public goods include national defence and law enforcement.

Our own understanding of the public good (note the singular) is complementary to the economics public goods definition, but not identical. For the purposes of our discussion in this book, we define the public good as an aspirational direction toward which we as a society seek to move. (Another possible name for it is the "common good.") "Public" indicates the intended target or beneficiary: society, the general public, the citizenry writ large. "Good" is normative, indicating that this direction is positive, an improvement rather than a degradation of the status quo. The public good, then, is a state of improved societal well-being, and activities done "for" the public good are activities that benefit society (the general public, the collective) by advancing societal well-being.

What is perceived to benefit society will vary with circumstances, context, and needs. Indeed, Dorn's study of American higher education between the eighteenth and twenty-first centuries traces how postsecondary understandings of "the common good" shifted from "civic-mindedness" in the post-Independence period to "practicality" in the antebellum and Civil War periods to "commercialism" in the Reconstruction period until the end of the Second World War, and to "affluence" in the postwar period (2017, 3–4). As societies evolve and change, so too does the public good.

So, what is Canada's current public good? It is our position that, as the country moves forward through the 2020s and toward the mid-twenty-first century, Canada's public good is defined by three pressing imperatives. We need innovative solutions to Canada's wicked problems. We need action on equity, diversity, inclusion, and decolonization. And we need skilled knowledge workers with specific talents to make those first two outcomes occur. We will explain these three imperatives in detail in chapter 2.

What Do We Mean by "Arts Graduate Education"?

This is a book about the potential of arts graduate education. But the term "arts" can be defined in different ways. In some definitions, "liberal arts" encompasses a number of science fields; we have even seen engineering included in at least one definition of liberal arts, a breadth of the term most would reject. University structures provide somewhat more direction, but only in small measure. Most Canadian universities have faculties (or, in a small number of cases, colleges) of arts (e.g., McGill University, University of British Columbia) or of arts and science (e.g., University of Toronto, Queen's University, University of Saskatchewan), while others have different organizational divisions, such as humanities and social sciences (e.g., Memorial University), social science(s) (e.g., University of Ottawa, Western University), humanities (e.g., McMaster University, York University), or a variety of creative names and combinations (e.g., the Faculty of Public Affairs and Faculty of Arts and Social Sciences at Carleton University, and the Faculty of Arts and Faculty of Native Studies at the University of Alberta). These organizational distinctions are not important for our argument and overall vision, although they can be quite important for the implementation of the vision.

Nevertheless, while there are some variations at the margins, there is a general consensus that the "arts" comprises academic disciplines that fall within the social sciences and humanities, but that are not associated with a profession. These include:

- social sciences such as anthropology, economics, geography, linguistics, sociology, political science, and psychology;
- humanities such as literature/English, modern languages, history, and philosophy; and
- disciplines that work at the intersection of social sciences and humanities, such as women's and gender studies, and Indigenous studies.

The disciplines we identify here are not exhaustive, but they provide a clear indication of the academic space of which we speak. We recognize that some disciplines—such as geography, psychology, and linguistics—bridge the arts and natural sciences with their different branches and subfields, and so we include them in our definition of the arts while recognizing that only some parts clearly fit.

Our definition of the arts disciplines deliberately excludes fine arts and performing arts. These programs encompass studio arts, visual arts, drama, dance, design, music, and other disciplines. While we greatly value the fine and performing arts, our focus is exclusively on the traditional liberal arts, specifically the social sciences and humanities. It is these liberal arts disciplines, focused on the creation and application of systematic knowledge about human endeavours, where we see the greatest potential for renewal and connection to Canada's public good imperatives.

Our definition of arts disciplines also—and perhaps controversially—deliberately excludes the professional areas of study within social science, such as management/business, education, public administration/policy, and social work. These disciplines and their associated programs are typically already tied to a particular understanding of societal engagement and contribution, with students explicitly taught a set of particular career-relevant skills. For decades, these programs have prepared students for positions and professional advancement in their area of study, primarily at the master's degree level. In chapter 4, we discuss how these professional programs tailored toward advanced professional practice are distinct from arts programs. Still, there is much to learn from these programs, and in chapter 8, we explore how arts professional doctoral programs might develop alongside traditional PhDs.

Now that we have clarified what is and is not included in our definition of arts, let's build to what we mean by arts graduate education. Graduate education in Canada encompasses master's and doctoral-level programming. Thus, when we speak of arts graduate education, we are focused on master's and doctoral programs in the traditional liberal arts—that is, the social sciences and humanities.

Undergraduate and graduate education are designed and delivered differently, and these differences are important. There has been no shortage of discussion about the purpose of arts education—by which most people mean arts undergraduate education. Pundits and the general public alike have long questioned, bemoaned, and debated the value of liberal arts education. Parents worry that their child's study of, say, history does not lead to a clear career path. Faculty counterargue that a student's education in, say, anthropology, will equip them not just with important understandings of culture and societies, but also with career-relevant skills.

These debates, while interesting, are limited in that they inevitably focus implicitly or explicitly on undergraduate students, or at least do not consider the distinctive category and context of graduate students. They highlight the value of developing broad thinking and critical inquiry skills for such students, which can then be applied to and refined to fit a variety of careers. Some even argue that arts education should not be too specialized—it is "training for life" rather than for a specific job (Anders 2017).

There is no similar conversation that focuses clearly on arts graduate education. But there should be. Arts graduate education, thoughtfully and purposefully developed, has the potential to go far beyond the valuable but more generic arts undergraduate contributions. As we explain in chapter 3, the graduate student population and its needs and potential are distinct. The graduate student experience is different. The funding relationship between universities and graduate students is often different. The expectations of graduate students, who are older, already possess an undergraduate degree, and may have spent time outside of the university between degrees, are different. And, importantly for our arguments, the potential direct contribution of graduate students to Canada's public good is much greater.

But how can arts graduate education contribute to Canada's public good, and, quite frankly, why should arts faculty, chairs, programs, and deans engage in the change work needed to do so? We are glad you asked.

How—and Why—Arts Graduate Education Can Advance Canada's Public Good

Postsecondary education, including graduate education, benefits both individual students and society as a whole. But these benefits are portrayed in different ways, and that leaves an important gap that *For the Public Good: Reimagining Arts Graduate Programs in Canadian Universities* seeks to fill.

Earlier in this chapter, we talked about private and public goods. Higher education in any discipline is often presented as a utilitarian private good for individuals, and rightly so. Postsecondary education correlates with many individual-level benefits, such as increased income, higher status or prestige, improved health outcomes, and greater life expectancy (Frenette 2014; Statistics Canada 2020). Yet emphasizing these compelling individual benefits can lead to a particular understanding of higher education that many chafe against. A narrow focus on the individual student's "return on investment" leads to a consumer model of education, reducing the goal from intellectual discovery and growth to "job training." This in turn sparks conflict between those (mostly in the university) who resist such a narrow approach and those (mostly outside the university) more supportive of it.

The exact benefits of arts research can also sometimes be fuzzy. For example, medical researchers can link their work to lives saved and better health outcomes, while engineers can point to new and improved technologies and buildings. The arts cannot always draw such direct links, leading to questions about their relevance to addressing societal issues. In turn, some argue that the most important impacts of the arts are indirect and conceptual (Fecher et al. 2021)—shifting frames and dimensions of thinking, and challenging existing assumptions.

The difficulty in sometimes pointing to "direct" benefits to society from the arts means that governments and others have sometimes explicitly prioritized certain programs, mainly in STEM, that produce "hard skills" linked to specific industries and employer demand. These are then justified as investments in what society—and the economy—need. In contrast, other programs—e.g., the arts—are seen to only benefit individuals who wish to study them, with any societal benefits being more tangential and ephemeral—and thus less worthy of public support and scarce tax dollars. For example, in 2020 the Australian Commonwealth government announced it would keep fees lower for STEM-related programs while charging more for other programs in the arts, where there was less perceived employer demand (Karp 2020). This decision was explicitly justified as allowing those who really wanted to study the arts to do so, but at their own expense.

Arts educators have fought back against the above by arguing that arts education also produces many benefits for society, such as increased civil involvement, higher rates of charitable giving, and a more informed electorate. But these tend to be presented in broad, relatively undefined ways. Again, arts education is sometimes said to "prepare students for life" more than for a specific job. We agree that it does prepare students to act as informed and engaged citizens. But students still need a job after they graduate.

Part of the difficulty may be the connection between student learning and student employability. The connection is strong in most STEM disciplines. Engineering students study engineering subjects, after which they are licensed and hired as engineers. The link is often not as strong in the arts; students may study sociology, but there are few "sociologist" jobs in the world, outside of universities. The link is not exact. ("Mathematician" is also not a common job title, while "psychologist" or "economist" is.) But our point is that, as mentioned above, STEM subjects are generally more likely to produce "hard skills"—specific competencies and knowledge in their degree programs that are desired by specific employers in specific industries. In contrast, the arts produce broader and more transferable skills—soft skills—that are not always specifically linked to either specific subject learning or specific jobs.

This fuzzier connection between degrees and specific professions in the arts also creates challenges in tracking outcomes systematically. Arts graduates end up in a wide range of different types of jobs in different industries and sectors, often outstripping the ability of labour market data to keep up. There are countless career success stories from arts graduates, but they are often exactly that, stories—narratives of how individuals found a particular fit between their education/skills and an employer or market need (see, for example, the 2019 TRaCE McGill narratives, which are individual stories of PhD students from all disciplines and how they found meaningful careers, and the 2021 Council of Canadian Academies' *Degrees of Success* report that combines high-level data with individual career narratives from doctoral graduates). These stories are inspiring and even exciting. But they remain centred on individual accounts, often with an element of serendipity and luck that led to happy individual outcomes that are not generalizable to graduates overall.

We see a gap here, one that arts graduate education is uniquely positioned to fill. Arts graduate education has the potential to achieve both individual-level benefits for students and the broad society-level benefits listed above. But it can go beyond these to achieve more specific collective goals. Specifically, we believe arts graduate education is uniquely positioned to be reimagined to advance Canada's public good by producing graduates who are able to apply advanced skills to address Canada's most vexing human-based problems and challenges, and on a more systematic basis, beyond individual serendipitous outcomes. Thus, we are arguing very specifically for greater attention to not just arts education or arts research in general, but arts graduate education.

We see the proposed connection between Canada's public good and arts graduate education as being a win-win. As we will show in later chapters, there is definite room for improvement in the current system. Benefits include improved outcomes for arts graduate students, improved status for arts disciplines within Canadian universities, and increased appreciation of arts research within Canadian society.

Arts programs have long been under pressure to justify their relevance to universities and societies. But increasingly they need to justify their existence to students themselves, amid accelerating pressure from the rest of society. Universities Canada writes, "Concern about the future of the liberal arts is not new. What is new is the serious decline in liberal arts enrolment at Canadian universities in recent years, particularly in certain regions, and the abundance of attacks on the value of the liberal arts in media commentary" (2016, 3).

This is a more pressing problem for the humanities than for the social sciences. For some time now the humanities have been described as being "in crisis." While part of the concern lies with enrollments—a topic we will get to soon—a larger issue is the perceived value of humanities research and scholarship. Hanlon (2022) argues that "the humanities have a credibility problem....the public doesn't seem to trust that we are engaging in real, methodical scholarly inquiry—or, at least, that such inquiries amount to much more than informed or pretentious opinion-making." A study of how the humanities are described in American journalism finds that the societal relevance of the humanities is often unclear: "the humanities struggle to be perceived as capable of bridging scales, of zooming in to the individual human scale while also zooming out to the societal scale. How the humanities help people move step by step from the minute experience of reading a book or attending a class, for example, to larger social and world action, and then back again in a round-trip of local-global engagement is not at all obvious" (Liu et al. 2022, 27).

Social science research faces fewer challenges. Canadians of a certain age will recall some upset in 2013 and 2014 when then-Prime Minister Stephen Harper took to disparaging sociology (Singh 2014), but generally speaking, the social sciences do not appear to draw the widespread skepticism and disdain experienced by the humanities. This also plays out with respect to student enrollments. In his analysis of Canadian undergraduate enrollment trends from 1992–93 to 2019–20, Usher (2022) finds that the social sciences have experienced significant total enrollment growth over the past twenty-five years, while enrollment in the humanities has fallen dramatically—with the exception of philosophy, which has generally held steady.

However, total enrollment is not the same as relative enrollment, and it is here that the arts disciplines overall are in particular trouble. Simply put, STEM and health enrollment growth is outpacing other areas, including the arts. Usher (2022) writes, "Basically, over the past 30 years or so, STEM and health programs have gone from educating a little over one in four undergraduate students to educating a little over four in ten today. Non-STEM/health fields grew quickly in the period 2000 to 2010, but since about 2010, effectively all growth has come on the STEM/health side." As STEM and health programs are both growing quickly and are more expensive to offer, arts programs face challenges in maintaining university resources, including tenure-stream faculty positions, graduate student funding, and other supports.

Again, this is a more acute concern in the humanities disciplines. Together, a lack of appreciation of humanities scholarship amongst the general public (and possibly university leadership) along with declining enrollments contribute to long-standing concerns about the future of the humanities. As Schmidt (2018) wonders, "The question is how much space any of the humanities can ultimately take up in a university." These are not new concerns; Jay (2014) reports that articles about the crisis of the humanities go back to the 1920s. Indeed, reflecting on the "permanent crisis" of the humanities, Reitter and Wellmon write, "Whether or not they are fully aware of it, for politically progressive and conservative scholars alike, crisis has played a crucial role in grounding the idea that the humanities have a special mission. Part of the story of why the modern humanities are always in crisis is that we have needed them to be" (2021, 3).

Social sciences are less likely to be declared "in crisis," and there is greater variance between disciplines. Some, such as psychology, are generally doing quite well, at least in terms of student enrollments. But, overall, they are in the same boat as the humanities—falling behind in both student and societal interest, and under pressure to demonstrate their continuing relevance, especially in terms of public support and investment.

It is our belief that reimagining arts graduate education and tying it explicitly to Canada's public good can benefit arts programs by more clearly defining the value of arts research and education to universities, policymakers, and potential students. Universities Canada writes, "there is urgency for universities and arts faculties to better rebrand and communicate the value of a liberal arts education, and to reframe its relevance in today's diverse society and innovative economy" (2016, 6). Linking Canada's public good to arts graduate education can serve as this rebranding and reframing.

Why We Are Writing This Book

For the Public Good: Reimagining Arts Graduate Programs in Canadian Universities is a call to action. We are writing with the intention of inspiring action among four key audiences. Ideally, this book will prompt some of these key individuals—hopefully you, dear reader— to become champions for change.

The first audience is our peers: university-based academics in social science and humanities disciplines in Canada involved in delivering or designing arts graduate education. At present, we believe that only a small number of this group is thinking—really thinking—about the costs and benefits of our current graduate education model, much less about how it could be reimagined to the benefit of students and society alike. We aim to increase the number of arts faculty actively engaged in this discussion at this time. If this is you, we thank you for thinking about this issue and encourage you to challenge your colleagues and peers to do the same.

Our second key audience is university leaders and program development specialists, particularly those involved in graduate education as provosts, deans (of both arts and graduate studies), associate and assistant deans, department chairs and heads, and graduate chairs and directors. These individuals have the direct ability to lead change— by starting conversations, creating incentives for action, or updating policies in ways that require arts graduate programs to shift practices to meet the needs of twenty-first-century students and society. If this is you, we are excited about your potential to create meaningful transformations in your university. We believe the information in the chapters ahead will empower you to move forward.

In this book, we also speak directly to policymakers and policy advocates as our third audience, including those in provincial ministries responsible for postsecondary education, federal policymakers at the Social Sciences and Humanities Research Council of Canada (SSHRC) and those involved in conversations about future skills, as well as advocacy organizations (like the Federation for the Humanities and Social Sciences), think tanks (such as the Business/Higher Education Roundtable), and university-based graduate student associations. As *For the Public Good: Reimagining Arts Graduate Programs in Canadian Universities* makes clear, the current arts graduate education challenge is not entirely one of universities' making. Universities have been rational (we hope) actors, responding to policy incentives and requirements. Meaningful change in arts graduate education will not—indeed, cannot—occur without addressing problematic policy. If you are a policymaker, we urge you to consider both the direct and indirect consequences of policy for arts graduate education in your jurisdiction and to identify options for better policy moving forward. If you are a policy advocate, whether within an organization or simply as an informed citizen, we invite you to draw upon the material presented in this book to challenge governments to do better.

Our fourth audience is current arts graduate students. Although they may not benefit personally from reforms to graduate curriculum, graduate students are often engaged in conversations about program requirements and curriculum reform. Although our primary purpose isn't to offer advice to current graduate students about how to navigate their programs (see Berdahl and Malloy 2018 for this), they may find some guidance in the three talent imperatives we argue are important to realizing the potential of arts graduate education. Much as we hope that students are being invited to play a meaningful role in conversations around arts graduate education, it is our view that the onus is not on them to drive change; rather, it's up to faculty members, administrators, and policymakers to embark on reform in consultation with students. If you are a graduate student engaged in these conversations or hoping to inspire changes for the students who come after you, we invite you to consider the proposals we set out and reflect on how these might have affected your graduate experience if they were already in place.

Our goal is that *For the Public Good: Reimagining Arts Graduate Programs in Canadian Universities* will provoke discussions among individuals working in academia, university administration, higher education societies, and provincial and federal governments. And, if we may dream, we hope that these discussions will prompt some bold leaders (be they faculty members or deputy ministers) to take the meaningful action that Canada needs to realize its potential.

Canada and its arts graduate students deserve this.

It is time for arts graduate education to move beyond simply addressing university financial needs and idiosyncratic faculty and student interests to explicitly focus on addressing the Canadian public good. This in turn requires a clearer articulation of the specific value of arts graduate education in building the skills and abilities of students. This is needed for Canada, for students, and for the arts disciplines themselves as we seek to protect their very existence.

In the chapters ahead, we lay out a systematic way of thinking about and structuring arts graduate education to advance Canada's public good. In chapter 2, we define Canada's current public good needs and identify how arts graduate education is well suited to meet these needs. In chapter 3, we explain why reimagining arts graduate education is necessary from the graduate student perspective, using data to demonstrate that the current system is not benefiting students. This is followed by chapter 4, in which we explain why our current programs persist despite their problems. In chapter 5, we explain how current graduate degree structures function, and how they could function better.

By this time, you will be wondering how we can create this magical arts graduate education that advances Canada's public good. In chapter 6, your patience is repaid, as we lay out a high-level vision for a reimagined arts graduate education. We find this vision compelling and exciting, and we believe you will, too. Chapter 7 provides a more focused explanation of that vision, and chapter 8 works through examples to provoke your own thinking and imagination.

This is the point where most books end: vision, generic "someone should do something" call to action, and then see you later. But as we outline in chapter 4, there are reasons why change is hard, and achieving the vision requires careful attention to implementation. For this reason, chapter 9 provides actor-specific steps to move arts graduate education forward to fulfill this mission of the public good. We explain why faculty and units, universities, and governments all have a role to play, and how each can act. To get to our reimagined state, Canada needs a path forward, and chapter 9 lays out that path. We conclude in chapter 10 with a brief pep talk to encourage you—yes, you—to take action, and suggest your easy first step to make necessary changes. As a bonus, in Appendix 3, we offer concrete suggestions for faculty members who want to work toward change through their own supervisory practice.

A few words about us before we proceed. As a team of authors, we bring both common and distinct strengths to this project. We are all political scientists whose research and teaching focus on Canadian politics, and we each have strong backgrounds in public policy processes and institutions that are critical to this study. We also bring considerable university administrative experience, from three different provinces and distinct postsecondary policy regimes and from four universities. Lisa Young served as associate dean and then dean of graduate studies at the University of Calgary; she was also extensively involved in rethinking graduate education through the Canadian Association of Graduate Studies, where she cochaired the Task Force on the Future of the Dissertation. Loleen Berdahl and Jonathan Malloy in turn bring experience as long-time heads of their academic departments, along with other considerable administrative experience in their universities. Jonathan Malloy brings expertise from his role as associate dean (research and graduate) at Carleton University's Faculty of Public Affairs. Loleen Berdahl brings additional public policy background from her previous work as the director of research for the Canada West Foundation and from her role as executive director at the Johnson Shoyama Graduate School of Public Policy, co-located at the University of Saskatchewan and the University of Regina.

We also bring strong related original research knowledge to this project. We actively study graduate professional development in Canada, with support from a SSHRC Insight grant, and have published peer-reviewed scholarly articles on this topic (see Berdahl and Malloy 2019; Berdahl, Malloy, and Young 2020; Berdahl, Malloy, and Young 2022, Casey et al. 2023). Berdahl and Malloy coauthored a previous book on graduate education entitled *Work Your Career: Get What You Want from Your Social Sciences and Humanities PhD* (2018); written for

PhD student readers, it is highly complementary in its vision to rethink graduate arts education in Canada.

Collectively, we look very much like the modal Gen X arts faculty member: pale. We entered the academy at a time when "diversity" was synonymous with gender, and our careers have in some ways been shaped by those conversations. We embrace calls for the academy to better reflect the diversity of Canada in its composition and in what and how it teaches. But we acknowledge that we are making this case from positions of privilege, and have sought to learn from BIPOC colleagues and members of other equity-deserving groups as we have refined our arguments. As political science professors whose research has focused primarily on Canada, we are acutely aware of the relative absence—until recently—of Indigenous voices in the academy and the public realm, and we place a high priority on creating space to remedy this absence. We take seriously Tuck and Yang's (2012, 3) admonishment that "the easy absorption, adoption, and transposing of decolonization is yet another form of settler appropriation," and we acknowledge how challenging—but essential—the process of decolonization in the academy will be. Tuck and Yang also remind us that "there is a long and bumbled history of non-Indigenous peoples making moves to alleviate the impacts of colonization" (2012, 3). With this in mind, we call for arts graduate programs to create space for Indigenous scholars to guide this work. You will see this commitment in the chapters that follow.

This book is important to us. As committed university educators with recent experience in academic leadership and graduate education programming, we see a strong need to spark a conversation about graduate education in the social sciences and humanities. The conversation needs to be wide ranging, addressing curriculum, program design, and the public policy that structures graduate education. As political scientists focused on Canadian politics and public policy, we are uniquely equipped to analyze the incentives and restrictions that structure universities' choices and behaviours around graduate education. As seasoned academics with leadership experience, we have firsthand understanding of the power of ideas and culture to shape academics' decision making within those institutions. As researchers, we have undertaken studies that inform our perspectives on the problems to be addressed and the direction for change.

And, possibly most importantly, as supervisors and instructors of arts graduate students ourselves, we are well aware of the untapped potential of Canada's arts graduates. We care deeply about our students and their futures. We care deeply about Canada and about its future. And we believe you do as well.

So, let's hop to it, shall we?

Three Imperatives to Advance Canada's Public Good

We started For the Public Good: Reimagining Arts Graduate Programs in Canadian Universities with the bold claim that graduate education in the arts has an important role to play in contributing to Canada's public good. We believe that arts graduate education can be reimagined to help advance Canada's societal well-being. In this chapter, we outline three pressing imperatives for Canada's public good:

- The Wicked Problems Imperative—Canada needs innovative solutions to Canada's wicked problems.
- The Equity, Diversity, Inclusion, and Decolonization (EDID) Imperative—Canada needs to take action on equity, diversity, inclusion, and decolonization.
- The Talent Imperative—Canada needs skilled knowledge workers with specific talents to make those first two outcomes occur.

For each of the above imperatives, we believe arts graduate education can play an important role in preparing researchers and practitioners to serve as leaders. The wicked problems imperative, EDID imperative, and talent imperative inform our vision of how Canada's arts graduate programs could evolve to contribute more explicitly and directly to the public good.

In this chapter, we explain these three imperatives and their potential connection to arts graduate education in detail. We must note at the outset that these imperatives and our linking of them to arts graduate education will raise ideological objections from some readers. For example, some readers may feel embracing the EDID imperative is an act of "wokeness"; other readers (or perhaps the same readers) may feel that tying graduate education to addressing wicked problems and/or providing advanced skills training degrades the noble purpose of higher education. In our opinion, it is both possible and necessary to address the three imperatives in ways that allow for diversity of thought and preservation of the true value of the arts. Aligning with Canada's public good can and should be a positive evolution of the role of arts graduate education.

Canada's Wicked Problems Imperative

Every day, the news reminds us we live in challenging times. Climate change produces weather catastrophes. Malign forces, internal and external, are putting democracies under pressure. Communities are divided on how they should respond to a global pandemic. All of these—and other pressing issues—can be understood as "wicked" problems.

Rittel and Webber introduced the terminology of "tame" and "wicked" problems in 1973. Tame problems are well defined, can be separated from other problems, and can have tidy solutions. Tame problems are the realm of science:

> The problems that scientists and engineers have usually focused upon are mostly "tame" or "benign" ones. As an example, consider a problem of mathematics, such as solving an equation; or the task of an organic chemist in analyzing the structure of some unknown compound; or that of the chess player attempting to accomplish checkmate in five moves. For each the mission is clear. It is clear, in turn,

whether or not the problems have been solved. (Rittel and Webber 1973, 160)

Tame problems are not necessarily easy; their solutions may be highly complex and difficult to achieve. But these problems are unambiguous and clear, as are their solutions, once discovered.

Wicked problems, in contrast, are ill-defined, interwoven with other problems, and do not have tidy—or even lasting—solutions. Wicked problems are slippery: people argue about how to define and measure the problems, how to resolve the problems, and how to measure success. The goals, terminology, and proposals shift and change over time as new information, new circumstances, and new stakeholders come into play. Wicked problems are challenging because they inherently engage with social values. Wicked problems are the domain of public policy: "Wicked problems...include nearly all public policy issues—whether the question concerns the location of a freeway, the adjustment of a tax rate, the modification of school curricula, or the confrontation of crime" (Rittel and Webber 1973, 160). They are also the domain of society, of how we coexist and function together, both formally and informally.

Wicked problems cannot be addressed without understanding humans and human societies. Consider the big issues of our times: climate change, income inequality, environmental sustainability, housing affordability and homelessness, economic growth, public health. There is no shortage of wicked problems facing Canada, and the vast majority require deliberate, thoughtful attention to human behaviour and governance.

As we outlined at the start of this book, the COVID-19 pandemic made this exceptionally clear. While scientific knowledge of the virus and how to combat it steadily grew, more concerning and harder to solve was the refusal of many people to cooperate and take appropriate measures based on the scientific evidence. Similarly, as a society, we know the science behind climate change. The real challenge is understanding why many refuse to recognize and respond to the science.

Canada's wicked problems imperative requires an understanding of how social, environmental, and economic issues depend upon and are informed by human behaviours, systems, and institutions. Let's be clear: we are very supportive of STEM research and education, and do not want to take away from progress in those areas. But they are insufficient to address the challenges that Canada faces and will face in the decades ahead. Often "the science" does not tell the whole story. It regularly misses important dimensions, especially involving equity and diversity, or overestimates its predictive power and need for future corrections.

Scientific determinism and rigidity enable us to deal with tame problems. Dealing with Canada's wicked problems requires knowledge that can flourish in areas of ambiguity. Rittel and Webber (1973) argue that societies require a different, more nuanced approach to deal with wicked problems. It is our position that these are arts' problems to solve. There is no shortage of potential linkages between the arts disciplines and these grand challenges. The potential contribution is significant.

Arts scholarship exists to find pathways for societal and human progress. It asks us to consider what truly is the public good; to understand both our shared and diverse values; and to advance conflict resolution and reconciliation, especially for our most deep and divisive issues. Humans and human societies are extraordinarily complicated. The arts disciplines are all about exploring and explaining those complications. As the Institute for the Public Life of Arts and Ideas writes, "the humanities develop a critical, historical, and case-based understanding of value that helps us determine why we should undertake certain courses of action in preference to others and why we should keep assaying the consequences of past events, formations, policies, and imaginings" (2013, 4). The same applies, in our opinion, to the social sciences.

Arts complements science, challenges science in important ways, and leads in ways that science cannot. Arts graduate programs, reimagined to explicitly connect to the wicked problems imperative, have the potential to advance Canada's public good by embracing the complexity, irrationality, and messiness of human societies and their problems. Arts graduate research can advance our knowledge. Arts graduate education can increase the number of individuals able to lead or collaborate on real-world solutions.

Riddell (2021) argues that a renewed commitment to solving wicked social problems is essential to fulfilling the moral contract universities have with the broader society. This is a challenge for the entire university, but perhaps more so for the arts disciplines, whose expertise is not always sought when wicked problems present themselves. Research and scholarship in the arts disciplines have a direct bearing on the wicked problems Canada faces. As the Institute for the Public Life of Arts and Ideas writes, "the world of the 21st century needs high quality humanities research and teaching now more than ever....the kinds of knowledge borne of the humanities can contribute to clearer, more historically informed, and more ethical understandings of problems that face modern Canada" (2013, 1). Again, we believe the same is true of the social sciences.

Many graduates of master's and doctoral programs in the arts disciplines are already playing important roles in addressing Canada's wicked problems. They are in leadership roles in the public service and the private sector; they are researchers whose work informs public policy. Whether researchers or practitioners, they are engaged in this important work.

But many had to build their own bridge from their graduate education to the role they now play and develop their competencies independently. To make the most of the pool of talent in arts graduate programs, we need to ensure that curriculum and research bring students in contact with wicked problems and scaffold their understanding of how humanities and social science research can engage with them. We need to be sure that they are ready to engage as productive members of multidisciplinary teams, and not just as lone scholars. And we must help students to articulate the ways in which their knowledge and skills equip them for this important work.

Canada's Equity, Diversity, Inclusion, and Decolonization (EDID) Imperative

Some of the most profound challenges facing Canada in the twenty-first century centre around questions of equity, diversity, inclusion, and decolonization.

We are experiencing a moment in which Canada's colonial past is being recognized and its harms identified. Statues are being toppled and institutions renamed. The 2015 report of the Truth and Reconciliation

Commission of Canada challenged Canadians to look squarely at the Canadian state's efforts to erase Indigenous Peoples through forced assimilation in residential schools—among other ways—and the role of churches in carrying out this policy. Reconciliation offers hope for Indigenous resurgence, as Indigenous people "reclaim what has been stolen from them whether it is their land, language, cultural artifacts, traditions, teachings, and even their perspectives on our collective history…[and] non-Indigenous people gain a deeper understanding and appreciation for Indigenous perspectives that have been hidden from our collective consciousness for far too long" (Blu Waters et al. 2022, 156).

Meanwhile, population growth driven by immigration is making Canada's non-Indigenous population ever more ethnically diverse. Canada's self-image as an egalitarian multicultural society is coming under growing pressure as evidence mounts that intersecting patterns of sexism, discrimination, and racism make the "Canadian multicultural dream" elusive for many.

Canada faces an EDID imperative to address inequities, conflicts, and resentments stemming from our colonial past and to meet the forward-looking challenge of building a radically diverse society. Universities are both vehicles for addressing this imperative and subjects for reform and change themselves. Writing about the Indigenization of universities, Gaudry and Lorenz (2018) establish a spectrum, with Indigenous inclusion at one end and decolonial Indigenization at the other. The former entails increasing the presence of Indigenous students and faculty, who "bear the burden" of Indigenization as they are expected "to adapt to the intellectual world view, teaching and research styles of the academy" (Gaudry and Lorenz 2018, 220). Decolonial Indigenization demands what Gaudry and Lorenz call a "wholesale overhaul" of the university, aiming to "unsettle and dismantle settler colonialism" (2018, 223). A version of this spectrum applies beyond Indigenization to addressing other sources of systemic racism. At a minimum, universities can become more diverse in the composition of their student and faculty complements. But meaningful change comes when those institutions become the site of diversification of perspective and worldview in ways that transform the academy and the communities it serves.

There are three dimensions to the EDID imperative. The first is to come to terms with our colonial history and chart a path of decolonization. As political science professors who did their graduate training in the 1990s, we each were taught and went on to teach about Canada's "two founding groups" and the politics of language and culture that dominated for 150 years afterward. Like for so many Canadian academics, our conceptions of the political foundations of the country largely glossed over the violent, genocidal reality. As Mahoney writes, "our origin story is incomplete and misleading. In 1996, the Royal Commission on Aboriginal Peoples wrote in its report, 'A country cannot be built on a living lie.' This lie, I argue, is in the story of Canada's origins and it must be corrected if we are to become the nation we think we are and create the necessary conditions for reconciliation with Canada's first peoples" (2016, 29).

The term "decolonization" refers to more than removing the colonizer's authority. Rather, as Leblanc writes, decolonization "requires the resurgence and recentering of Indigenous life and land…at the same time that it requires a step away from the liberal state…and the willingness of non-Indigenous peoples to step aside and to be open to transformative change" (2021, 357). To embark on truly decolonial Indigenization is ambitious and must be authentic. It will certainly be contested.

Canada's journey of truth and reconciliation will be lengthy. Arts graduate education has a significant role to play in ensuring that Canada's colonial history and its consequences are widely understood among people in leadership positions across government and the private and not-for-profit sectors where many arts graduates build their careers. Not all will endorse the project of decolonization, and those who do will vary in their approaches. A reformed arts graduate education must itself embrace decolonization and prepare arts graduate students to engage in society-wide debates and negotiations.

The second dimension of the EDID imperative is to fulfill the promise of Canada's commitment to multiculturalism by improving racial equity and inclusion. Established as a national policy in 1971, multiculturalism was originally intended to provide support for Canada's cultures, help overcome barriers to full participation, promote interchange among cultural groups, and help immigrants to learn English or French (Wayland 1997, 47). It was intended to be a source of national identity that defied the existence of a "dominant" culture, but in practice became a way for Canada's Anglo-Saxon dominant culture to remain "unmarked and invisible, a non-hyphenated de-ethnicized 'Canadian-Canadian' norm in comparison with which all other practices and identities are constructed as 'multicultural'" (Winter 2005).

Even before the COVID-19 pandemic, it was evident that multiculturalism had not produced the egalitarian society it promised; the stresses of the pandemic, which laid bare racism and inequalities, prompted mobilization focused on addressing these. As Lei and Guo (2022) observe, "racialized communities today demand not only recognition of their heritage culture, or more conversations about diversity, but also a heightened awareness and better social mobilization capability to demand immediate action and change for equity and social justice."

In the coming decades, diversity will become an even more central demographic reality in Canada. A Statistics Canada study (2022a) projects that, by 2041, immigrants will comprise between 30 percent and 34 percent of the Canadian population, up from 22 percent in 2016 and marking "a record-high level since the 1867 Canadian Confederation." The study also projects that by 2041, some 40 percent of the Canadian population will be part of a racialized group, and the figure will be substantially higher in many urban areas.

The growing diversity of the Canadian population poses a profound challenge to Canadian institutions, to move beyond superficial multiculturalism toward authentic equality and inclusion. Arts graduate education is well positioned to contribute to meeting this challenge, as arts disciplines develop the critical tools to understand the challenges and their potential remedies. Arts graduate students must be prepared to manage and lead these challenges. Further, arts graduate programs themselves must be inclusive of the growing diversity of the Canadian population, both in their composition and in their curriculum and pedagogy.

Universities, including arts graduate programs, play a key role in the Canadian immigration system. One path to permanent residency in Canada is through admission to a postsecondary institution, followed by an application to stay in Canada. Roughly half the graduate students who came to study in Canada between 2000 and 2014 became landed immigrants within a decade (Choi, Crossman, and Hou 2021). Arguably, much of the international student demand for admission to graduate programs in the arts and other disciplines at Canadian universities is influenced by the possibility of remaining in Canada. This raises some thorny dilemmas as Canada scoops up well-educated ambitious young people from elsewhere in the world. To the extent that some graduate programs, faced with declining domestic student demand, are replacing domestic students with international ones in order to preserve their program, there may be reason for concern. Nevertheless, in admitting and educating these newcomers to Canada, arts graduate programs have the potential to equip these individuals to attain positions that allow them to employ their education and talents for Canada's public good, should they wish to stay, or for their home country's public good, should they wish to return there.

The third dimension of the EDID challenge is to understand equity in a multi-dimensional—or intersectional—way. Social movements of the 1970s brought about profound changes to gender roles and heralded a new era of acceptance for LGBTQ2S+ Canadians. Some of these changes remain contested, and even some that have been normalized—like women's participation in the paid workforce—have not yet resulted in full economic or other equality. Other sources of identity, including social class, education, and age, also produce privilege and hardship. Intersectionality is a way of understanding the complexities of social location. It is an idea that is widely shared among progressives and contested by conservatives.

Working with and through these three dimensions will require awareness, sensitivity, and bravery. Canadian businesses, governments, and society writ large will need to find ways to acknowledge colonial and racist histories, structures, and interests, and to move Canada beyond these legacies.

This will be uncomfortable and at times ugly work. Confronting colonialism, racism, and other forms of systemic discrimination forces us to look inward and challenge our understanding of the world. Decolonization demands a fundamental rethinking of teaching, research, and program administration. It throws into question the established ways of knowing that underpin inquiry in many arts disciplines. The scholars best positioned to lead the conversations are in short supply and have many demands on their time. There are many potential objections to the work, from within and beyond the academy.

But Canada's EDID imperative is to get this work done despite its challenges. Education at all levels has a large role to play. Again, universities are both vehicles for change and subjects of necessary change themselves. Success on the EDID imperative front requires conscious, deliberate attention to education, including postsecondary education. And as many of the leaders of tomorrow will enroll in graduate education, these priorities are increasingly pressing in graduate programs.

Arts disciplines are already advancing Canada's EDID imperative. Understanding colonialism and its legacies are the "home domains" of arts disciplines such as history, sociology, political science, anthropology, and literature, and are a central focus of many interdisciplinary areas of inquiry, like Indigenous, women's, and Black studies. The theoretical tools and empirical understanding of social difference and conflict are a central preoccupation of many of the arts disciplines. Writing in 2013, the Institute for the Public Life of Arts and Ideas argued:

> The humanities foster understanding across lines of national, ethnic, racial, and gender difference, which is an urgent requirement in an increasingly global world. To take one central example, critical humanities work has been foundational for the advances made by women over at least the past sixty years. The humanities make it possible to address—critically and historically—first-order questions about value, justice, ethical practice, and the principles of human dignity that must guide policy decisions and technological development and implementation. (3)

Arts graduate education in particular has the opportunity and responsibility to advance the EDID imperative. Arts graduate students conduct original research, learn advanced skills, and go on to hold leadership roles in our governments, corporations, and society.

If arts graduate students aren't advancing the EDID imperative in Canada, who will?

Canada's Talent Imperative

Canada needs talent. Advanced talent. Talent beyond what students obtain at the undergraduate level. Every discussion of the "future economy" emphasizes the importance of human capital. This seems counterintuitive as increasing numbers of tasks are being automated. Yet in a global knowledge economy experiencing unprecedented technological innovation and disruption, the role for humans is evolving—and more critical than ever.

Canada's talent imperative is to address the opportunities and challenges that cannot be handled by automation, bots, and artificial intelligence. These are areas that require individuals who have the ability to bridge issues of globalization and cross-cultural understanding to balance environmental sustainability and societal inequality, to navigate political polarization and institutional processes, and to deal with the realities of human behaviour—to name just a few things. As Aoun writes, "a computer can model climate change, but it takes human beings to devise and enact policies to stem it" (2017, 43).

Moving forward, universities must prepare students to meet Canada's needs, in practical ways. This requires deliberate attention to the development and refinement of the career competencies and skills that society needs and expects of university graduates. As RBC writes, "Young people are entering the world of work just as it's being radically transformed, but they're stuck with the same old career model — that's Canada's quiet crisis" (2018, 25). Skills gaps are costly for Canada. According to the Conference Board of Canada, "The unrealized value of skill vacancies in the Canadian economy rose from $15 billion in 2015 to $25 billion in 2020" (FSC-CCF 2022, 4).

Lists of requisite career competencies for the current and future labour market frequently emphasize specific skills related to human interaction, analysis, digital technology, and technical skills. While there is an abundance of grey literature in this field not grounded in primary research (White et al. 2022), a Canadian study by RBC (2018) based in primary and secondary research argues that Canada's future economy needs critical thinking and management skills ("solvers"), analytical skills ("providers"), emotional intelligence and complex problem-solving skills ("facilitators"), technical skills ("technicians" and "crafters"), and basic skills ("doers").

Skills and competencies lists are constantly evolving and can get to a level of specificity that sits uncomfortably with a broad discussion of arts graduate education. Indeed, a key strength of the arts disciplines is its breadth and flexibility. For that reason, instead of speaking of talent in terms of "skills," we prefer to use the language of literacy development.

For the purposes of our discussion here and in the chapters that follow, we build on and adapt the three "new literacies" that Aoun (2017) identifies as critical for our technology-driven world: human literacy, data literacy, and technological literacy. While arts undergraduate education should introduce these literacies, arts graduate education offers the opportunity to deepen this development to produce sophisticated advanced practitioners. Let's look at each of these three literacies.

Human Literacy

Human literacy is built upon a foundation of knowledge about—no surprise here—human societies, behaviours, and institutions. In our view, it encompasses the following talents:

- *The ability to work successfully in complex and diverse teams, and across cultures.* This includes sociodemographic diversity (race, culture, gender, nationality, language, neurodiversity, ability and disability, generations), disciplinary diversity (engineers and nurses and historians, oh my!), and diversity in general personality styles. Human literacy requires cultural agility and understanding, seeing past differences to find commonalities and valuing the ability of different viewpoints to address a problem from myriad vantage points.
- *The ability to communicate effectively in multiple formats.* These include written and oral communications, of course, but also non-language-based images such as infographics, data visualization, and storyboards. Effective communication requires the ability to empathize with one's audience, the ability to inspire others, and an understanding of the power of storytelling and narrative.

- *The ability to make connections.* This involves identifying and facilitating connections between ideas, between contexts, and between people.
- *The ability to motivate and lead.* This involves working with others to drive change, regardless of one's official role in a team, and understanding and working within institutional contexts. Anders (2017) argues that the ability to "read the room" is a critical career skill; to this we would add the ability to work within and navigate processes, rules, and structures. Emotional intelligence and change management skills factor highly here.
- *The ability to act ethically and with empathy.* This involves not being an asshole. In today's world, that is a talent. Training in ethical frameworks and development of emotional intelligence are key to this ability.

Human literacy is strengthened through education that advances understanding of how and why humans think and act in the ways they do, be it individually, in groups, or in societies. This includes knowledge about cultures, group identities, histories, and values. It includes knowledge about cognition and emotion, cognitive biases, and the power of storytelling and narrative. It includes knowledge about inequality, societal biases, and institutionalized privileges and disadvantages. These topics lie at the centre of arts education. While arts graduate programs may not use our exact words as learning outcomes, through their content training and evaluation practices, arts graduate education develops the capacity of students across all of these human literacy talents. There is opportunity, as we will discuss in later chapters, to do so more effectively and explicitly.

Aoun argues that human literacy is the most important of the three new literacies: "Even in the robot age—or perhaps, especially in the robot age—what matters is other people. Human literacy equips us for the social milieu, giving us the power to communicate, engage with others, and tap into our human capacity for grace and beauty" (2017, 58–59). Human literacy encompasses key skills gaps in Canada. According to the Conference Board of Canada, "The six most highly valued skill vacancies are active listening, critical thinking, reading comprehension, speaking, monitoring, and coordination. Vacancies related to each of these skills currently cost the Canadian economy $1 billion or more annually in unrealized value owing to unfilled job vacancies" (FSC-CCF 2022, 4).

Simply put, human literacy is the key area in which arts graduate education is positioned to significantly contribute to Canadian talent capacity.

Data Literacy

Aoun defines data literacy as "the capacity to understand and utilize Big Data through analysis" (2017, 57). However, we suggest a broader understanding of data literacy that includes but goes beyond large-scale quantitative data to encompass qualitative data and the use of mixed methods and multi-methods approaches. It is also different from technological literacy, described below. Data literacy, in our view, encompasses the following talents:

- *The ability to use data analysis software tools.* This includes statistical programs and qualitative analysis programs and the ability to learn and use new analytical software tools as they emerge.
- *The ability to gain insight from data.* This includes asking the right questions of data, separating "signal from noise" within the data, and making connections within and among data sources. In Aoun's words, "by understanding both interpretation and context, data literacy enables us to find meaning in the overwhelming flood of information pouring from our devices" (2017, 57). Anders writes, "Practically every organization is wrestling with the information age's awkward disparity: too much data, not enough clarity. It takes training to feel at home with mountains of incomplete, haphazardly organized information, to be confident you can distill everything down to a few powerful insights" (2017, 37). And RBC writes: "Being able to draw inferences, make unexpected connections and identify overarching trends is a competitive edge. In the 21st century...you can't get anywhere without analytics" (2018, 26).
- *The ability to assess data sources critically.* This includes selecting the proper data sources to answer questions; assessing measures

and samples for bias, incompleteness, and error; and placing data sources in proper context. We agree with Aoun that "the purpose of data literacy...is to give us the tools to read the digital record and also to *understand when we ought to look elsewhere*" (2017, 58; emphasis added).

"Data" has traditionally been a tricky concept in the arts, often relegated to the quantitative side of social science, such as survey research. The digital humanities have expanded the boundaries and methodological tools of humanities disciplines to incorporate technology and large-scale data into their inquiries, and Big Data in particular holds exciting possibilities for the use of very large bodies of information and tools of analysis (Schiuma and Carlucci 2018).

But, as signalled above, we argue for a broader expansion that emphasizes qualitative as much as quantitative data, and both smaller and capital-B Big Data. This captures what is actually happening across the board in arts graduate education, and the key skills that students are, or should be, acquiring. The social science disciplines share an emphasis on using data and analysis to answer questions, whether through quantitative data literacy (e.g., economics, psychology), qualitative data literacy (e.g., anthropology), or both (e.g., political science, sociology). The humanities may place more emphasis on analyzing singular items of information, but while scholars still visit dusty libraries and archives, they may be collecting data to be analyzed by advanced software, and libraries and archives themselves are being rapidly digitized for much greater access and analytic opportunities. Furthermore, it is probably the humanities more than any other field that most critically reflects on the use of data and its normative implications.

"Data literacy" thus emphasizes both the direct use of data but also reflections on the use of data, and this is where the arts disciplines have the greatest value. As Carlucci, Schiuma, and Santarsiero argue, "Working with any kind of data entails some drawbacks such as privacy and trust, as well as intellectual property and copyright" (2018, 23). And Milligan and Warren write: "The ever-expanding world of digital tools requires the development of a critical infrastructure through which to find, process, and analyze these sources....We thus need to be increasingly rigorous in questioning, interrogating, and challenging the tools that underlie our research" (2018, 70). This goes beyond the exciting but specialized world of Big Data to encompass much of what the arts disciplines do on an everyday basis: generate and collect data, analyze it, and reflect critically on its use.

Thinking about data literacy in this broad frame helps us to understand the value to students and their future employers of the ability to work with data, broadly defined. This should ideally involve comfort and familiarity with data-analyzing technologies, as we explore below with technological literacy. But data literacy is also the ability to separate signals from noise, and to critically reflect on how and why data are used. This bigger picture is essential. As Milligan and Warren write, "researchers have to be nimble in their thinking and create their solution instead of finding a tool that is the solution. Tools become outdated and dramatically change and algorithms shift. An understanding of underlying principles becomes more important" (2018, 71). Again, arts can have the edge here. To conclude, data literacy is an area in which arts graduate education is positioned to significantly contribute to the Canadian talent imperative.

Technological Literacy

Technological literacy is defined by Aoun as "knowledge of mathematics, coding, and basic engineering principles" (2017, 55). This does not mean that everyone needs to be engaged in software programming or building robots, but rather that people have "a grounding in coding and engineering principles, so they know how their machines tick" (Aoun 2017, xix).

Technological literacy, in our view, encompasses a number of talents:

- *The ability to complete basic coding and programming tasks.* This includes working in syntax and applying logic to create solutions. RBC writes, "Few young Canadians will need the type of coding proficiency required to work in Silicon Valley, but most will need a healthy dose of digital fluency and comprehension" (2018, 21).
- *The ability to apply numeracy skills.* To quote RBC again: "Like it or not, numbers are here to stay...the ability to factor quantitative and

spatial information into your decision-making...adds up to career success" (2018, 21).
- *The ability to employ design thinking.* This includes needs assessment and problem definition, creative problem solving, solution testing, and project management.
- *The ability to identify areas for process improvements.* This includes opportunities for automation and efficiencies.

Technological literacy might not seem like a natural space for arts graduate education—at least not yet. But it is useful to consider the potential for the arts to "[push] students to explore the social dimensions of our machines, including the ethical implications of technological change" (Aoun 2017, 106). As with data literacy, the use of technology itself is an important area of reflection, but it is strongest when the analyst has their own good grasp of the technology in question. It is also valuable to consider how technological skills might enable arts graduate students and scholars to address long-standing questions of disciplinary interest. The use of digital archives and network analysis tools, for example, may present new approaches that build students' technological literacy.

The Conference Board of Canada writes, "One notable skill for which the value of vacancies is low is programming. This may be surprising given that digital skills are frequently cited as being in short supply. This can be explained by the fact that relatively fewer jobs require detailed knowledge of programming languages or a strong background in computer sciences" (FSC-CCF 2022, 7). However, it is the combination of technological literacy with human and data literacy that is most effective, and arts graduate education is powerfully positioned to play a stronger role here. To again quote the Conference Board of Canada, "combining skills creates synergies...the value of an individual skill may be conditional on the presence of complementary skills" (FSC-CCF 2022, 8). Human literacy is paramount, and data and technological literacy are essential companions.

Bringing the Imperatives Together

The three public good imperatives are interrelated. Wicked problems affect groups differently, depending on their social location, so their solutions must take into account questions of equity, diversity, inclusion, and decolonization. Canada's colonial legacy is, in itself, a wicked problem. Understanding how to approach and address wicked problems requires talent—individuals trained in human literacy, as well as individuals trained in data and technological literacy. And an approach to talent development that is not inclusive will be limited in its utility.

Arts graduate education has the potential to deliver on all three public good imperatives. We can reimagine our programs to focus research on wicked problems and their untidy solutions. We can challenge our students to see the connection between their understanding of humanity and their potential to help develop real-world solutions to wicked problems. We can prepare them to work across cultures and disciplines. We can make our programs stronger by ensuring they recruit from broader pools, create an inclusive environment, and produce a diverse cohort of graduates. Arts graduate education can, and in many important ways already does, train students to be advanced knowledge workers in all three of the "new" literacies.

To be clear, we are not suggesting that all arts graduate programs need to do all of these things. We are not arguing for English MA programs that teach students to use coding to connect analyses of Faulkner to anti-racist harm reduction strategies in rural Manitoba. (But that would be very cool, wouldn't it?) But we *are* asserting that most, if not all, arts graduate programs can do some or even many of these things, and that doing so more deliberately would be to Canada's benefit.

In this chapter, we have laid out the exciting potential of arts graduate education to serve the public good, and the three imperatives of how and why it must do so. In the next chapter, we outline the present state of arts graduate education and why it is not serving current students well. Together these build the case for change.

Canada's Arts Graduate Education Problem

We started For the Public Good: Reimagining Arts Graduate Programs in Canadian Universities by arguing that universities play an important role in advancing Canada's public good. In chapter 2, we argued that this public good at present consists of three imperatives: the wicked problems imperative, the EDID imperative, and the talent imperative. And we argued that, with some reimagination, arts graduate education has a considerable opportunity to move Canada forward on all three imperatives. The reimagined arts graduate education can be seen as being for and in the public good.

We see some big achievable dreams here. What's in it for Canada is hopefully clear: better solutions to our wicked problems, advancement on issues of inclusion and reconciliation, and a more robust supply of the highly qualified personnel that Canada's economy requires.

But what's in it for the arts and for universities? Simply put, why should arts faculty, graduate committees, department chairs, and deans go through the effort to reimagine graduate education to realize this potential? Why should graduate deans, provosts, and university staff support them in these efforts? And why should university boards, national granting councils, and policymakers demand that they make these efforts and make their own changes to facilitate success?

Reimagining arts graduate education requires a lot of work and change, mostly but not exclusively within universities. Change is difficult in most contexts, and particularly so in large and complex institutions such as universities. Our personal experiences as university faculty members, leaders, and senior leaders mean that we deeply understand the challenges that come with the aspiration to align arts graduate education with Canada's public good.

So why should universities bother? The answer is that universities have a major problem of their own to fix. Quite simply, Canada's arts graduate students are not thriving.

If arts graduate programs were flourishing, we would see rising demands for admission, good times to completion, high completion rates, robust levels of student satisfaction, and strong student mental health. Post-graduation employment rates would be high, reflecting a general recognition of the value placed on graduates of these programs.

Instead, we find flagging demand for some programs. Long-standing problems—notably lengthy times to completion and relatively low completion rates—are made more pressing by the emerging evidence of the difficulties some graduates face when they transition to the workforce. Students' mental health is getting worse, and their satisfaction with their programs declines the longer they're enrolled.

If all was well, we wouldn't be writing this book.

Once again, we want to stress that there is much to be celebrated in the dedicated mentorship many faculty members offer arts graduate students and in those students' achievements and contributions to knowledge. Our point is not to denigrate those acheivements and contributions, but rather to assert that program reforms could help to harness this dedication and students' talents more effectively, lessening some of the stresses and frustrations both students and faculty experience.

In this chapter, we lay out the problem that needs to be solved. By the chapter's end, we hope to have convinced you that if Canada's universities, arts graduate programs, and arts faculty members are going to meet their promises to arts graduate students, we can't keep doing what we're currently doing.

Arts Graduate Student Data: Student Experience and Outcomes

Let's set aside the public good idea for a moment. Arts departments often promote their graduate programs in terms of the private benefits to individual students. Completing an arts graduate degree allows students to deepen their knowledge and understanding in an area of interest. Program websites often suggest, explicitly or implicitly, that students will benefit from personal growth and satisfaction. Program materials may state outright that arts graduate education will help students further their careers, though the level of specificity will vary.

In recruiting arts graduate students, departments are inviting individuals to devote years of their lives and forgo earning potential, and often assume student debt, for the pursuit of advanced study. Whether a student is motivated by a passion for the subject or a desire to launch a career, or both, an arts graduate education is presented to them as a private good.

So, before we move into later chapters outlining our vision of advancing arts graduate education for the public good, let's first assess whether arts graduate students are currently receiving the benefits they have already been promised, implicitly or explicitly. Are students thriving in their programs? Are students thriving after their programs?

Unfortunately, despite the tens of thousands of students entering Canada's many arts graduate programs every year, and a mass of graduates, we have surprisingly little systematic data either from institutions or government on how arts graduate students are doing in their programs and afterward. This itself is a big deficiency. We are making promises to students and yet often cannot reliably prove their fulfillment or track our performance. But the data we do have in Canada is not encouraging. These data strongly suggest that the system of arts graduate education does not live up to its private good promise.

Completion Rates and Time to Completion

If all were well in arts graduate education, most of the students who started a degree would complete it. And they would finish in roughly the time that the degree was supposed to take—one or two years for an MA, and four or five years for a PhD. These are the typical program lengths advertised on arts graduate program websites and the typical lengths of scholarships and teaching and research assistant funding available within Canadian arts graduate programs.

We suffer from a striking lack of data about what happens after a graduate student enrolls in an arts master's or doctoral program at a Canadian university. Although universities track this data, most do not make it public.

Highly dated information from a 2003 Canadian Association for Graduate Studies (CAGS) study reported on outcomes for a cohort of students admitted to Canadian universities in 1992. It found that about seven in ten master's students in the humanities and social sciences completed their degree, and only about half of doctoral students. While master's completion rates were only slightly lower for arts students than those in other disciplines, there were substantial differences at the doctoral level, with arts PhD students being much less likely to complete their degree. For those students who did finish, times to completion were longer in the arts disciplines. On average, arts PhD students were registered for sixteen semesters before graduating, as compared to fourteen semesters for those in the physical and life sciences (CAGS 2003).

While a lot can change in two decades, more recent data give reason to believe that the patterns from the CAGS study are still roughly accurate. For instance, the University of British Columbia (UBC) reports its completion rates and times to completion publicly (a best practice that we encourage all universities to adopt). At the time of writing, the UBC website (2022a) indicates a 75 percent completion rate for students in its PhD program in English, with a mean time to completion of 6.27 years. For political science, the completion rate is reported to be 77 percent, and average time to completion is 6.88 years (UBC 2022b). For economics, 60 percent of students graduate, and the mean time to completion is 6.18 years (UBC 2022c). Looking beyond a single institution to a single discipline, the Canadian Historical Association (CHA) completed a study of history doctorates between 2016 and 2022 and found that the mean time to completion was 6 years and 7 months (2022, 9–10).

If the available data are reflective of broader patterns, the time to completion data present at least two causes for concern at the doctoral level:

- *Labour market opportunity costs.* A student who takes two or three years to complete a master's degree, and then another five or six to complete a PhD has devoted almost a full decade to graduate education. For some students, this is a decade well spent: they emerge with knowledge and skills that prepare them for meaningful work in the future, and they have been financially supported while contributing to knowledge through their research. For others, as we will discuss further, it involves an increasingly miserable experience that postpones launching a career and mires them in a sense of unfulfilled ambition. They have sacrificed years of their lives, often very formative years, for little benefit.
- *Program promises versus reality.* Most Canadian arts doctoral programs offer funding to students for four years, or five at the outside. Many universities set the maximum time for completion of a PhD at six years, so the many students who extend beyond that time have to apply for an extension to their program. Simply put, there is something wrong with a degree structure that is claimed to be possible to complete in four years, but that takes more than six. (Master's completion times on their own are less concerning; it appears that most MA students finish within two years, since their program requirements are shorter and more fixed, and they do not fall into the yawning abyss of a doctoral dissertation.)

What about the completion rate data? Data here are very limited. One study of a single university's history program found that 18 percent of doctoral students discontinue (Smith-Norris and Hanson 2018), but these numbers may be low. It is unrealistic to assume that completion rates need to be 100 percent. Some students may depart programs for even better opportunities; their studies may lead directly into relevant career work such as co-ops and internships that set them up for success, but mean less time for their programs; many will start a family or otherwise have more important personal priorities that slow their academic progress; and, of course, some simply don't meet program standards and must withdraw. (These exceptions may be one reason why universities are reluctant to share completion data, or do so with heavy conditional explanations.) But even all those exceptions still leave a significant margin of students. If one-quarter to 40 percent of arts graduate students are not completing their program, it should cause us to ask, why is that the case and what are the costs to students, universities, and society?

At an individual level, we can celebrate when a student decides a program is not for them and withdraws from a program ill-suited to their talents, interests, or aspirations. This is particularly true when the student makes that decision relatively early in their program. But in practice, some exits from PhD programs come after five or more years. Such departures represent a great personal cost for students. As the CHA writes, "some students may start a Ph.D. program and withdraw within a year or two, realizing that the program was not for them. More concerning is slow attrition—students who withdraw years after completing all program requirements except the dissertation. These students have sacrificed many years of their lives in studying without finishing their degrees" (2022, 7). While the decision to leave a PhD program may well be a great relief, and may indeed lead to better things, it still comes with the stigma of "quitting" or "giving up," and there are almost certainly associated mental health costs. MA dropouts are less costly, but they still represent lost time and effort, on the part of both students and institutions.

Time a student spends working toward a degree is time not spent doing something else, and this brings us back to the public as well as private good. The student bears the opportunity cost of education, while the economy bears the opportunity cost of time absent from the workforce. Lengthy times to completion are costly to students and to society. And degrees abandoned are fiscally costly both to the student and to the university, and emotionally costly to students.

If we are going to meet our promise to students, we can't keep doing what we're currently doing.

Student Well-Being

One of the most important and growing issues in higher education is attention to the mental health of students. There is a growing body of evidence about the mental health toll of graduate education in humanities and social science disciplines. A survey of over 60,000 American undergraduate and graduate students found that humanities and fine arts graduate students were more likely than their peers to experience mental health challenges and seek treatment for them (Ketchen Lipson et al. 2015). A survey of PhD students in economics departments in the United States used clinically validated surveys to measure mental health status. It found that:

> 18% of graduate students experience moderate or severe symptoms of depression and anxiety—more than three times the population average—and 11% report suicidal ideation in a two-week period. The average PhD student reports greater feelings of loneliness than does the average retired American. Only 26% of Economics students report feeling that their work is useful always or most of the time, compared with 70% of Economics faculty and 63% of the working age population. Depression and symptoms of anxiety increase with time in the program: 25% of students in years 5+ of their programs experience moderate or severe symptoms of depression or anxiety compared with 14.5% of first-year students. (Barreira, Basilico, and Bolotnyy 2018, 1)

While there will be moments of stress or anxiety when completing a demanding academic program, this should not be a permanent condition experienced by students. And unfortunately, mental health challenges are found within all programs and at all levels across the university.

But we are particularly concerned about arts graduate students because many of their stress and mental health challenges follow directly from the structure of their program. We are concerned about the extent to which stress is unintentionally built right into the current design of arts graduate programs. Their largely unguided "on your own" nature—particularly once PhD students get to the dissertation writing stage—and uncertain career outcomes, especially related to the extremely competitive academic job market, are a recipe for mental unwellness. For some arts graduate students, these structural stresses are compounded by other exacerbating factors related to their program, such as toxic supervisors, financial insecurity, and student debt. Simply put, the mental health stresses of the graduate student experience—and particularly the PhD experience—are disproportionately experienced by arts students.

It's further concerning when mental health challenges increase over time in programs, as the research focused on PhD students in economics demonstrates. This is not a case of "it gets better." For many arts graduate students, uncertainty about direction, struggles with motivation, and unexpected research challenges result in lengthy periods of limited productivity, extending the process by months or years and ultimately reinforcing the cycle of discouragement. As funding runs out, the need to find employment solely for income then also stretches further their time in the program, causing them to repeat the cycle and/or resulting in a decision to withdraw entirely.

Although mental health challenges can be experienced by any student working on a graduate degree, we suspect that students from equity-deserving groups are more likely to face mental health challenges. As Ayres observes, writing about the experiences of students from racialized groups, "Lack of role models, and people to confide in who understand what you are going through can further exacerbate this. Further, exposure to both racism and microaggressions can be incredibly harmful, consolidating impostor feelings and feelings of not belonging" (2022, 107–108). Versions of the same patterns apply to Indigenous students, international students, women, LGBTQ2S+ students, neurodiverse students, and students with disabilities. And when these sources of identity intersect, the strains on mental health can be all the greater.

This should be a wakeup call for all arts faculty members. Arts graduate students are not doing well. The human cost of how we are currently offering graduate education in the arts disciplines is far too high.

Student Funding

In universities offering both MA and PhD programs, funding packages tend to be more generous for PhD students than master's students. Some universities have developed funding policies that guarantee a minimum annual stipend for PhD students, but not for master's students. For example, in 2021, UBC established a policy that requires all PhD students receive at least $22,000 per year for the first four years of their degree (UBC n.d.-a).

Due to the length of PhD programs, there is greater concern about the funding packages for PhD students. There is often a misalignment between the duration of funding packages and average time to completion, with packages of four to five years being the norm for PhD students and time to completion being one, two, or more years longer. There can also be significant gaps between the size of funding packages and cost of living, although there are many students who are substantially funded through the first four years of their degree—for instance, the University of Toronto (n.d.) reports that the actual net income for domestic PhD students in their first four years in humanities and social science programs in 2020/21 was in excess of $30,000.

Often, however, the duration and amounts of funding leave many PhD students scrambling to pay rent and grocery bills through sessional teaching, teaching and research assistant positions, and employment outside of academia. The CHA's study of history doctorate programs in Canada found that university funding packages range from two to six years in length and from $0 to $27,000 in value. The CHA estimates that the most generous funding package is almost $9,000 below the cost of living (2022, 24). And, the CHA notes, international students in most provinces must pay additional costs for private medical insurance and at some institutions pay higher tuition rates.

Beyond university funding, students can apply for SSHRC funding, provincial funding (when available in their province), and other random scholarship options. Some of these funding opportunities are not available to international students, and most are highly competitive. For instance, in 2021, the success rate for SSHRC doctoral scholarships and Canada Graduate Scholarships was 43 percent, although in reality the proportion is much lower as universities are limited in the number of applications they are permitted to submit (SSHRC 2022a).

The CHA raises concerns about how funding differences impact students' opportunities for success in their program:

> Three classes of PhD students emerge, with important implications on income and workload: (a) those who hold a CGS or Vanier scholarship. They earn a livable wage through scholarship income alone and can forgo TA work to get on with their research and writing; (b) those who receive a lower-value federal or provincial grant. They can approach a livable wage if they continue to supplement their scholarship income with TA work, even if that might detract from research time and travel; and (c) those who have not (or who have not yet) won an external scholarship. They earn less than a livable wage, all while their income is significantly tied to TA work which takes away from research—if students can even afford to travel for research. (2022, 30)

The CHA further writes,

> To complete their studies, PhD students require adequate funding. If students are required to self-fund their History PhD programs (to whatever extent), they must either draw on their family's savings or borrow money. This is a significant barrier for many prospective students, it is particularly so for first-generation students, racialized students and Indigenous students, who are least likely to have the family financial resources to support their studies. Given the dire need to diversify our profession, the lack of funding must be considered a serious equity issue. (2022, 28)

This is a concern for all arts programs.

Student Debt

Not surprisingly given the limited funding packages available to them, many of Canada's arts graduate students are graduating with high levels of debt. The most recent Statistics Canada data found that in 2015, 43 percent of humanities master's students and 51 percent of "social and behavioural science and law" master's students graduated with student debt (median debts, respectively, were $11,638 and $19,750). At the doctoral level, 51 percent of humanities and 50 percent of social and behavioural science and law students graduated with debt (with median debts of $25,431 and $27,689, respectively) (Galarneau and Gibson 2020, 4).

The arts doctoral debt levels stand in contrast to the national average. In reference to Canadian graduate students as a whole, Galarneau and Gibson write, "The proportion of doctorate degree holders with student debt also decreased steadily between 2000 and 2015, from 45 percent of those who graduated in 2000 to 36 percent of those who graduated in 2015. This relatively low proportion of graduates with student debt may be linked to the fact that many doctorate students receive funding through scholarships, fellowships, awards or prizes, or work as research or teaching assistants" (2020, 2–3). PhD debt is thus particularly an arts problem, and it goes against the trend in other disciplines.

Career Readiness

While education has value in itself and some pursue graduate degrees primarily in a quest for knowledge, most graduate students are motivated by a desire to further their careers, inside or outside the academy. Since career outcomes are less readily defined in the arts disciplines, professional development that allows students to identify and hone the skills that will allow them to build a successful and meaningful career is important. This is particularly true for doctoral students, as many will be in their thirties (or older) by the time they enter or re-enter the non-academic labour force.

FIGURE 3.1 **Reason for Pursuing a Degree**

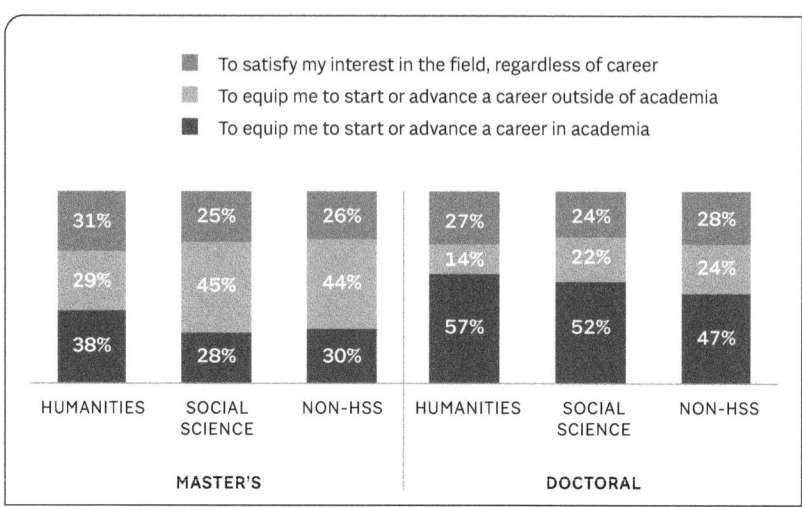

Source: Calculated from the *Canadian Graduate and Professional Student Survey: 2019 Summary Report* (see CRIEVAT 2019). Question wording: "What was your primary reason for enrolling in your program?"

Do arts graduate students believe their program is preparing them for their career? To gain some understanding of this, we analyzed data from the 2019 Canadian Graduate and Professional Student Survey (CGPSS; CRIEVAT 2019), a regular national survey of Canadian graduate students conducted once every three years by participating universities. The CGPSS survey instrument is copyrighted by the U15—Group of Canadian Research Universities Data Exchange—and the Canadian Association for Graduate Studies (CAGS) acts as a trustee of the anonymized data set. The 2019 CGPSS survey, conducted between January 9 and May 8, 2019, can be found at CAGS (2023). Survey invitations were sent to the full universe of eligible students, and a total of 63,077 responses was received (see CRIEVAT 2019 for the full details, to which we thank CAGS for giving us access).

Again, the data are not terribly encouraging. They demonstrate that the majority of doctoral students, and a non-trivial proportion of master's students, are pursuing their degree to equip them to start or advance a career in academia. This is particularly true in the humanities

FIGURE 3.2 **Arts Master's Students' Evaluations of Career Preparation (Percent Evaluating as "Good" or "Excellent").**

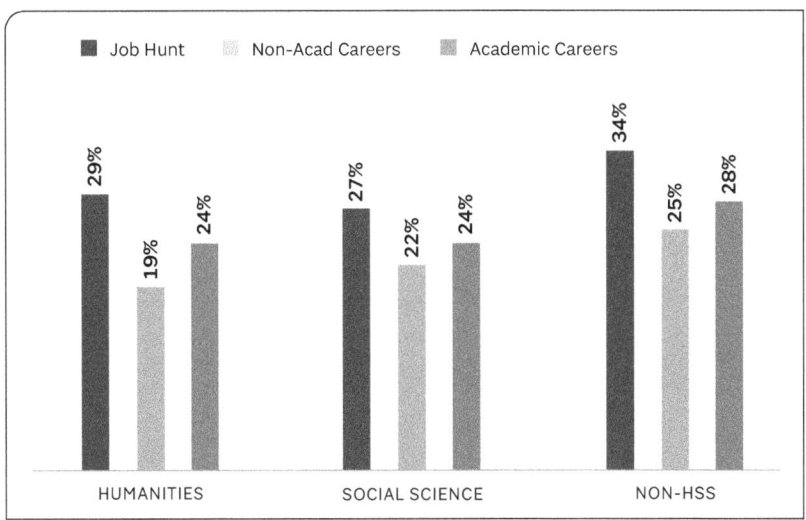

Source: Calculated from the 2019 *Canadian Graduate and Professional Student Survey* (CRIEVAT 2019). Question wording: "How would you rate the quality of the support and training you received in these areas?" Job Hunt: "Advice/workshops/tools on job searching (CV prep, interview skills, etc.)"; Non-Academic Careers: "Advice/workshops/tools on career options outside academia"; Academic Careers: "Advice/workshops/tools on career options inside academia."

disciplines, as Figure 3.1 shows. This strong focus on an academic career is a cause for concern, given the mismatch between the number of PhD graduates and the academic jobs available in most disciplines.

For arts master's students, less than one-third surveyed considered that the training and support they received around their eventual job search was of "good" or "excellent" quality (see Figure 3.2). Less than one-quarter considered the support and preparation they received for either non-academic or academic careers to be of high quality. It is noteworthy that students' satisfaction with the preparation for academic careers was slightly higher than for non-academic careers. This is particularly striking when we consider that most master's students do not go on to do a PhD, much less pursue an academic career.

Although they spend more time in their graduate program, survey results show that arts doctoral students are even less positive

FIGURE 3.3 **Arts Doctoral Students' Evaluations of Career Preparation (Percent Evaluating as "Good" or "Excellent").**

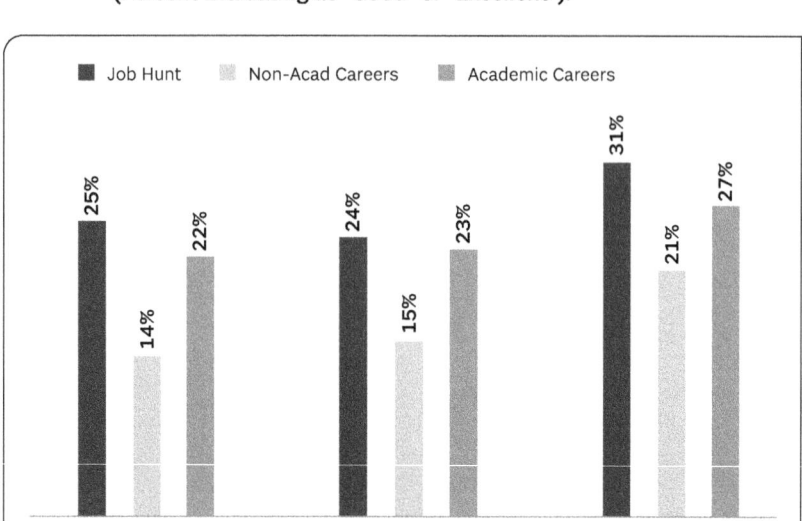

Source: Calculated from the *Canadian Graduate and Professional Student Survey: 2019 Summary Report* (see CRIEVAT 2019). Question wording: "How would you rate the quality of the support and training you received in these areas?" Job Hunt: "Advice/workshops/tools on job searching (CV prep, interview skills, etc.)"; Non-Academic Careers: "Advice/workshops/tools on career options outside academia"; Academic Careers: "Advice/workshops/tools on career options inside academia."

than master's students about their career preparation. Only one-quarter rated the preparation they received for their job search or for academic careers as "good" or "excellent," and that figure dropped to only 15 percent for non-academic career preparation (see Figure 3.3). When we look more closely at the data, breaking it down by the student's year in their program, we find that students nearing the end of their program (in year four and beyond) were ten percentage points less likely to rate either academic or non-academic career preparation as good or excellent.

Arts doctoral students' evaluations of the preparation they have been offered to develop specific skills valuable in academic (and some other) careers were more positive. Figure 3.4 shows that over 40 percent offered a positive evaluation of their preparation for teaching, and over 30 percent offered a positive evaluation of their preparation to meet

FIGURE 3.4 **Arts Doctoral Students' Evaluations of Academic Career Preparation (Percent Evaluating as "Good" or "Excellent").**

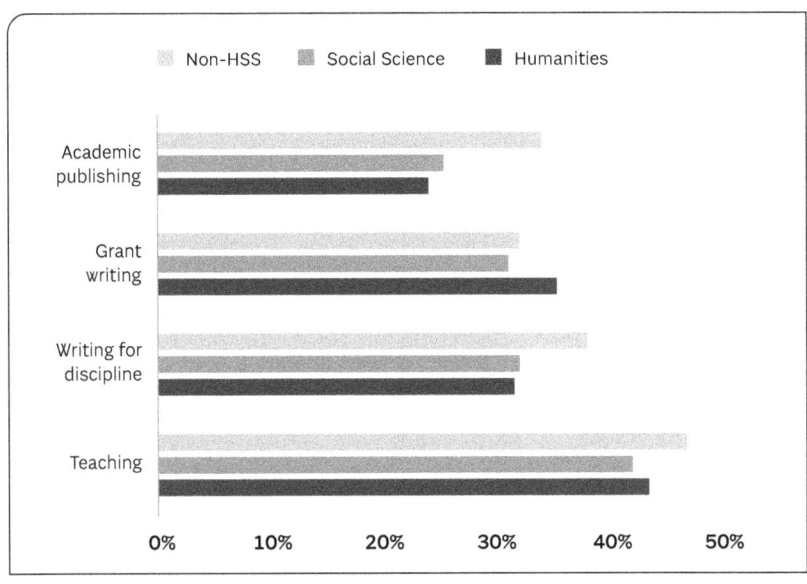

Source: Calculated from the *Canadian Graduate and Professional Student Survey: 2019 Summary Report* (see CRIEVAT 2019). Question wording: "How would you rate the quality of the support and training you received in these areas?" Academic publishing: "Advice/workshops/tools on publishing your work"; Grant writing: "Advice/workshops/tools on writing grant proposals"; Writing for discipline: "Advice/workshops/tools on standards for academic writing in your field"; Teaching: "Courses, workshops, or orientation on teaching."

standards for writing in their discipline and for grant writing. While these are more positive results, it is interesting to note that doctoral students in other disciplines were more positive than arts graduate students in almost all of their evaluations.

The bottom line is that arts PhD programs are falling short in preparing their students for their future career. This signals an enormous problem. Students are spending years of their lives in arts graduate programs but are not being offered good preparation for their subsequent careers, academic or otherwise. This is not an arts-only problem, but it is still an arts problem.

Career Outcomes

We have seen that arts graduate students do not feel confident in their preparation for careers. But what are their actual career outcomes? Again, the data are discouraging.

We will start with Statistics Canada data examining the employment status of 2015 graduates three years after graduation, in 2018 (Reid, Chen, and Guertin 2020). These data show that for both humanities and social science graduates (note that the grouping includes law), the rates of permanent employment for students three years after graduation decrease with educational level (see Figure 3.5).

We will give you a moment to let that sink in.

How do arts graduates compare with those in other disciplines in terms of employment post-graduation? Well, the national rates for 2018 (which include the arts) are 86 percent for those with a bachelor's degree, 86 percent with a master's, and 63 percent with a PhD. Thus, the arts are performing fine at the bachelor's level, are below average (and perhaps pulling down the average) at the master's level, and are a bit split at the doctoral level. PhD employment is complicated by a pattern of academic precarity in the form of sessional teaching, limited-term appointments, and postdoctoral fellowships. Reid, Chen, and Guertin (2020) report that in 2018, three years after graduation, 23 percent of national doctoral graduates across all disciplines were working in a postdoctoral role; when these individuals were removed from the analysis, 76 percent of national doctoral graduates reported being in permanent employment. Even if we assume that the arts doctoral graduates not working in a postdoctoral role have permanent employment at exactly the national rate—a bold assumption, perhaps, but fair enough to make our point—the pattern of lower employment rates as the level of education increases holds.

The Statistics Canada data do provide a measure of good news: arts graduation education does increase a graduate's likelihood of working in a career related to their field of study (see Figure 3.6). Again, the numbers for holders of doctorates may reflect precarious academic employment. Finally, we note that for humanities graduates in particular, feeling overqualified for one's job increases with education, with 41 percent of humanities PhD graduates surveyed feeling overqualified—a full

FIGURE 3.5 **Proportion of Graduates of 2015 Working in Permanent Jobs in 2018.**

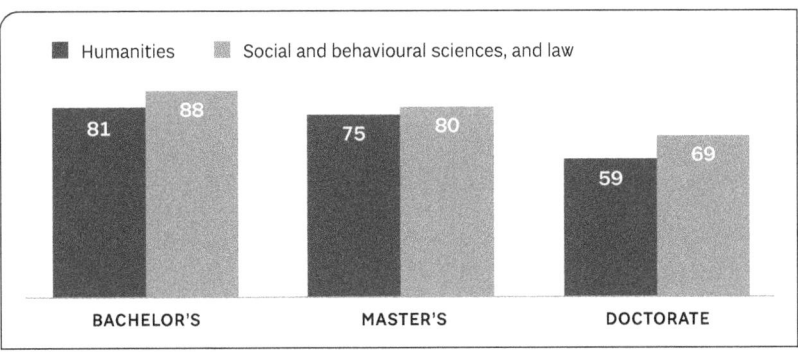

Source: Adapted from *Labour Market Outcomes of Postsecondary Graduates, Class of 2015* (Reid, Chen, and Guertin 2020).

FIGURE 3.6 **Proportion of 2015 Graduates Who Reported Working in a Job or Business Related to Their Field of Study in 2018.**

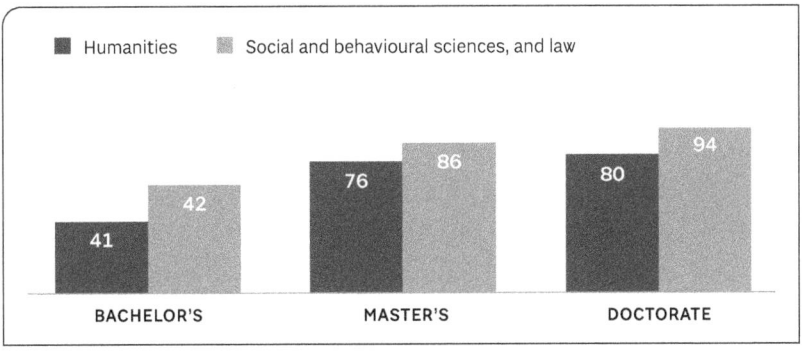

Source: Adapted from *Labour Market Outcomes of Postsecondary Graduates, Class of 2015* (Reid, Chen, and Guertin 2020).

seventeen percentage points above the national average of 24 percent, and considerably higher than any other individual disciplinary category (see Figure 3.7).

FIGURE 3.7 **Proportion of 2015 Graduates Who Felt Overqualified for Their Job in 2018.**

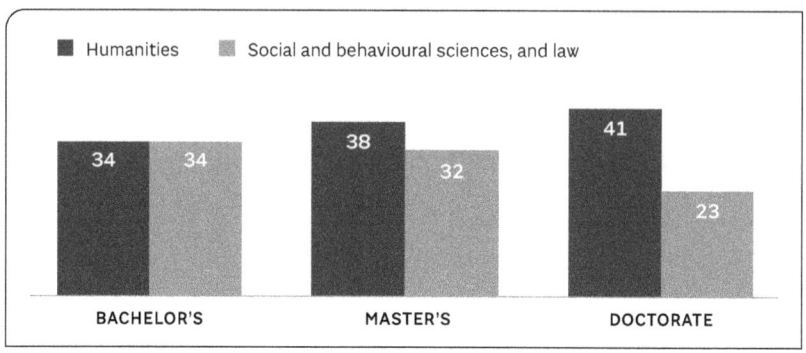

Source: Adapted from *Labour Market Outcomes of Postsecondary Graduates, Class of 2015* (Reid, Chen, and Guertin 2020).

Let's now focus on arts PhD students and their *academic* employment outcomes. From our analysis of the Statistics Canada data, we know that over half of PhD students in humanities and social science disciplines report being motivated to pursue an academic career. And as we just said, to the extent that they have received career mentorship during their program, it is likely to have been focused on the academic career route. So how many actually get permanent academic jobs?

The best available data on career outcomes for PhD graduates tells us that, at best, just over one-third of newly-minted PhDs will end up in a tenure-stream academic job within five years of graduation. Both the University of Toronto and UBC have undertaken comprehensive analyses of where their PhD graduates are employed. Toronto's 10,000 PhD project went looking for all its PhD graduates between 2000 and 2015, and located over 85 percent of them (Reithmeier et al. 2019). For both humanities and social science PhDs, 36 percent of the located graduates were employed as a tenure-track professor (Reithmeier et al. 2019). UBC's PhD career outcomes study, which covered 2005–2013, located 91 percent of its graduates (UBC Graduate and Postdoctoral Studies 2017). It reports that 50 percent of its arts PhD graduates were working in higher education; of those, 48 percent were in a research faculty position, 17 percent were in a teaching faculty position, and the remaining 35 percent were working in another higher education role. Thus, 32.5 percent of UBC's total arts PhD graduates were in a faculty position at the time of the study, with 17.5 percent working in another position—many in postsecondary education.

The University of Toronto and UBC PhD outcomes data showing roughly one-third of arts PhD graduates in a tenure-stream position likely represent the high end of arts PhD faculty placement rates, as they are two of Canada's top universities, ranked very highly internationally. For other institutions, the number is probably lower. To provide a different perspective that includes a variety of institutions, the 2022 CHA study provides discipline-wide data. It found that between 2016–17 and 2021–22, Canadian universities posted 87 tenure-steam history positions. In the same time period, Canada had 562 history PhD graduates. As of fall 2022, 58 of the 562 (10 percent) held a tenure-stream academic appointment (CHA 2022).

The bottom line is that the vast majority (somewhere between 67 and 90 percent) of Canada's arts PhD graduates are not ending up in a tenure-stream position. This should not be a surprise to anyone who has sat on a humanities or social sciences hiring committee. Except for a few specialized areas, it is common for an academic job advertisement to receive dozens or even hundreds of applicants, each holding a shiny new (or not-so-new) PhD. Consequently, even if its exact extent is unclear, the general problem of output greatly exceeding demand is clear.

Many arts PhDs do end up working in higher education in other roles. In the University of Toronto study (Reithmeier et al. 2019), 32 percent of found humanities PhDs and 24 percent of found social science PhDs were employed in postsecondary education, but were not on the tenure track; as noted above, UBC arts PhDs had a rate of 17.5 percent. Careers for PhDs in higher education beyond the professoriate include sessional lecturers (the precarious workforce of academia), limited-term positions, postdoctoral fellowships, and so-called "alt-ac" positions in student affairs, research services, and the like.

The contingent teaching provided by PhDs as sessional lecturers or in limited-term positions resolves university teaching needs at a low cost for programs, but at a high cost for individuals. Temporary teaching work can start out as a good thing; the opportunity to teach a course as a sessional instructor or in a limited-term appointment gives recent PhD graduates an opportunity to gain teaching experience. But this often turns into long-term contingent work, at low pay—less than $10,000 to teach a 12-week course at most institutions—and with limited job security; even with unionized seniority rights, getting more work depends entirely on whether a program needs a temporary instructor again the next year. Many PhD graduates find themselves patching together a living teaching courses at several institutions, with no benefits and little predictability. Limited-term appointments offer more security, but not long-term security, and often require individuals to make frequent cross-country moves along with their family, possibly without coverage of moving expenses. Some recent PhD graduates find themselves unable to move because of their partner's employment in the location where they studied or for other family-related reasons. For women, who tend to be seen as default caregivers, this can be a particularly acute dilemma. As each year of precarious teaching passes, the likelihood of being hired into a tenure-stream position wanes, as few are able to maintain an active publishing program while teaching heavy loads at multiple institutions.

The employment of arts PhD graduates as long-term sessional instructors or itinerant limited-term faculty is an issue that provokes the most angst for arts PhD students and graduates, and rightly so. And while this problem is found across the disciplines, it is more prevalent in humanities and social science departments (Rajagopal 2002; UBC Graduate and Postdoctoral Studies 2017; Reithmeier et al. 2019). A cynic might argue that universities are deliberately flooding the academic job market with a growing number of PhDs in order to create a large pool of qualified personnel who enjoy limited bargaining rights, thereby decreasing their instructional costs. While we do not subscribe to this conspiracy theory, we can't deny the reality of a substantial number of PhD graduates spending years as precariously employed sessional instructors. The problem is not intentional; it is systemic. Universities sit atop a cyclical system that brings in students seeking an academic career, and then retains them as precarious workers. This is ethically troubling.

FIGURE 3.8 **Median Employment Income of 2015 Graduates Who Were Working in a Job or Business in 2017.**

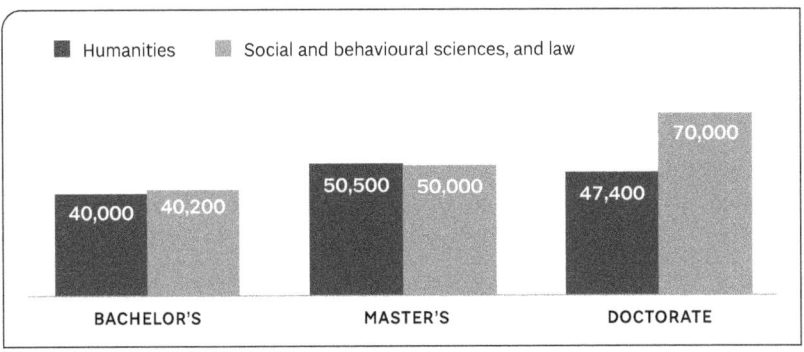

Source: Adapted from *Labour Market Outcomes of Postsecondary Graduates, Class of 2015* (Reid, Chen, and Guertin 2020).

Financial Return on Investment

Let's set aside careers themselves and talk about money. Do students receive a good financial return on investment (ROI) for their graduate programs? Stated another way, are arts graduate students earning considerably more after obtaining their graduate degrees than they would have if they had ended their studies with a BA?

Statistics Canada data provide an opportunity to consider employment earnings. Reid, Chen, and Guertin (2020) report on the median earnings in 2017 of employed 2015 graduates. The results show that both humanities and social science (and law) graduates with a master's degree enjoyed a roughly $10,000 advantage over those with a bachelor's in humanities or social science (or law). But while social science (and law) PhD graduates had a $20,000 advantage over those with a master's degree, humanities PhDs enjoyed no earnings advantage over humanities graduates with a master's, and only a $7,000 advantage over those with a humanities bachelor's degree (see Figure 3.8).

Are these income advantages a reasonable ROI for a two (or more) year master's degree? Are they reasonable for a six (or more) year PhD?

What happens to our ROI assessments when we build in consideration of graduate student debt and time outside the workforce?

Evidence from another data source provokes similar questions about the ROI of arts graduate degrees. The *Degrees of Success* study (Council of Canadian Academies 2021) analyzed data from the Educational and Labour Market Longitudinal Program, which is a collection of data on graduates of publicly funded postsecondary institutions, linked to tax information provided by the Canada Revenue Agency. The analysis found that humanities PhD graduates had an average annual income of under $50,000 in the first year after graduation, and an average income of about $70,000 five years after graduation (Council of Canadian Academies 2021, 109). Social science PhDs fared somewhat better, with an average income of about $60,000 in the first year, and $75,000 after five years. The analysis also shows outcomes for master's graduates in these disciplines. For both sets of graduates, the annual income of master's graduates was about $10,000 lower than that of PhDs, growing to a $20,000 difference for humanities graduates. Of course, averages can hide wide variability in incomes. As the report notes, "It is clear that a significant number of graduates have earnings well below the low-income measure in Canada. For example, for Ph.D. graduates in the humanities, the 10th percentile group (which represents about 300 people) earns on average $7,700 one year after graduation, growing to $19,300 by year five" (Council of Canadian Academies 2021, 110). For reference, Canada's Official Poverty Line in 2015 ranged between $32,871 and $40,777 (Canada 2018).

Again, these data should force us to pause and think about what we are doing in our arts graduate programs. While there are many graduates who achieve financial stability post-graduation, the non-trivial number who do not are a source of concern. This is particularly the case because it is often universities that benefit from these graduates' willingness to work for low wages as sessional instructors.

Student Satisfaction

How satisfied are arts graduate students with their education? Figure 3.9 shows the average score, on a scale from 1 to 5, where 1 is poor and 5 is excellent, of graduate students' satisfaction with the quality of their

FIGURE 3.9 **Graduate Student Satisfaction by Discipline and Degree (Means /5).**

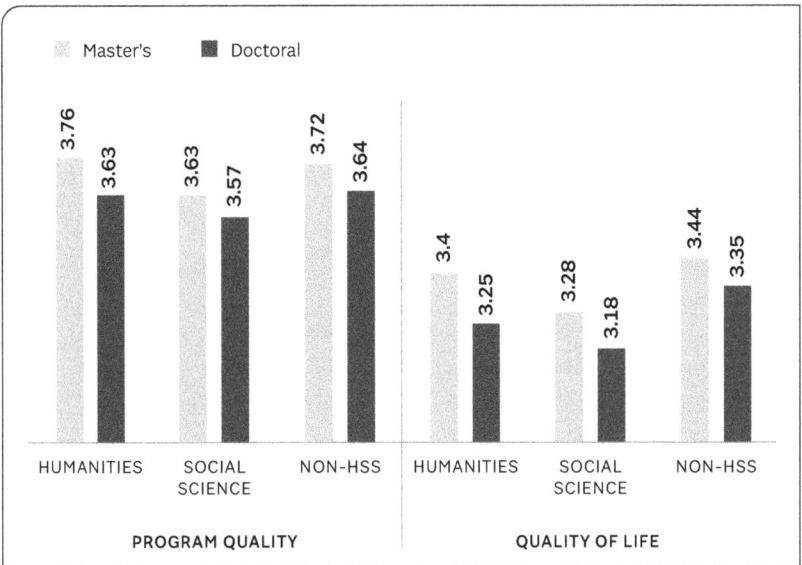

Source: Calculated from the *Canadian Graduate and Professional Student Survey: 2019 Summary Report* (see CRIEVAT 2019). Question wording: "Overall, how would you rate the quality of your graduate/professional program at this university?" and "Overall, how would you rate the quality of your student life experience at this university?"

graduate program and student life at their university, as found by the 2019 CGPSS (see also CRIEVAT 2019).

Here, the news is relatively good. When asked to provide an overall evaluation of their academic program, the majority (around 60 percent) of arts graduate students said the quality was "very good" or "excellent," and arts graduate students were no less satisfied than graduate students from other fields of study in this regard. Doctoral students were less satisfied than master's students, and when it came to quality of life, arts graduate students reported being less satisfied than did other graduate students.

When we break down patterns further, we find modest differences that give us an inkling that not all is well. Women surveyed were consistently a little less positive in their evaluations of their program and the quality of student life at their university than were men. International students were consistently more satisfied than domestic students. Among domestic students, BIPOC students were consistently a little less satisfied than non-BIPOC students. And student satisfaction was shown to decline ever so slightly each year a student was enrolled in their program. These patterns are troubling and in contradiction with most universities' goals to promote equity, diversity, and inclusion within the university.

Summary of Student Experience and Outcomes

Together, the student experience and outcomes data present many reasons for concern about the current state of arts graduate education. Times to completion are long. Program incompletions are common. Career preparedness is weak. Student well-being is strained. Debt levels are rising. Career outcomes are unclear. Return on investment is modest. Student satisfaction can be improved.

The chief counterargument to this is that graduate students are adults and informed customers. Choosing to enter graduate school is, or at least should be, a mature decision. And students self-select between academic and purely professional programs; if they just want a job, they apply to an MBA or similar program. Graduate school is ultimately an intellectual project, right? Can it ever be reduced to a utilitarian mission of jobs and money?

Perhaps. But this brings us to the question of student demand. And what we see is that students are beginning to doubt the value of an arts graduate education in ways that should concern arts faculty and leaders committed to preserving the arts disciplines in Canada.

Arts Graduate Student Data: Student Demand

The story of student demand for arts graduate programs is…complicated. It is possible to use the existing data to argue that student demand for arts graduate programs is robust, as total arts graduate program enrollments have grown over the past twenty years (see Figure 3.10; Statistics Canada 2022b). But it is important to consider some nuances to this interpretation.

FIGURE 3.10 **Total Enrollments in Arts Graduate Programs, 1992–93 to 2019–20.**

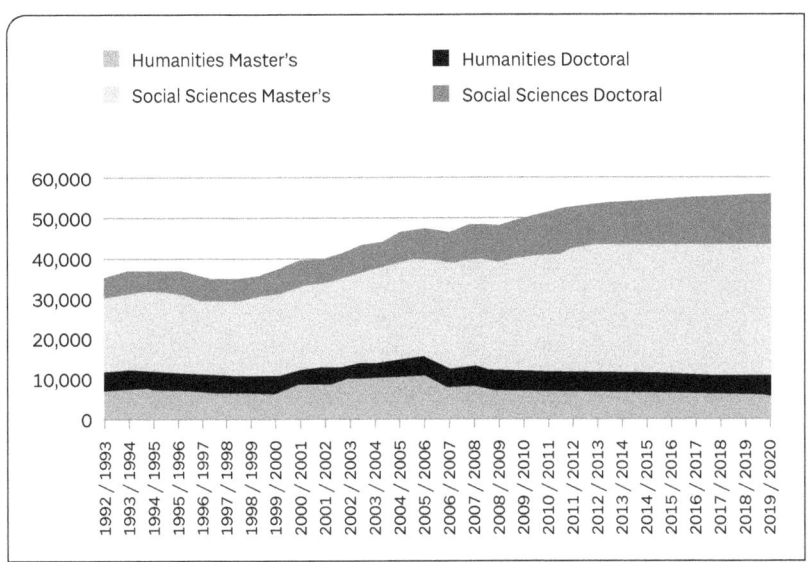

Source: Adapted from Statistics Canada, Table: 37-10-0018-01 (formerly CANSIM 477-0019), "Postsecondary Enrolments, by Registration Status, Institution Type, Status of Student in Canada and Gender" (see Statistics Canada 2022b).

First, there are important differences to note between the social science and humanities disciplines. Total enrollment in social science graduate programs is growing: between 1992–93 and 2019–20, enrollments in social science master's programs increased by 80 percent and enrollment in social science doctoral programs increased by 149 percent. But enrollment in humanities graduate programs has stagnated: over the same period, enrollment in humanities master's programs declined by 19 percent while enrollment in humanities doctoral programs increased by a modest 7 percent.

Second, while arts graduate enrollments have grown in absolute numbers, they have declined as an overall proportion of total Canadian graduate education numbers (see Figure 3.11; Statistics Canada 2022b). This is because overall Canadian graduate education numbers have

FIGURE 3.11 **Graduate Enrollments by Disciplinary Grouping, 1992–2019.**

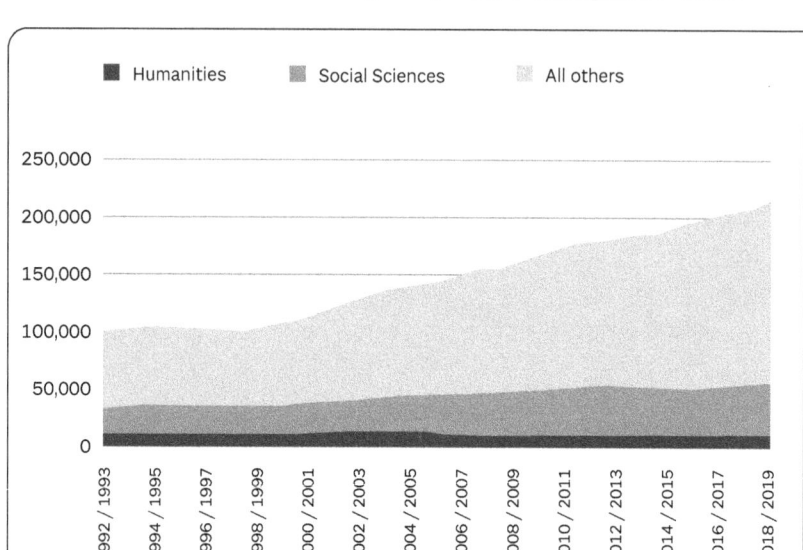

Source: Adapted from Statistics Canada, Table: 37-10-0018-01 (formerly CANSIM 477-0019), "Postsecondary Enrolments, by Registration Status, Institution Type, Status of Student in Canada and Gender" (see Statistics Canada 2022b).

grown faster than the growth of arts disciplines. While one in every three graduate students in 1992–93 would have been an arts student, by 2019–20, it was one in every four. The picture is bleaker for the humanities. Because the humanities graduate programs saw only modest changes in program enrollments during a period of robust overall graduate enrollment growth, humanities graduate programs have declined considerably as a proportion of Canadian graduate education. In 1992–93, 12 percent of all graduate students at Canadian universities were in the humanities; by 2019–20, this figure had plummeted to 5 percent.

Considering both absolute and relative numbers is a good reminder that an increase in enrollments doesn't necessarily reflect an increase in student demand. Rather, we can think about universities' demand for graduate students. As we will discuss in chapter 4, pressures from governments, universities, and academic units have all resulted in the creation of "places" for graduate students, often with associated funding support. Thus, increased enrollments in the social sciences and maintained total enrollments in the humanities may reflect institutions' own creation of student demand: students are responding to incentives and funding offers and deciding to enroll. The bottom line is this: we built it and some students showed up (albeit considerably fewer than showed up for the non-arts graduate programs).

Another way of understanding the actual demand for arts graduate education in Canada is by contrasting domestic and international enrollments. These work very differently. As a general rule, universities prioritize domestic applicants because it is much easier to put together a competitive funding package using public money. As noted above, most external sources of funding—SSHRC scholarships and provincial graduate scholarships—are available only to domestic students. Thus, while international students may be as talented and capable as domestic students, they are more expensive for universities.

And yet, international arts graduate student numbers are increasing. Indeed, arts graduate enrollments are increasingly dependent upon international students (see Figure 3.12; Statistics Canada 2022b). At both the master's and doctoral levels, and in both the humanities and the social sciences, international students have become a larger proportion of the students enrolled in these programs.

Again, there is value in considering the social sciences and humanities separately. As noted earlier, total humanities master's enrollments fell over the period of 1992–93 to 2019–20, while humanities doctoral enrollments increased modestly. The data indicate that the small growth in humanities doctoral enrollments can be attributed entirely to increasing international enrollments. International students increased dramatically in PhD programs outside the arts (from a low of 18 percent to a high of 40 percent), but even in the arts disciplines, they increased to 20 percent of PhD students in the social sciences and 25 percent in the humanities.

Another way of looking at this is to think about where enrollments are growing or shrinking. Over the time period covered in this data, domestic enrollment in doctoral programs in the humanities decreased

FIGURE 3.12 **International Students as a Percentage of Graduate Enrollments, 1992–93 to 2019–20.**

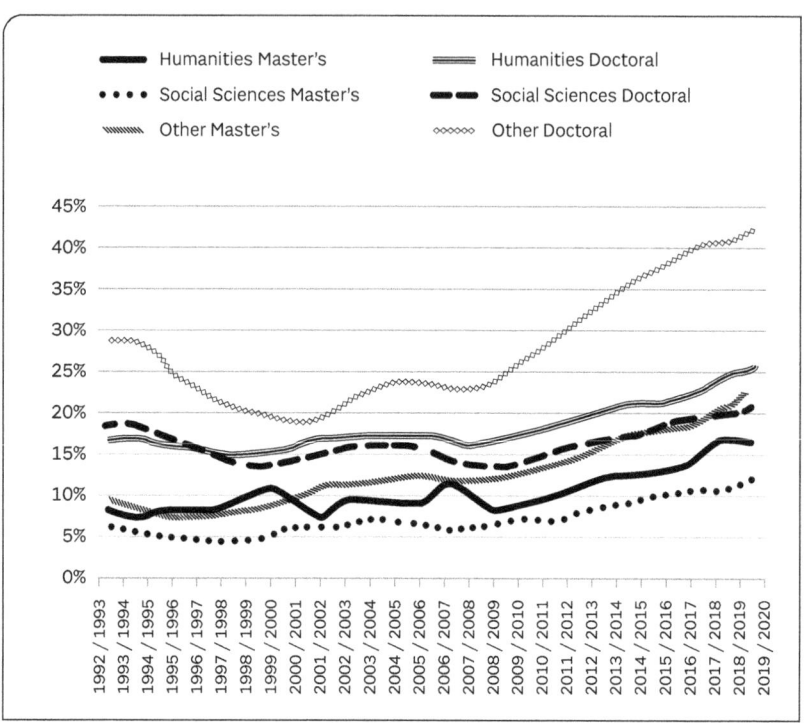

Source: Adapted from Statistics Canada, Table: 37-10-0018-01 (formerly CANSIM 477-0019), "Postsecondary Enrolments, by Registration Status, Institution Type, Status of Student in Canada and Gender" (see Statistics Canada 2022b).

by 5 percent (from 3,492 to 3,327), while international enrollments increased by 64 percent (from 702 to 1,149) (Statistics Canada 2022b). The only growth in enrollments came through the increasing numbers of international students. In the social sciences, enrollment growth for doctoral students was divided relatively evenly between the domestic (a 140 percent increase) and international (a 190 percent increase) groups.

The increasing reliance on international arts graduate students to meet universities' demand for graduate students—seats that need to be filled, research that needs to be done—is a strong indicator that domestic student demand for arts graduate programs is declining. This is very clear in the humanities data, as the dependency of humanities arts graduate programs on international students is undeniable. In the social sciences overall, domestic demand has continued to increase, but anecdotal observations suggest that much of the social sciences' growth in demand is in psychology and economics, two disciplines that are growing in popularity, while some other social sciences have remained constant or declined.

Putting the data points together—specifically the decreased relative proportion of arts graduate programs and the increased reliance on international students to meet university goals—it is difficult to use the available data to convincingly argue that Canada is experiencing strong student demand for arts graduate programs.

We can only speculate about the reasons for stagnant or declining domestic demand for arts graduate programs. In part, these reflect the overall popularity of various disciplines, as a decline in undergraduate numbers will almost certainly result in a decline in graduate numbers. Arts graduate programs also compete with professional master's degrees in areas like public policy, public administration, and management that offer professional development and career preparation explicitly in their curricula.

What is clear is that most arts graduate programs as they are currently offered are not being overwhelmed with domestic student interest. This is a signal that all is not well. We need to give serious thought to why demand is tepid, and to the "value proposition" these programs offer to potential students and the ones who do enroll.

Why Arts Graduate Education Needs to Change

All of us who are involved in arts graduate education can point to success stories. Students who have produced exemplary research. Alumni who have gone on to success in academic or non-academic roles. Lives that have been enriched through the study of the humanities or social sciences at an advanced level.

But the data presented in this chapter tell us that those success stories are not universal—and possibly are uncommon. Too many students start but do not finish their degrees. Those who do finish often spend too long as students. Many are dissatisfied with their experience and most feel under supported when it comes to career preparation. And a substantial proportion of the graduates—particularly of doctoral programs—struggle to find appropriate, well-compensated employment when they graduate. MA students are somewhat better off, or at least less vulnerable. But they are subject to many of the same pathologies, particularly if they aspire to then enter a PhD program.

We firmly support learning for learning's sake, discovery, and similar lofty goals. We see value in arts graduate education as a private good. And the accumulation of private goods can be understood to provide a public good. For example, a 2008 report argued that graduate study contributed to the American economy through "increased tax revenues, greater productivity, increased workforce flexibility, decreased reliance on government financial assistance, and improved ability to adapt to and use technology" (Council of Graduate Schools 2008, 6).

But as the data we have presented in this chapter illustrate, arts graduate education's claim to be a private good is open to scrutiny. The private benefits relative to the private costs for individual students do not present a clear win for students.

Further, graduate education cannot be simply a private good. Public dollars are used to support arts graduate education in Canada. Unlike most professional graduate programs, arts graduate education does not cover its costs primarily through tuition fees, which are kept relatively low and similar to undergraduate programs. Furthermore, a large proportion of arts graduate students receive funding for their programs through scholarships or research and teaching assistantships for which rates of pay are highly subsidized. This is different from, say, an MBA program where tuition is much higher and funding much less (or non-existent), on the expectation that graduates will rapidly recoup the value of their investment by landing a well-paid job directly related to their program. In the arts, the private payoff is often much less certain, yet the public investment is considerable.

Canada is investing in arts graduate education. The public should benefit from this investment.

And yet while arts graduate education has tremendous potential to advance the public good, Canada's current system has tenuous ties at best to any notion of a public benefit. This is not to say the system is not public-spirited; in fact, a great deal of arts teaching and research is dedicated to discussing what constitutes the public good. But much of this is abstract and does not equip students with specific tools and skills to truly pursue that good. Instead, the system produces the following pathological results:

- Graduate students serve as essential assistants for the research of faculty, who in turn are heavily incentivized to build RAs into their projects. However, the linkage with the rest of their graduate program is weak, and RA training is primarily focused on building skills for elusive academic careers.
- MA programs range widely in structure and requirements, even within disciplines. Canada is unique in its widespread standalone MA, yet there is no consensus on the purpose of the MA, except as a middle ground between undergraduate and doctoral study. Programs tend to be built around the idiosyncratic interests of faculty or students, or both.
- Every year, PhD arts programs produce far more doctoral graduates than there are available faculty job openings, even though evidence overwhelmingly shows most PhDs aspire to academic jobs. Conversations about non-academic career paths for PhDs have been going on for decades. While attitudes have shifted to be more supportive of non-academic career outcomes, there is little evidence of systemic change.
- In general, arts graduate programming often exists to serve other institutional objectives, at considerable public cost, rather than the interests of students themselves or the societies that underwrite their education.

The faculty and staff delivering arts graduate education may consider their programs to be public-spirited. But the current system often does not seem to be serving any clear purpose or good, public or private, including and most especially for students themselves. It perversely lacks both sufficient structure and sufficient flexibility to serve students well, and in turn serve the public good.

We're not claiming to be the first to recognize this problem. Nor are we the first to argue for change. But we are arguing for much more ambitious change than the two conventional solutions that are often discussed.

The first conventional "solution" is simply to reduce the number of graduate admissions and programs, particularly at the doctoral level, given the apparent overproduction of PhDs. But this is not happening; in fact, the number of programs is still growing. We explore the full reasons for this in chapter 4, but fundamentally this is a collective action problem. Individual universities, units, and faculty have no incentive to cut back on their production of graduate students, and in fact have many incentives to continue increasing them, even if more and more they have to cast the net internationally, as discussed.

Consequently, the second and much more common "solution" is to expand the focus of programs, again particularly at the doctoral level, to include more attention to non-academic careers. This has taken many forms. The most important is an expansion of professional development programming at all levels of the university (i.e., at both unit and graduate faculty levels) to better equip students for non-academic career paths. Units and disciplines have also slowly—sometimes very slowly—moved to embrace and celebrate graduates who have ended up in non-academic careers. Programs have sometimes been made more streamlined to move graduates through faster, and there is an increasing openness to different types of dissertations and "knowledge production." Some of these latter changes are also tied to making graduates more competitive on the academic job market; for example, many arts PhD programs have adopted the widespread STEM dissertation model of producing a set number of individual publishable papers.

These are admirable changes. But they are reactive, not proactive. Again with special reference to the PhD, those in charge of doctoral programs are faced with the clear evidence that many or most of their graduates will not be getting an academic position, and they realize they need to equip them for a broader range of careers. But there is little or no fundamental retooling of the structure and purpose of the PhD itself—much less a cutback in PhD production, as noted. And there is limited capacity and expertise within these graduate programs to even offer the add-ons intended to repurpose the graduates.

Nor is there overwhelming evidence that there is an exclusive market for arts PhDs outside of academia. In other words, while many PhDs are able to find a good non-academic career, it is not clear that there is a specific demand for PhDs in most non-academic fields. In fact, many hiring managers may see the PhD as a liability, rather than an asset. Many programs are admirably scrambling to help their graduates find jobs anywhere they can, but mostly as a reaction to the deficiencies of the academic job market. The core academic job focus of the PhD remains paramount, and is perpetuated and sustained by forces we will outline in chapter 4 that encourage universities and departments to maintain and even expand their supply of doctoral students, even if future job prospects are uncertain. And meanwhile, the MA drifts—perhaps in less dire trouble than the PhD, but still underperforming and not serving students as well as it could.

Canada's arts graduate education status quo should be unacceptable to everyone.

4

How We Got Here, and Why We Feel Stranded

We have presented evidence that arts graduate education, with its primary focus on developing the next generation of the discipline, is failing to meet the needs of students, institutions, and the public. We have made the case that arts graduate education can make important contributions to the Canadian public good and that this potential is not yet being realized.

In short, the status quo is not working.

This is not due to a lack of caring or effort. We know that our colleagues, the faculty members who teach and supervise arts graduate students, consider this to be among the most important work they do. And they do it with great dedication. Our colleagues who take on the challenge of leading graduate programs work tirelessly on behalf of students. And the students who enter our programs are full of promise.

So where are things going wrong? How did we get into this situation in the first place, and why hasn't change occurred already? These are important questions, because if we don't understand the systems and processes that created our current arts graduate education reality, we can't fix it.

In this chapter, we explain how the arts graduate education system in Canada has evolved incrementally and erratically in response to many different forces and demands, almost all of them pushing for one thing: growth. This prevailing growth mindset has created incentives for expansion without purpose. In most cases, the only overriding principle is growth itself—growth in the number of programs, and the number of students in those programs. This growth mindset has combined with curricular inertia. Degree structures and curricula are slow to change; copying is more common than differentiation. The result is that we are trapped in a growth mindset where the number (but not the diversity) of arts graduate programs increases, along with enrollment, even when there is evidence of a mismatch between the number of graduates and the demand for their services post-graduation. And no one is doing much to fix it.

There are many incentives to create and expand arts graduate programming, and relatively few to curb or even coordinate it. Programs do close—or get closed, involuntarily—in times of crisis and austerity. But even then, growth is sometimes seen as the solution out of crisis. The current state is not simply because of ignorance or neglect, though admittedly those are also factors. Instead, much of it reflects the environment in which arts graduate programs have been established and operate.

To understand this tendency toward uncoordinated growth and limited curriculum change, we start at the most general level, with Canadian governments, both provincial and federal. We then go on to talk about the environment of the contemporary Canadian university. And finally, we delve into the incentive structures that shape arts faculty members' work. By moving from the macro to the micro, we can understand how the various parts fit together (Figure 4.1).

Following from this, we focus on the challenge of change. We argue that a combination of path dependency, incentive structures, and a lack of vision have combined to bring us to this place. Fortunately, in this seemingly grim analysis we can identify the tools required for meaningful change to occur.

FIGURE 4.1 **Layers of Actors.**

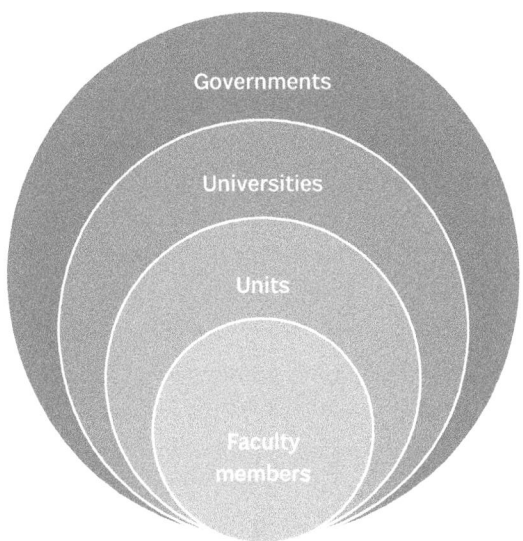

The External Environment: Government Policies and Their Effects

In Canada, unlike in some other countries (most notably the United States), postsecondary education is almost exclusively run through public institutions, including universities, colleges, and polytechnic institutes. While Canadian universities are autonomous institutions and not part of government, they are accredited and overseen by provincial governments, and in part funded by provincial and federal governments.

This means that governments have a large role to play in how Canadian universities function. Universities are both affected directly by government policy and are themselves treated as instruments of public policy to achieve larger ends. And yet, the public policy framework shaping Canadian universities is fractured with many different players.

As a federal country, Canada has an exceptionally strong division of labour between the federal and provincial governments when it comes to universities. While postsecondary education is not explicitly mentioned in the constitution, provinces are clearly assigned responsibility for "education," which over time has become understood to include higher education. Gradually this has come to mean that matters related to university institutions are exclusively under provincial jurisdiction. In most practical ways, there are ten different postsecondary systems in Canada, one for each province (as well as three more modest-sized systems for each territory), each with its own approach to managing these postsecondary systems. And yet, the federal government still plays a major role in indirectly influencing universities by funding research, including graduate research, and by funding students (Cameron 2004; Lang 2022). This has had significant implications for the development of graduate education in Canada.

Because public policy underpins the graduate education situation, policy decisions can offer a partial explanation for the patterns of enrollment, resistance to curricular reform and innovation in degree structures, and limited adaptation to changing labour force outcomes for graduates.

Provincial Funding: Incentives to Growth

Over the past two decades, provincial government transfers to universities (in real dollars) have increased from about $10 billion annually to $15 billion (HESA 2022, Figure 4-1, 50). Most of that increase came before 2008; since then, provincial funding has been flat. This aggregated number hides variations among provinces. For instance, over the past ten years, Ontario's real funding for its postsecondary institutions has declined by 17 percent, but this has been largely offset by Quebec's increase of 17 percent over the same period (HESA 2022, Figure 4-2, 51).

Provincial funding models differ. In some provinces, the funding of each individual university is based on historical patterns and/or short-term decisions and factors. But in other provinces, particularly Ontario for many years, funding is distributed by a highly developed formula approach that creates incentives and/or penalties for each institution. Enrollments are usually the most important factor in these formulas, with money being given or perhaps taken away from universities based on the number of students. In fact, a 2015 study observed that "Very little of the MTCU [Ontario Ministry of Training, Colleges, and Universities] funding model is distributed based on performance or outcomes other than enrolment" (HEQCO 2015, 7). More recently, Ontario moved to a "corridor" model that caps overall funding at a maximum number of spots, but this was after years of employing a funding formula that strongly incentivized enrollment growth (Deller, Kaufman, and Tamburri 2019).

While government transfers have remained flat, universities' revenue from tuition has grown (HESA 2022, Figure 3-5, 44). The balance between provincial funding and tuition revenue has long been shifting to create increasing institutional reliance on tuition dollars, though it differs considerably by province. While in most provinces the ratio between tuition revenue and traditional public funding is more balanced, in Ontario, this ratio is close to 70:30—that is, universities depend far more on tuition than government funding (Council of Ontario Universities 2023, 4). (This does not take into account other types of funding, especially research funding and philanthropy, which we will discuss.) The bulk of revenue growth for institutions has been in international tuition. In fact, HESA observes that "100% of all new money in Canadian higher education since 2011 has come from international tuition fees" (2022, 41).

At the same time as provincial funding changes have made universities more reliant on tuition dollars, provinces have taken a strong interest in controlling tuition fees, at least for domestic undergraduate students and students in non-professional programs. Tuition caps for programs such as law and medicine as well as for professionally oriented master's programs like the MBA have been significantly relaxed in recent years, leading to much higher tuition fees than for "academic" programs, on the assumption that graduates will move into high-income jobs. All provinces regulate tuition levels, usually placing maximum caps on how much domestic tuition can increase annually. There are substantial variations across provinces, with Newfoundland and Labrador and Quebec maintaining domestic tuition fees that are less than half the amount in most other provinces (HESA 2022, Figure 5-2, 60). In some instances (notably Ontario in the 1990s and Alberta in 2019), provincial governments have coupled making significant cuts to universities' operating grants with allowing significant tuition increases. In 2019, the Ontario government ordered universities to cut domestic tuition by 10 percent and froze it at that level for the next five years. Outside of these exceptional circumstances, provinces tend to allow small annual increases to tuition fees.

While provincial governments closely regulate domestic tuition fees, they tend not to regulate the tuition charged to international students. Consequently, international tuition rates are orders of magnitude higher than domestic tuition rates for most programs of study. This creates significant incentives for universities to enroll international students. While there are strong provincial controls on raising domestic tuition fees, universities are generally free to increase the number of students by accepting more, including more international students who typically pay higher tuition fees.

Enrollment growth, then, can be seen as a rational response by universities to their fiscal context. To fulfill their mandates and strategic visions and to ensure sustainability, universities must focus on the bottom line. Due to the difficulties of cutting costs given the fixed and growing expenses associated with largely unionized workforces and tenured faculty, universities focus on increasing revenue. Due to tuition fee caps, universities are limited in what they can charge for their programs. But they can recruit more students. This combination of factors makes growth the default for most universities. Provincial policies that control tuition but not enrollments in most programs (and even incentivize enrollments through formula funding) create incentives for universities to constantly expand enrollments, taking in more students to maintain revenue growth while hoping to contain costs through economies of scale.

This is particularly the case for arts education, which is typically cheaper to deliver than science and engineering programs that require laboratory space and equipment (these extra costs are often incorporated into funding formulas, but not necessarily into tuition rates). The marginal costs of expanding arts undergraduate and graduate programs are low.

Moreover, expanding arts graduate programs can itself be a cost solution for arts undergraduate expansion, as it expands the supply of low-cost graduate student teaching assistants available to service undergrad teaching. The broad funding model of Canadian universities—particularly in Ontario, where universities rely more heavily on tuition than government transfers—pushes universities to deliver courses to large numbers of students in a cost-effective manner. The financial sweet spot is a small number of faculty or contingent instructors delivering lectures to large numbers of undergraduate students, whose work is then graded mechanically or by an army of graduate teaching assistants.

Moving from the broad picture of funding arrangements to the more concrete incentives facing universities, it is possible to point to instances where provincial governments have incentivized growth in graduate student enrollments particularly. In 2005, the Ontario government announced its "Reaching Higher" plan for postsecondary education, which included new funding to increase graduate enrollments in the province by 12,000 students in 2007–08 and 14,000 by 2009–10. The province funded constant growth in graduate enrollments from that time until 2016. As a result, between 2005 and 2015, enrollment in master's programs in Ontario increased from approximately 20,000 to 37,000, and Ontario PhD enrollments increased from approximately 11,000 to 19,000 (Looker 2018, 20–21). In its 2018 reforms to its funding formula, the government of Quebec amended its funding formula to move from a grant of approximately $23,000 per full-time PhD student to approximately $42,000 (Bouchard St-Amant et al. 2020). Bouchard St-Amant et al. argue that "an increase in PhD enrollment can be expected, despite placement problems that may (already) exist" (2020, 12).

Overall, then, the actions of provincial governments have tended in the direction of encouraging enrollment growth, including in graduate education. And in some instances, provincial action has explicitly and directly incentivized growth in graduate education. In contrast, there are few cases of incentives the other way, rewarding restraint and presumably quality over quantity. And as mentioned, when governments do make broad austerity cuts, new growth and the revenue it represents may be seen as the solution to the problem.

Provincial incentives for university growth may be changing. In recent years, provinces such as Ontario and Alberta have become more interested in "performance-based" funding. While there are different models here, the common theme is a move away from either historical funding or enrollment-based formulas. Instead, universities are to be incentivized to focus on distinctive areas of strength and their quality and impact, including career readiness of graduates. Mostly arising only in the late 2010s, these ideas are relatively fledgling, and it is too soon to determine their impact. While performance-based funding is widely found in the United States for public universities, there are various models. These universities also operate within a larger system of private institutions, making it difficult to transfer firm lessons to the Canadian context.

Provincial Approvals: Oversight Without Coordination

Provincial governments have authority and oversight over all postsecondary credentials offered within their borders. Provincial policies on creating, reviewing, and discontinuing university programs vary (Universities Canada n.d.), but new degree programs generally require approval from provincial quality councils and governments, sometimes including direct sign-off by the relevant government minister. Even decisions to close degree programs typically require provincial approval. (Saskatchewan is a notable exception to these practices.)

In addition to evaluating the merits of each proposal for a new degree program, the provincial ministry responsible for advanced education has the authority to determine whether it makes sense within the provincial postsecondary system to offer a new degree program. This might take the form of a "system review" (as in Alberta and BC) or involve consideration of whether the program duplicates others, and if so, whether duplication is warranted (as in Ontario) (Duklas 2015).

For those of us who are concerned that Canada might have too many arts graduate programs on offer (or at least too many of a certain kind), this sounds like good news. But in practical terms, the system is flawed.

First, by definition, the system being considered is the provincial one (except in Atlantic Canada where this function has been assigned to the Maritime Provinces Higher Education Commission). This works reasonably well when considering whether it makes sense for Manitoba to have two programs training physicians, or whether there should be more than one institution educating social workers in Alberta. But it arguably has not been effective in addressing the cacophony of MA and PhD programs in arts disciplines. As arts graduate programs often do not require new funding from a provincial ministry, the only meaningful check on program proliferation is the case universities make to forecast provincial demand or employment for graduates. Sadly, some hand-waving and optimism are often enough to move a program through, especially since it is often easier to produce data about student demand (through existing applications and enrollments in related programs) than post-degree employment, which is more difficult to track. And while new program proposals might comment on the national landscape, by virtue of being focused on the unit of the province, there is no effective mechanism for asking how many MA or PhD programs in a particular discipline Canada needs.

The second issue, somewhat ironic compared to the above, is that provincial oversight can make it difficult to change and adjust programs. Provincial governments decide whether new programs can be offered or old ones closed, and may even have authority to approve or reject major changes to an existing program. There is good reason for government to provide this kind of oversight, as it ensures the overall quality of credentials. (The alternative is some kind of arms-length accreditation body, as in the United States.) But it adds an often-daunting bureaucratic layer to experimentation. Many good innovations have been stopped in their tracks by the question, "Wouldn't the approval have to go to the province?" From the perspective of the academic proponents of a new program or set of significant program changes, waiting months (possibly many months) for provincial approval of a set of program changes that have gone through multiple levels of discussion and approval within an institution is the bureaucratic cherry on top of a sundae of paperwork. This encourages sticking to familiar models and tinkering within them, even if there is increasing evidence that they are not working. While this issue applies to all levels and areas of education, it has special resonance for arts graduate education, which is so clearly in need of change.

Federal Funding: Incentives for Graduate Research

The federal government has no authority to approve programs or regulate universities (except in narrow ways generally not related to education). Federal involvement in research, however, allows the federal government to shape universities through the funding of researchers and research projects themselves, leapfrogging over institutions and programs. This includes graduate students who receive funding both directly through federal scholarships and indirectly through faculty who hire graduate students with their federal research grants.

There is a long history here. While in the 1950s the Government of Canada gave direct grants to universities, provincial governments objected to this infringement on their jurisdiction, preferring unconditional block grants that allowed provinces to spend funds across a range of policy areas. The federal government thus retreated to directly funding individual researchers and projects only, not institutions (see Cameron 2004). The federal role in research was augmented in the 1990s and early 2000s, as the government made major new investments in Canadian research infrastructure, primarily through universities. The Canada Research Chairs program and the Canada Foundation for Innovation were introduced at this time, while existing programs, most notably the three major academic grant agencies in Canada (the Social Sciences and Humanities Research Council, or SSHRC; the Natural Sciences and Engineering Research Council, or NSERC; and the Canadian Institutes of Health Research, or CIHR, together known as the Tri-Council), were bolstered with new funding.

Most of this federal activity engaged with institutions and individual researchers and was designed to not directly infringe on provincial jurisdiction on education—that is, actual classroom learning. Nevertheless, the implications for graduate education were significant, since much of the new research funding went to support labs and personnel, creating a strong faculty demand for graduate students to populate them. Tri-Council funding of graduate scholarships also increased in this period, combining federal strategies of scholarships and research to bolster graduate programming.

This federal funding influence means that national granting agency decisions have been consequential for the direction graduate education has taken in Canada. And unfortunately, despite their active involvement in the same space, coordination between the two orders of government in Canada is limited, including or even especially with respect to graduate education. The result is that the federal government shapes graduate education in ways that are unconnected to either provincial or institutional planning and priorities.

This lack of coordination creates competing dynamics in graduate education (Young 2019). For example, a university or province may want to cap its overall number of PhD programs and students. However, its researchers will still directly receive federal grants, much of which goes to fund graduate research assistants; individual students can also receive federal scholarships. This creates pressure from faculty to maintain or expand graduate programs regardless of overall institutional or provincial priorities, especially if individual students will be well-funded by federal scholarships and/or faculty research dollars.

What does all of this mean for arts graduate programs? For the vast majority of arts researchers, including graduate students, SSHRC is the relevant funding council. Its funding priorities have had the following implications for programs:

- *Domestic student focus.* The eligibility requirements for SSHRC grants incentivize arts graduate programs to try to recruit domestic students, as only citizens and permanent residents are eligible for most scholarships.
- *Independent student research model.* While the two other councils have moved in the direction of supporting graduate students largely indirectly through faculty members' grants, SSHRC has continued to offer the bulk of its graduate student funding directly to students through scholarships (CFSR 2017, 83). This incentivizes arts graduate programs to maintain the more traditional model of independent student research, rather than integration into faculty-led research teams. Indeed, in a 2015 review of the doctoral scholarship program, SSHRC concluded

that holding a scholarship "allowed students to spend more time on their own independent research, free from the demands on their time that comes with some other types of funding, such as research or teaching assistantships" (18).
- *Master's program changes.* SSHRC's willingness to include major research papers as constituting a "significant research component" (NSERC 2023) has likely contributed to the transition away from master's theses, particularly in Ontario.
- *Doctoral program conservatism.* Even while recognizing that not all the graduate students it funds will follow an academic career, SSHRC has only used its influence modestly to tackle the issue. The objectives for its doctoral scholarship program include helping students to successfully complete their degree, allowing them to focus more on their research interests and gain opportunities for international research experience. Concerns about the mismatch between academic jobs and numbers of PhD graduates were addressed with a generic recommendation that students be given professional skills training (SSHRC 2015).
- *Limited attention to diversity.* Until relatively recently, EDID considerations were absent as specific funding criteria. In 2022, the council announced a pilot initiative to offer a top-up to master's scholarships for Indigenous students (SSHRC 2022b).

All of these point to the importance of SSHRC's scholarship program in shaping arts graduate education. Thinking of the three imperatives that drive our public good argument—wicked problems, EDID, and talent—we see affinities with SSHRC priorities…up to a point. In recent years, SSHRC has accelerated its interest in tackling specific social issues, often with an equity dimension, outside of the traditional disciplinary boundaries that guide much of its existing activity. In 2018, working with Policy Horizons Canada, SSHRC identified sixteen "emerging global challenges" such as "working in the digital economy," "truth under fire in a post-fact world," and "building better lives across the gender spectrum" (Policy Horizons 2018, 11). These in turn have driven special funding opportunities such as the Knowledge Synthesis Grants, which in 2022 prioritized research on gender-based violence and the "shifting dynamics of privilege and marginalization" (SSHRC 2022c). Furthermore, SSHRC funding decisions in all programs have increasingly emphasized the importance of training "highly qualified persons" (HQPs) as a key criterion for obtaining grants.

The challenge remains, though, that these programs are funding individual faculty and graduate students, not graduate programs themselves. They may spur coordination at the institutional level, but more through serendipity and entrepreneurial activity rather than organized coherence. As we think about the potential for transformational change in chapter 9, we will return to the role SSHRC could play.

Lack of Governmental Coordination

So, universities are incentivized by both the provincial and federal governments to grow their graduate programming across the board—though not necessarily in the same direction. The lack of federal-provincial coordination can be seen as both a strength and a weakness. From the point of view of universities, it can be an advantage, allowing them to draw from both levels of government and perhaps even play them off against one another. However, as Cameron writes, "The financial participation of both orders of government certainly increases the resources available to postsecondary institutions and students, but the manner of their joint participation complicates their lines of accountability and inhibits the capacity of either order of government to pursue innovative policy alternatives" (2005, 285).

There is also a lack of interprovincial coordination. In higher education, like with most other areas, there are substantial variations in the provinces' approach. For example, the number of universities in a province only loosely correlates with population size—despite having generally similar populations, Nova Scotia has ten university-level institutions, while Manitoba has three and Saskatchewan two. Ontario and Quebec also have very differently organized systems from each other.

Yet, despite its varying systems, Canada has remarkably similar universities. There is a high degree of institutional isomorphism in Canadian postsecondary institutions (Trotter and Mitchell 2018; Weingarten 2021). While some Canadian universities have a long history and charming ivy-clad stone buildings, many others were founded relatively recently (and have the brutalist architecture to show for it). Founded to serve the needs of a region or city, universities like the University of Calgary and Brock University were established in a period of rapid expansion, often as the only university in town (or in the case of Simon Fraser University and York University, as "the second university" created explicitly to handle overflow from an older local institution), and are thus encouraged to be all things to all people. As they were created explicitly to serve local growth, growth naturally became the default for these institutions, and their dominant mode for decades after their founding.

Furthermore, many Canadian universities, both old and new, that began as undergraduate-focused institutions have over time expanded into "research intensity" and graduate programming—and sometimes quite rapidly. Canada's sense of fairness and its formidable geography each contribute here. Why should universities like Laval University and the University of Toronto retain a monopoly on graduate programming? Why should a student have to leave St. Catharines or Saskatoon to pursue a PhD in psychology? Only a few small Canadian institutions have expressly stuck to an undergraduate-only mission. Instead, Canadian provincial governments have adopted (or been persuaded to adopt) the position that almost all universities are entitled to a graduate education profile. And while growth is across the board, the easiest way to establish this profile is in the arts disciplines, which unlike science or engineering require few new capital resources in the way of buildings, lab space, and other infrastructure.

The unintentional result is an array of programs that (may) make individual local sense but do not contribute to a sense of national coordination. There is modest cooperation in some professional postsecondary areas—for example, the tightly regionalized organization of veterinary schools in Canada. But there is no larger infrastructure to share information and coordinate. Imagine, for example, an initiative to decide how many graduate programs in sociology are needed in Canada. We're not necessarily saying that's a good idea or an answerable question. The point is that Canada lacks the capacity to even address it.

Taken as a whole, the complex government funding and regulatory landscape in Canada encourages the proliferation of graduate programs that are similar to one another as well as enrollment growth within those established programs. Provincial funding policies incentivize universities to grow their way out of financial problems by creating more programs and recruiting more students, with arts programs typically offering the best immediate short-term returns. Federal research funding powerfully incentivizes research-based graduate education, providing a welcome shower of money to individual researchers that can be passed on to graduate students, but is largely unconnected to provincial priorities or even individual institutional ones. While in STEM there is typically at least a strong connection between a student's research job and their own thesis or dissertation, arts graduate students receive their own direct funding for their individual projects, often with little connection to the projects of their faculty supervisors even if they are also assisting on the latter.

Public policy plays a significant role in shaping graduate education trends. Yet the policies are often not well-coordinated, and they often incentivize the pursuit of revenue through growth over academic objectives and coherence. The result is both widespread expansion of graduate education, but also drift and lack of direction in the system. This combines with factors within universities, to which we will now turn.

The Internal Environment: The Contemporary University and Its Context

The muddling and sometimes incoherent state of arts graduate education makes even more sense when we consider how it is driven by internal factors within the contemporary university. Canadian universities—like their counterparts elsewhere—are colonial in origin, oriented toward constant growth, caught up in an international game of rankings, and increasingly focused on research. While the individual quality of their offerings can be good, in the sense of well-qualified instructors, up-to-date digitized libraries, and academically rigorous and rich curricula, their quality assurance processes do not encourage or facilitate fundamental reconsideration of overall structures and a larger consideration of what truly constitutes "quality" beyond the way things have always been done. It is not completely correct to say that Canadian universities are "slow to change"—sometimes they can adapt quite rapidly, but only if they are incentivized (or firmly pushed) to do so. And these incentives are again largely about growth.

Colonial Institutions

Among the ways that Canadian universities perpetuate the status quo is their very slow change from their origins as colonial institutions that have long produced and reproduced social and economic privilege. Over time, there has been a gradual broadening of participation, as class, gender, racial, and other barriers to admission and inclusion have broken down. The student body is certainly more diverse, although there are huge variations between programs and types of diversity. But, as institutions, Canadian universities are still led mostly by white men (Diversity Gap Canada 2019), and the faculty complement is not representative of the diversity of Canadian society. Increasingly, institutions are trying to overcome their origins, with varying degrees of enthusiasm and authenticity. The appointment of senior leaders and adoption of strategic plans to pursue equity, diversity, inclusion, and (sometimes) decolonization signal what might be the beginning of a gradual shift in these large organizations. We'll repeat: gradual.

Much of this change takes the form of Gaudry and Lorenz's (2018) "inclusion," placing the onus on "newcomers" to the university to adapt to the existing structures. Deeper structural changes, such as decolonization, are much less common and usually face significant institutional barriers.

As with all social institutions, changing attitudes at the individual level is one thing, while confronting problems at the systemic level is more challenging and more likely to spark resistance and outright denial that there is any problem at all. This could obviously be a book in itself (and here we would refer readers to some of the already excellent books on this subject, e.g., Ibrahim et al. 2022; Henry et al. 2017). Those who have achieved individual success within universities are often resistant to the idea that their achievements were in part a product of privilege, rather than purely related to merit. Efforts to decolonize or otherwise reform curriculum to make it more inclusive are sometimes seen as undermining a discipline, or as casting aside great scholarship. The status quo rolls along, because it serves a lot of existing interests well, even if those beneficiaries don't realize their own privilege and that it does not serve others as equitably.

Arts graduate education is in a curious spot here, as while some arts graduate programs are clearly products of the colonial university, others have been formed in opposition to it, and some programs are very explicitly built on or have been reoriented around anti-colonialism and anti-racism principles. Most fall somewhere between these two extremes. The beauty of universities is that they can accommodate this diversity in perspective and orientation. But even those graduate programs formed in opposition to colonialism are housed in a colonial institution whose rules and practices may feel oppressive to some students. They also still may follow some of the other pathologies of arts graduate programs, such as an overemphasis on training for academic jobs and a limited focus on other types of career training and readiness. And these programs tend to be "bottom-up" creations driven by faculty interest and dedication, rather than created as institutional priorities (in fact, befitting their origins, they are often likely to have a built-in anti-institutional emphasis, perhaps with a creation story of how the program was established despite a lack of institutional support). In general, EDID agendas are generally a sidebar to the "real" priorities of universities, which remain overwhelmingly around growth, particularly in research prowess and activity.

Internal Competition: Growth is Always Good

As with external public policies, internal factors within Canadian universities lead to the ongoing prioritization of graduate programs and yet to limited coordination or overall vision for them, including around equity-driven goals. In fact, universities depend on a steady inflow and robust graduate population simply to keep many of their other processes going.

Graduate students play multiple roles in modern, complex universities, often serving as students and employees simultaneously. Graduate research assistants are vital for most research projects. Graduate teaching assistants are crucial for delivering mass undergraduate education efficiently, and teaching assistantships are a primary form of funding for graduate students, especially in arts disciplines. Most perversely—although we do not believe by deliberate design—universities depend on part-time contract instructors to deliver much of their teaching, and the primary pool for those instructors are PhD students and recent PhD graduates. Graduate students are thus deeply embedded in making universities work on a daily basis, typically with no ceiling to their possible capacity and utility. A larger supply of graduate students is almost always better for university operations, particularly as undergraduate enrollments rise.

Internal structures typically also encourage graduate education. If provincial funding formulas incentivize increased graduate enrollments, this will almost certainly be built into internal budget models, rewarding faculties and departments for expanding graduate programs and taking in more students. This might be through variations of "responsibility-based" budgeting that specifically incentivize units to take in more students, or through other less explicit reward structures. And even if unit budgets are not linked to enrollments, units with graduate programs typically enjoy more prestige and standing within the university, especially the more that the university prizes research intensity. Competition is rampant within universities, as departments and programs compete for resources, and graduate education is a key area in which units jockey for position.

Graduate education is more decentralized than undergraduate education, especially in the arts. While undergraduate recruitment and admissions are usually central university operations, departments are usually the primary actors in graduate admissions, reviewing applications and making admission and funding decisions. And while a typical undergraduate arts student takes a range of courses from different programs and disciplines, graduate students normally take all their courses within the unit and usually work as a TA or RA within the unit. All this encourages insularity amid the perpetual growth. Each unit sets its own course in graduate education, and the institutional incentives inevitably prioritize bringing in and retaining as many students as possible, at times even competing with other units for the same prospective students.

In short, at all levels of the university, graduate education is characterized more by growth rather than meaningful coordination. There are many factors driving this growth and yet few controls or incentives to direct or curb it.

The Rankings Game

In addition to being competitive within themselves, Canadian universities also exist in a competitive external environment. They compete with each other for finite research dollars and the student enrollments that translate into tuition revenue. Institutions also compete for prestige in the form of reputation and rankings, which in turn further contributes to their ability to compete for those research dollars and enrollments. All this has further implications for the direction of graduate education.

We have seen how provincial funding formulas incentivize enrollment growth across the board, and how federal research programs further encourage faculty and institutions to prioritize graduate students. Graduate enrollment and research intensivity are also critical for success in university rankings and reputations. Within Canada, fifteen of the oldest and most prestigious universities are self-organized as the "U15," which describes itself as "an association of fifteen leading research universities" that was formed to "advance research and innovation policies and programs for the benefit of all Canadians" (U15 n.d.)—in short, explicitly prioritizing research. The only other cross-provincial organized group of universities, the Maple League, comprises four small institutions (Bishop's, Mount Allison, Acadia, and St. Francis Xavier universities) with little or no graduate programming at all. In general, all but the smallest undergraduate and private (mainly religious) institutions' strategies include commitments to grow their research footprint and profile, and research and graduate students are inevitably closely intertwined with one another.

The most prominent and familiar ranking exercise in Canada, the long-standing *Maclean's* rankings, does distinguish between three categories of universities: medical-doctoral (roughly the U15); comprehensive; and primarily undergraduate, with a wide set of criteria beyond research intensity and primarily focusing on the undergraduate experience. However, the more influential rankings are international, including the Times Higher Education World University Rankings, the QS World University Rankings, and the Shanghai Ranking, and these are based almost exclusively on research intensity—the quantity of research publications produced, the rate of citations of that research, as well as criteria such as the number of Nobel Prize winners on the faculty (see Hazelkorn and Mihut 2021).

Scoring high on these rankings is critical for Canadian universities for two major reasons. The first is their validity for domestic audiences, especially provincial governments. While provinces may not formally incorporate international rankings in their funding formulas, a high international ranking certainly assists institutions in their efforts to encourage further investment from the provincial government. It also holds obvious appeal for philanthropic donors.

The second and even greater imperative to score high on rankings is their appeal for prospective international students (Hazelkorn and Mihut 2021, 8), who, as we have seen, are increasingly important for university revenue. These applicants must select universities based on limited information, so recognized international rankings are a valuable guide. The irony is that most rankings are research based rather than teaching based, and are thus imperfect or even misleading indicators of the actual student experience, particularly for undergraduates. Yet they are critical for attracting international student enrollments, signalling the long-term value and prestige of the degree they would earn. And the best way to prevail with rankings is to invest in and prioritize research—and, by extension, graduate programs.

In short, universities are here again heavily incentivized to build and expand graduate programming to advance their research prowess, for reasons unconnected to the quality and coherence of the programs themselves.

Quality Assurance: Everything's Fine

As self-governing entities, universities have to maintain quality assurance processes. These are intended to maintain the standards of credentials offered by the institution. At the level of the academic unit, they take the form of unit reviews and program or curriculum reviews.

These are normally driven by central administration, in the case of unit reviews, and/or perhaps by the university's teaching and learning centre in the case of curriculum reviews; these may in turn be shaped and determined by provincial quality assurance frameworks.

In theory, quality assurance is a crucial tool to ensure the continuing health and excellence of academic programs. Typically, they begin with an elaborate "self-study" conducted by the unit, including extensive commentary on institutionally generated data about enrollments, graduations, student satisfaction, and faculty productivity. Curriculum reviews focus on identifying the overarching learning objectives of a degree program and mapping course requirements against this. External reviewers—established colleagues from other institutions—are then brought in to review the self-study, meet with the unit, interview deans and others, and write a report with assessments and recommendations. All of this is done on a cyclical basis, typically every five to seven years.

These quality assurance processes should, ideally, give units an opportunity to step back and think critically and creatively about what they are doing, and to be energized and held to account. In reality, though, quality assurance is often clumsy and time-consuming, and tends to reinforce the status quo and isomorphism in program design.

It's a lucky coincidence if a scheduled review comes at a time when a unit is actively looking to reinvent itself, and when its leadership has the time and energy to do the necessary heavy lifting. Most of the time, however, a review is an arduous and dreaded burden for academic administrators who already have more than enough work. For many (perhaps most) department chairs and program directors, there is a temptation to view the whole process as a time-consuming inconvenience, and to approach it with the objective of minimizing disruption and change. Human nature being what it is, units tend to seize reviews as an opportunity to voice general grievances and lament resource shortages, to little effect.

Bringing in external reviewers may have the unintended effect of encouraging homogeneity across units within a discipline. In essence, external reviewers are there to say, "I come from a well-respected sociology department. This department I'm reviewing might consider moving in the direction of my and other sociology departments." As Skolnik observes, quality assurance processes constitute a "centralized, visible and potent mechanism for promoting conformity in academe" (2010, 12).

At the same time, there is no central direction to this conformity. For some non-arts disciplines, most notably engineering and health professions, quality assurance is tied to accreditation of the program by external professional bodies. In these fields, accreditation is a vital designation that allows the program to exist and have its graduates' professional credentials legally recognized. Accreditation formulas, set by the external bodies, are typically rigorous and set out what students should be studying and how much (including minimum numbers of hours in the classroom or labs). Assessors then apply this common template to yield their assessments of program quality. While accreditation can encourage innovation, its primary function is to certify that the program is working well and up to standard.

In contrast, arts disciplines that are not tied to specific professions lack such templates and externally regulated bodies capable of setting and enforcing them. There may be a general consensus on broad topics that should be covered, especially at the introductory level, but a great deal of assessment is subjective. This leaves considerable leeway for the interpretations and idiosyncrasies of individual reviewers, and they may in turn be deferential to a unit's particular way of doing things, since there is no clear external standard beyond the reviewer's own knowledge and experience. In short, quality assurance can produce both homogeneous groupthink and erratic outliers, and yet still certify that everything is working well.

Conducted within the context of the institution, unit reviews look at the quality of academic offerings, but often do not look at the broader environment in the rest of the university or beyond. An MA program in linguistics that has maintained its enrollment in the face of declining applications by recruiting international students is not placed in the context of multiple competing programs at the same university or at other institutions in the province or nationally. And while a review can look meticulously at program curriculum and teaching processes, it is much harder to assess students' career outcomes once they leave the program, beyond imperfect survey data or anecdotes. Reviews are also usually divorced from actual resource and budget discussions, so reviewers typically recommend improvements, such as hiring more faculty, that do not take wider factors into account—and their reports are often ignored for that reason.

Thus, while quality assurance reviews are the one widespread instrument that encourages thinking about the goals and purposes of graduate programs, even the best processes offer little or no context of other programs and the university as a whole. In general, quality assurance and other similar processes discourage more than encourage innovation and diversity of programming. And they don't accomplish the function achieved by formal professional accreditation processes, which ensure consistency tied to students' acquisition of career competencies.

It does not have to be this way, and we do acknowledge that there are instances in which quality assurance processes have sparked innovation and set units on a new path. But these are exceptions, dependent on good timing and leadership. Following Skolnik's (2010) assertion that quality assurance processes should be seen as political processes, we note the agenda-setting function senior administration can play. Quality assurance should not be treated as a form of accreditation, certifying that everything is fine. Instead, if reviews and external assessors are set up with innovation in mind, and are tasked with creativity rather than conformity, the very processes that otherwise stifle innovation can encourage it. This innovation role for reviews is, however, underutilized. The later chapters in this book suggest some ways to proceed.

The Individual Actors: Faculty and Their Realities

The place where there is most likely to be thoughtful and nuanced reflection about graduate education and students, beyond the relentless quest for growth, is at the unit level and among individual faculty members. Faculty are central to the direction and delivery of graduate education. While faculty's actions are shaped and constrained by other actors that shape incentives and direction for them (refer again to Figure 4.1), for graduate education to be successful, faculty members who develop courses and deliver supervision in graduate programs must embrace (or at least accept) innovation. Faculty members also care deeply for their students' well-being, and many are well aware of some or most of the arts graduate student challenges we detailed in chapter 3.

So why aren't arts faculty members and departments driving graduate program transformation? The answer, we believe, lies in incentive structures and culture.

Academic Incentives: Research First

Reimagining arts graduate education takes vision and leadership. It requires skills in change management, knowledge of educational design, and understanding of university processes. And it takes time. In most arts academic departments, there are few if any brave faculty members seeking to take this task on.

Indeed, it is rational for them not to do so. The reward structures within their institution and their discipline favour scholarly publication in high-impact venues. Tenure, promotion, and merit pay standards prioritize research activity heavily above other factors, including educational leadership and service. Department chairs face considerable demands on their time and energy, and struggle to maintain their personal research trajectories while in the role. Graduate program chairs are typically asked to manage existing programs rather than reimagine them. There are few or no incentives for individual faculty members to lead change themselves. And universities rarely provide departments with incentives to work together toward change, except under pressure in times of austerity.

There are also disincentives for faculty to drive graduate program change, as their own research and thus career success relies on maintaining the graduate program status quo. The adage "publish or perish" is long-standing, but more novel for arts disciplines are the growing emphases on obtaining external grants to receive tenure and promotion, grants that primarily fund graduate students, and attracting and completing graduate supervisions, previously more exclusively a STEM practice.

Increasingly, funding agencies are creating incentives and supports for "mode 2" research, in which knowledge production is "a mode of collaboration between scientific and societal stakeholders" (Fecher et al. 2021, 5) and research impact is measured not only through citation counts but also through measures of impact on public conversation and policy. This could help change incentives in the direction of the public good as we envision it, particularly with connection to the wicked problems imperative. But the extent may not be enough to overcome the barriers to change. Arts faculty members engaged in this type of research may be more amenable to orienting graduate programming toward the public good imperatives we outlined in chapter 2. But they may also be cautious, as they are aware that the academic world is still organized to value traditional measures of impact. This is particularly the case in the early stages of faculty careers, when individuals are advised to stick close to existing paths, creating habits and orientations that make it likely that they will keep doing so even after tenure and promotion.

We must note that the research-first incentive structures go beyond the universities. Granting agencies award research grants based on past research records and future research plans. Academic peers invite each other into interesting projects due to research synergies. Speaking invitations, media inquiries, requests to speak at parliamentary hearings or to professional bodies, and myriad other flattering and sometimes remunerated opportunities are all tied to one's research profile and expertise. (Try to substitute the word "teaching" for "research" in the above paragraph. It doesn't work.)

Given the balance of existing incentive structures, it makes sense for arts faculty to direct their attention to their personal research productivity rather than educational leadership.

Academic Culture: (Academic) Research First

Even apart from the overt incentives we've described, there is a general culture in academia that valorizes research, and specifically academic research. University faculty are overwhelmingly hired, tenured, and promoted based on their past research records, their ability to produce even more research, and their ability to train others (i.e., graduate students) to follow in their research footsteps. By design, many faculty members connect very strongly with the research mission of their university and, by extension, the research mission of their department's graduate programs.

It is reasonable to assume that this research focus among faculty members is intensifying over time, particularly in the arts. The oversupply of arts PhD graduates relative to available academic jobs means that the candidate pool for almost any arts faculty position is filled with applicants with stellar research records who aspire to research-intensive faculty positions, and hiring is primarily based on research prowess more than teaching potential. While institutions are increasingly experimenting with "teaching-intensive" faculty positions with limited or no research expectations, the massive supply of available arts PhD graduates means that research-intensive candidates are often still selected for teaching-intensive positions, and they accept them as the only academic jobs available to them, while still aspiring to research-intensive faculty positions.

For many arts faculty, working with graduate students is among the more enjoyable parts of their job. Undergraduate teaching in the modern university is a more ephemeral activity: students come and go, and they vary in academic ability and research promise. In all but the smallest institutions, personal connections between faculty and undergraduate students are sporadic and weak, from both directions. In sharp contrast, connections between faculty and graduate students can be quite strong. Graduate students are around for years, work closely with faculty members as TAs and RAs, and may share research interests with faculty members.

As most arts faculty have followed a traditional academic career path—BA, MA, PhD, academia—it is understandable that they see academia as the ideal home for promising researchers. Inevitably, faculty encourage the most promising MA students to go on to doctoral studies—and the students often need little encouragement since the culture of academic research is already so predominant. To the extent that careers are discussed with arts PhD students, faculty aim to prepare students for academic careers first. Of course, arts faculty are well aware of the challenging academic job market and that many of their PhD graduates are unable to find academic jobs. They are thus increasingly open to broader professional development programming focused on non-academic career paths—but only as a backup "Plan B." Whether intentionally or unconsciously, faculty tend to extend and perpetuate a research culture focused on academic research.

To be clear, academia's research-first culture doesn't need to lead to stagnant thinking on arts graduate education. The problem is academia's *academic* research-first culture. The assumption that advanced arts research skills are ideally or exclusively located within academia stifles creativity about graduate education and reinforces status quo programs. When one assumes that advanced arts research skills are as or even more valuable when located beyond academia, it is possible to reimagine arts graduate programs in exciting ways. Innovative arts faculty members can design graduate programs that tap into the richness of their disciplines to identify creative, nuanced responses to society's myriad human and human system challenges. Indeed, we desperately hope that innovative arts faculty members will take up our call to action and design precisely such programs to direct the arts' research mission toward making progress on wicked problems.

Why Change Is Hard

We have discussed the complex environment in which Canadian arts graduate education operates, and the different factors that tend to promote uncoordinated growth. We can sum these up, and the reasons why change is hard, as follows: path dependency, incentives, and lack of vision.

Path Dependency

The concept of "path dependency" is employed in many social sciences. In many contexts, it is used to mean that "particular courses of action, once introduced, can be virtually impossible to reverse; and consequently, political development is often punctuated by critical moments or junctures that shape the basic contours of social life" (Pierson 2000, 251). Pierson conceives of path dependency as resulting from "increasing returns." In this view, "the probability of further steps along the same path increases with each move down that path. This is because the relative benefits of the current activity compared with other possible options increase over time" (Pierson 2000, 252).

Graduate programming is path dependent—that is, it follows the same course it always has and is difficult to change in fundamental ways. It is more complicated and more decentralized than undergraduate education, with individual units carrying primary responsibility for most aspects. And when asked to consider change, academics often reply with variations on "this is the way we've always done it" or "this is how my PhD program was structured."

Innovation—leaving the existing path—is costly. It requires that time be spent designing and implementing changes—time that could be spent on other things with more tangible career benefits (read: academic research). And it entails the assumption of risk if the new program is not an improvement on the old one. Innovation is more likely to be siphoned off through separate professional degree programs, often in entirely different units, rather than radically retooling existing academic degrees.

Path-dependence theory suggests that change only occurs at "critical junctures"—where paths diverge or cross and a conscious decision has to be made about where to go. Change happens when the cost of doing the same thing becomes greater than the cost of change. These junctures—decision points—typically arise due to external shocks or "punctuated equilibriums," a financial crisis, a security threat, or something that upends conventional wisdom and processes and increases the cost of the status quo.

While individual units and programs may experience these—especially sudden and drastic financial crunches—graduate education as a system has had few or no "critical junctures." The closest has been the growing acceptance that too many PhDs are being produced for the academic job market. But this has been a gradual awakening over decades, not an abrupt realization, and so the PhD has fundamentally continued on the same path as always. If PhD programs were faced with declining numbers of applicants, it might provoke a sense of crisis. However, many programs facing a decline in domestic applicants have shifted to admitting from large pools of international applicants, thereby avoiding the potential critical juncture. And so path dependence continues.

Incentives

Academic institutions seek both money and prestige. These are, of course, mutually reinforcing. Money is needed to keep institutions going, and finding new and more revenue is always preferable to making unpleasant cost-cutting decisions. And higher prestige typically makes it easier to attract revenue.

As we have seen, many incentives combine to encourage growth in graduate student numbers. Provincial governments may reward universities for enrollment growth (or punish them for decline). Many international rankings schemes include graduate student numbers or proportion as a positive metric. These institution-level incentives are then incorporated into the institution's own internal incentive system, where graduate programs respond to them.

But even without institutional incentives, faculty members are individually incentivized to want to supervise graduate students. Grants, which facilitate their research and are necessary for career progress, are evaluated in part on the grantee's record of mentorship and supervision. And ambitious faculty members want to be in a department that has a graduate program. Tenure, promotion, and merit pay models all encourage faculty, directly or indirectly, to attract and supervise more graduate students.

These incentive structures only narrowly capture excellence. Provincial governments count students in programs, but may not pay as much attention to graduation rates and times to completion, and even less to the tricky question of post-degree employment.

And so, like rational actors always do, institutions, departments, and individual faculty members focus their attention on how best to respond to incentive structures, rather than thinking deeply about whether there are ways of doing things differently that would be better for all involved.

Lack of Vision

The final reason for a lack of change and innovation in arts graduate education—apart from the above reasons to just keep on doing the same thing—is the absence of a clear vision of where and how it should be changed. Many agree that arts graduate education is not working well. But there is no consensus on the source of the problem, or on how it should work instead.

As any dean of arts will tell you, arts faculty members are creative, even visionary, thinkers with strong views. But it would be a rare arts faculty council that would engage in a true debate about the fundamentals of arts graduate education to ask: what are we doing here? What kind of programming could we build? Instead, reform initiatives tend to focus on incremental change designed to fix the last problem that emerged.

For some, the solution is simply a lot more money, such as to create more faculty positions for those with PhDs. For others, it may be a radical downsizing in programs and student spaces (though rarely does anyone volunteer for their program to be the first to do so). More modestly, many are tinkering on the edges with piecemeal solutions, such as the growth in professional development programming. But no one is challenging the overall model with a clear and realistic vision to replace it. So, the status quo endures.

Exacerbating the Gap: Attitudes and Ignorance

At the beginning of the chapter, we noted that the current state of arts graduate education is not simply attributable to ignorance or neglect. But these are admittedly also present along with distorted agendas. People and organizations use and manipulate graduate education for their own ends—to hoard resources, build personal empires, or quite simply to exploit people and their labour and money. Or conversely, they don't think much about graduate education at all—they are distracted by other organizational and personal priorities. And after all, as long as enough students keep showing up and graduating, the system may seem to be working.

Optimism fuels arts graduate education. This is most evident in the decades of denial about the oversupply of PhDs relative to academic positions. For a very long time, doctoral students have been reassured of "a coming wave of retirements" and other factors that would restore equilibrium in the academic job market—or even create a surplus of positions.

Those reassurances have become less common over time, but have not disappeared entirely. More broadly, there is a great deal of vague faith in non-academic career prospects for those with arts PhDs, despite little evidence of an active demand across the board for PhDs outside academia, except in some specific fields. Finally, the standalone Canadian research MA seems to have persisted largely because everyone seems to assume it must be good for students, and it certainly serves the other institutional and faculty research objectives outlined above.

Like other areas of postsecondary education, arts graduate education is also affected by external political and policy agendas that distort the system, typically without fully understanding it. This is less evident in Canada than in some other countries, such as the United States, where postsecondary policy has become dangerously politicized, or the UK or Australia, where a stronger emphasis on "research performance" has further valorized research as the primary and perhaps only really worthy focus of graduate education. Still, and as we have discussed, calls to support programs only "where there is a clear job demand" tend to come from an excessively narrow viewpoint; they can also precipitate opposing reactions against "mere job training" and "anti-intellectualism." Neither is helpful to building and maintaining a robust system that prizes knowledge and serves students well.

Why Change Is Possible

It's crucial to understand these structural reasons for the gap between the current and potential state of arts graduate education, because only then can we properly understand how to change things for the better.

The impediments identified in this chapter make change challenging, but they do not make it impossible. With the right vision and incentive structures, we believe it is possible to reimagine arts graduate education for the good of students, faculty, and Canada. In the chapters ahead, we aim to help you believe it, too.

Canada's Arts Graduate Credentials

Realities and Possibilities

We began this book by laying out what we see as the pressing public good needs of Canada and how arts graduate education can respond to them through the three imperatives of wicked problems, EDID, and talent. But the previous two chapters have shown how and why the current arts graduate education system is falling short. The student experience is not what it could or should be, and the system is driven and shaped by structural forces often unconnected to the best interests of either students or Canada.

Change is clearly needed. And in this chapter, we begin laying the groundwork of what needs to be done to produce arts graduate education for the public good. The first step is understanding the framework of degrees and credentials that underlies arts graduate education. What is working? What is not working? This structural overview then sets us up for the following chapters, which lay out what arts graduate education should be doing and how it can serve the three imperatives and the public good.

To an outsider (and, let's be honest, to many insiders), graduate credentials are a confusing jumble. Only a relatively small group of academics and administrators really understand what is supposed to be the difference between a master of arts (MA) in political science versus a master of public policy (MPP), or a PhD in psychology versus a doctor of psychology (DPsy) degree. Even among degrees carrying the same official title, there can be a surprising level of variation; for example, some MA programs seem like mini-PhDs with their multi-year thesis projects, while other MA programs are entirely course based. Add to this an array of graduate diplomas, certificates, and micro-credentials, and the graduate credential space can seem hard to navigate—because it is.

If arts graduate education is going to evolve to realize its potential to serve Canada's public good and to better meet the needs of students, we need to start by reviewing graduate credential structures—the building blocks of the system. This primarily means degrees, the traditional credential of universities. There is increasing attention to the other types of graduate credentials mentioned above, and we will address them as well. But master's and doctoral degrees remain the core of graduate education, past, present, and—we believe—future. To build a coherent national system, we need a common understanding of the purpose of different degree structures, along with other credentials, and what each is set up to achieve. But right now, understanding is muddled. Clarifying purpose is foundational to considering how arts programs can be maintained, tweaked, updated, and/or transformed moving forward.

So, we're here to walk you through the logic of graduate credential structures, with a focus on the underlying purpose of each credential. We start by creating a typology of graduate degrees, noting both the current purpose of these degrees and our proposed redefined purpose for them. We further consider two key dimensions—research training and development, and career training and development—and how each type of degree differs on these, or should differ, in order to serve the degree's overall purpose. With this typology in place, we move to consider how arts graduate degrees can be thoughtfully tied to Canada's public good through explicit connections with the wicked problems imperative, the EDID imperative, and the talent imperative. We end the chapter by exploring graduate certificates and diplomas.

The Graduate Degrees We Have: A Typology

Graduate education consumes considerable time, energy, and money from faculty, students, and staff. So, what is the purpose of graduate degrees and the different types of degrees? To some extent, this information is available in public policy. The Council of Ministers of Education, Canada (CMEC) is an intergovernmental body in which provincial ministers of education discuss policy and undertake joint initiatives. In 2007, CMEC endorsed the *Ministerial Statement on Quality Assurance of Degree Education in Canada*, which included the Canadian Degree Qualifications Framework (CDQF) (CMEC 2007). The CDQF outlines degree standards, and in doing so distinguishes between the characteristics of the bachelor's, master's, and doctoral degree levels.

These guidelines apply to degrees across all disciplines. But they remain very wide, in part because of that need to span all disciplines, and they have been adopted and adapted in different ways by provinces and territories. This in turn leaves room for further adaptation by individual institutions. And as we explained in the previous chapter, governments and universities tend to encourage growth in all directions. Quality assurance and similar processes, unless guided by external accreditation, are not always successful in maintaining consistency across institutions. The result, as we will show, is that there can be considerable variance, especially for the master's degree.

Looking specifically at arts graduate degrees, we can identify two clear categories, academic and professional, and two degree levels, master's and doctoral. This produces four degree types: the master of arts, professional arts master's degrees, the arts PhD, and professional arts doctorates. This is the starting point for our discussions in this chapter. For each degree type, we consider degree purpose with respect to research training and career development. In doing this, we look back at the evolution of these degrees to try to understand how their fundamental purposes have evolved or blurred over time, with a view to helping faculty members to sharpen the focus of their graduate programs moving forward.

Master's Degrees

Canada's master's degree is a strange entity. It is more than a bachelor's degree, but less than a doctorate. Its name implies "mastery" of an area of study, but the proliferation of master's degrees and the variation in requirements across them highlight the subjectivity of that terminology. The academic master's is focused on subject-matter mastery and research preparation, while the professional master's is designed to prepare students for professional practice in some field. For all master's degrees, CMEC states, "Graduates will have the qualities needed for either further study in the discipline or for employment in circumstances requiring sound judgment, personal responsibility and initiative, in complex and unpredictable professional environments" (2007, 4). This leaves a lot of space for variation, so next we look more closely at how this works in the arts disciplines.

The Master of Arts (MA)

The MA is a research degree. As CMEC describes, "Research-oriented master's programs are typically for graduates of related undergraduate or professional programs in the field...the focus is on developing the research, analytical, methodological, interpretive, and expository skills necessary for doctoral studies or for leadership in society" (2007, 2). The MA predates professional master's degrees, and until professional master's degrees came along, the MA was the default choice for university graduates who wanted to distinguish themselves by demonstrating "mastery" and perseverance in their study area.

At present, the purpose of Canada's MA is poorly defined. In some cases, MAs seem to be designed simply to prepare students to continue onward to doctoral study (despite the low numbers of MA students who actually go on to become PhD students), while in other cases, MAs seem to be designed simply to provide students space to continue disciplinary study and postpone entry into the workforce—a "victory lap" after the undergraduate degree. Or more positively, a "leg up" in the competition for jobs. In many cases, the MA openly claims to do all of the above.

Given its vague and multiple purposes, it is not surprising that MA programs in Canada vary considerably in their requirements and relationships to adjacent undergraduate and graduate programs. Consider the following:

- *Length*: MAs can range from eight to sixteen months of study (i.e., two to four four-month terms). Workload requirements per term may be relatively similar, but the number of terms and total credit requirements are not standardized—much different than with undergraduate degrees. These requirements usually correspond to standards set by the university (or perhaps the provincial regulator), rather than the discipline—thus, while the requirements for a history MA program may vary considerably across the country, they will probably (although not always) closely resemble the standards for other master's degrees at the same institution.
- *Research Requirements*: Differing program requirements for MAs are also seen in research training and the wildly varying place of the master's thesis. The research focus of the MA has evolved over time. Originally, the research focus was signalled through the requirement that students conduct research and present a thesis for examination. Over the past several decades, however, many Canadian universities have relaxed the requirement of a thesis, offering students the opportunity to take more courses and fulfill the requirement of research through a major paper or some other mechanism. Thus, while the thesis was once widely required in most arts MA programs, it is now typically optional or even unavailable, replaced with less onerous "major research papers" or a pure coursework program.
- *Cross-Listing*: The supply of standalone master's courses—probably the best indicator that the MA is a distinctive and exclusive degree experience—varies considerably, usually depending on resources and the size of the program. In most universities, at least some MA courses are cross-listed courses—that is, master's courses are combined with either fourth-year undergraduate courses or PhD courses (and sometimes both). Larger well-resourced programs can typically offer a range of graduate-only courses (usually available to both MA and PhD students), although cross-listed courses will still be common as well. In smaller MA programs, there are

few or possibly no exclusive MA courses at all, with "graduate" courses simply being student spots in undergraduate courses. It is in fact rare to find a fully self-contained MA program that does not overlap with one or the other degree or both.

These variations add up to a massive number of training differences sitting beneath the same degree label. The credential "master of arts" can mean that the holder has completed two years of coursework followed by writing an original research thesis, has completed an intensive eight months of advanced coursework with no original research work, or has done work that lies between these two points. Within the coursework components, MA students have vastly different experiences: when MA courses are cross-listed with PhD courses, the MA program resembles the doctoral experience, whereas when MA courses are cross-listed with BA courses, the MA experience resembles an additional undergraduate year.

These variations are not wholly undesirable, as they are often tailored to specific contexts and allow students flexibility and choice. But they illustrate the lack of consensus about what a master's degree should entail in concrete terms, other than being more than a bachelor's and less than a doctorate. The master's degree sits uneasily between the other two degrees. Is the MA basically a fifth (and sixth, and sometimes seventh) year of undergraduate study? Is it preparation for the PhD? Is it something else entirely? And if it is many things, can they be reconciled?

The challenge of defining the MA is not limited to Canada, although there are national differences. In the United States, a bachelor's graduate aspiring to continue research-based academic study will go directly into a doctoral program; after progressing to a certain stage, they are commonly awarded a master's degree while they continue to progress on the PhD. The American MA's close ties to the PhD mean that, in the words of an American Historical Association study, "the master's degree is considered to be just like the doctorate, only less so" (Katz 2005, 46). And further, "Is there a way to describe the master's degree, in history or any other discipline, that is not inherently hierarchical, and that does not privilege the PhD as the preeminent credential?" (Katz 2005, 45). As we think about how to refine the MA in Canada, it is worth reflecting on the contemporary conversation about the MA in the United States. In *The New PhD: How to Build a Better Graduate Education*, Cassuto and Weisbuch

(2021, 284) argue for the revitalization of the MA as a more professionally oriented degree. However, this reflects the limited status of the American academic MA as largely an accessory to the PhD, compared to the long-standing standalone Canadian MA.

In the UK, there is a distinction between research MAs and coursework ("taught") MAs, with the research MA being more dominant. As an observer asserted in speaking of coursework MAs, "the M.A. student is neglected. There are many books on studying at undergraduate level; many on being a research student; but the M.A. is a poor relative caught in the middle" (Bennett 2014, xii). A meta-study of British "postgraduate taught education" (PGT) similarly observes that "most study of postgraduate provision has been about postgraduate research students, not PGT" (Bamber 2015, 223).

While Canada is not alone in having vaguely defined MA programs, this does not make the situation acceptable or desirable—for students or for universities. Canada has a long-standing distinctive model for the standalone MA, and a substantial proportion of its arts graduate enrollments are in the MA. We owe it to our students and ourselves to have a clear vision of what the degree is for. At present, we do not. Simply put, the purpose and structure of the Canadian master of arts program are not well thought out.

So, what should be the fundamental purpose of the MA? In our view, the purpose of the MA should be to prepare sophisticated generalists whose grounding in an arts discipline, ability to conduct basic research, and acquisition of skills have prepared them to make a meaningful contribution in the public, private, or non-profit sector, or to continue to a PhD. This purpose is achieved through both research training and career development.

In terms of research training, master of arts programs should, ideally, train students in research preparation. Programs should teach students to develop their own specific research skills and conduct basic research on their own or as part of a team. Research training might occur entirely through coursework or involve an independent research project scaled to the degree level. How this can be done will vary based on the discipline and area. For example, an economics or sociology student might work with an existing database to pursue an independent project for a course project; in contrast, an anthropology student might not be expected to pursue their own fieldwork, but instead be expected to synthesize existing studies.

With MA research preparation, the focus should be on developing the student's research skills, but not go as far as expecting them to produce an independent contribution to knowledge. While master's-level research preparation will situate a student well for doctoral studies, it has other meaningful potential outcomes. In a knowledge economy, research skills are essential across a wide range of contexts. The ability to synthesize and evaluate research findings, design research and evaluative instruments, and ground actions in research findings are the "generalist" skills that many potential employers identify as their reason for valuing students with arts backgrounds.

In terms of career development, master of arts programs are not tied to specific industries and as such should prepare students for entry into careers across a range of fields. The career path is undefined: a graduate with a philosophy MA, for example, might end up working in politics, public administration, the non-profit sector, communications, technology, academia, business, or something else. An MA program prepares students for general career success. Theoretical understanding is deeper than at the undergraduate level, research skill development is typically more advanced, and career competencies are ideally transferable across industries.

Professional Arts Master's

Professional master's degrees are designed to prepare students for professional practice. As CMEC describes, "Profession-oriented master's programs normally admit students holding baccalaureate degrees and provide them with a selection of courses and exercises intended to prepare them for a particular profession or field of practice or, if they are already involved in the profession or field, to extend their knowledge base and skills as professionals/practitioners" (2007, 2).

The prototype for many professional arts master's degrees is the master of business administration (MBA), normally a course-based program designed to launch careers in business and administration. Arts disciplines have followed the lead of the MBA and have developed professional master's programs related to their discipline or that draw upon multiple arts disciplines. The master of public administration

(MPA) has long been a public sector answer to the MBA, and more recently the master of public policy (MPP) has joined it as a professional degree for students interested in the policy sciences. Other more specialized degree offerings have been developed in everything from disaster and emergency management to philanthropy. These degrees normally offer a combination of social science or humanities content with the acquisition of administrative or managerial skills. These degrees are typically named for their subject matter, such as the "master of public service" or "master of philanthropy." Professional arts master's degrees tend to be relatively short (often one year), or are designed for part-time and/or distance delivery. Tuition fees tend to be high and are often comparable to the MBA.

The purpose of the professional arts master's degree is refreshingly clear: it prepares students for professional practice, whether in a regulated profession like social work or a more amorphous one like public policy. And this is, in our view, entirely appropriate. Students are attracted to these programs for professional training and career advancement, and these programs typically deliver on this promise.

The result is a different orientation toward research. Professional master's programs typically focus their research training on research literacy, which is foundational knowledge that allows one to be an informed consumer of research. A research-literate student should understand the research process, how to locate and critically read research, and the qualities of trustworthy research. Many (but not all) undergraduate programs teach basic research literacy. Professional graduate programs should go beyond these basics to prepare students to be competent in working with research—finding it, reading it, analyzing it, and developing strong skills of discernment in how to filter and digest it—so that they are able to engage in evidence-informed practice.

The career development role of professional master's programs is tied to specific industries, such as public administration (master of public administration), social work (master of social work), regional and urban planning (master of planning), or journalism (master of journalism). The career path is clear: upon finishing their graduate program, the student applies for employment opportunities directly in their field of study. Professional master's programs are often tied to accreditation bodies, such as the Canadian Association of Programs in Public Administration, the Canadian Association for Social Work Education, or the Canadian Institute of Planners.

In a professional master's program, students are being prepared to enter a specific field, and by extension, the program requirements are tailored to that industry. Content knowledge, theoretical training, and competency training are all directed toward ensuring the student is career ready for that industry by the time of graduation. Experiential learning is tied to that industry. It is all very deliberate, focused, and specific.

Doctoral Degrees

The doctoral degree is the highest degree awarded by universities. In contrast to the muddled state of the arts master's degree, the arts PhD is reasonably well defined in Canada. Students normally enter an arts PhD program after completing an MA, usually in the same or a closely related discipline. PhDs have traditionally been tied to a single discipline, although interdisciplinary programs are increasingly common. While professional arts doctorates are growing more common in other countries, they remain rare in Canada. Let's dive in for more details.

The Arts PhD

CMEC describes PhD programs as follows: "Research-oriented doctoral programs focus on the development of the conceptual and methodological knowledge and skills required to do original research and to make an original contribution to knowledge in the form of a dissertation" (2007, 2). While this description could lead to a number of directions, in arts graduate education this has taken the form of academic career preparation. Indeed, to the extent that arts graduate education in Canada has been coherent at all, it has privileged research and vocational education for future professors through the PhD. This spirit is captured in the idea of PhDs serving as "stewards of the discipline," to use a term proposed by the Carnegie Foundation for the Advancement of Teaching:

> the purpose of doctoral education, taken broadly, is to educate and prepare those to whom we can entrust the vigor, quality, and integrity of the field. This person is a scholar first and foremost, in the fullest sense of the term—someone

who will creatively generate new knowledge, critically conserve valuable and useful ideas, and responsibly transform those understandings through writing, teaching, and application. We call such a person a "steward of the discipline." (Golde and Walker 2006, 5)

Although there is now considerable discussion about "rethinking the PhD," it remains largely about supplementing—rather than fundamentally changing—a graduate program whose primary purpose is to educate the next generation of university faculty members in a discipline.

As with MA programs, PhD programs vary by country. American and Canadian doctoral programs are basically similar in structure, with three main parts: coursework, comprehensive examination(s), and the thesis/dissertation (the terms are used interchangeably). The chief difference is that there is more coursework in American PhD programs because their students are admitted after completing a bachelor's degree, while most Canadian PhD programs admit students who have completed a master's. In sharp contrast to the Canadian and American three-part PhD structure, British, Australian, and many European PhDs historically eschewed the first two parts entirely, going straight to the thesis. This is evolving, as coursework and even comprehensive exams are increasingly common in UK PhD programs.

Unlike the generally neglected master of arts degree, the twenty-first century has seen serious and ongoing discussion of the purpose and design of the arts PhD, both in Canada and internationally (IPLAI 2013; Cassuto and Weisbush 2021). The chief reason is simple: arts PhD programs are typically structured as vocational training for future professors, but there are too many PhD graduates relative to available academic jobs. Exactly how much so is contested and it can vary between disciplines and programs, and we lack consistent data. But regardless of the size of the gap, most students in surveys report that their primary aspiration is to become a professor (Casey et al. 2023; Desjardins 2012, 12), and many are willing to pursue this at great personal sacrifice. The result is growing numbers of highly trained research professionals working in a succession of temporary academic positions, such as limited-term academic appointments, postdoctoral fellowships, and sessional teaching contracts, many of which require them to move or commute regularly

(Desjardins 2012; Hewitt 2018; Anonymous 2022). Much of the conversation about "rethinking" the PhD has focused on ways to address the troubling career outcomes for graduates, generally by offering professional development alongside the PhD, while still maintaining PhD programs and enrollments.

So, what should be the fundamental purpose of the arts PhD? How could we balance the imperative to produce the next generation of "stewards of the discipline" with the compelling need to harness and develop the talent of these students to ensure they have successful and meaningful careers in a diverse range of settings?

We believe it is essential to think of the PhD as the paramount research degree, and that the research competencies that are developed in the degree are essential to meeting our public good imperatives. As such, the purpose of this degree must be to develop highly skilled research experts. Arts PhD graduates must be skilled researchers who are able to lead and conduct original research, train junior researchers, and mobilize research findings in a wide variety of venues. PhD programs that embrace these fundamentals throughout their curriculum will prepare graduates for both academic careers and research-informed work beyond the academy. In our view, then, the purpose of the arts PhD needs to broaden from preparing future faculty members to preparing advanced researchers.

In terms of research training, arts PhD programs emphasize theoretical and curiosity-driven research (or pure research) that may not have any immediate application. They also place a stronger emphasis on research contribution that advances theory and knowledge in the discipline and is disseminated and published through scholarly publications and outlets.

In terms of career development, arts PhD programs are not tied to specific industries, except academia itself. Given the realities of the academic job market, we feel it is important to go beyond academia and see the arts PhD as a research-intensive general career preparation program that trains "stewards of the discipline," some of whom go on to work in academia while others go on to work in other fields. The "stewards of the discipline" model necessarily demands some breadth of understanding of the discipline (or interdisciplinary area of study). The emphasis on creating new knowledge means that the PhD must prepare researchers. This dual purpose of developing subject-matter expertise and research capacity must remain at the core of PhD program design. While many PhD graduates will go on to roles that do not use their subject-matter expertise, the process of developing that expertise teaches them the skill of developing expertise, which can then be applied to other subject matter if or when needed.

Deliberately redesigning the arts PhD to prepare advanced researchers, only some of whom will become university faculty, will require changes to coursework to ensure there is sufficient rigorous research training. It will require programs to rethink the value and format of comprehensive exams. It will require programs to reimagine the format of the dissertation and the composition of dissertation committees. All of these "reimaginings" of the arts PhD are necessary and important.

Such an emphasis on rigour in research could lead to a decline in PhD enrollments, possibly accompanied by a growth in enrollments in professional master's or doctorate programs. This is an outcome that we think has merit, as we will discuss next.

Professional Doctorates

Professional doctorates hold a different title than PhD, such as doctor of education (EdD). According to CMEC, "Practice-oriented doctoral programs are of a more applied nature, relate to a professional or creative activity and, where there is an internship or exhibition requirement, may also require a dissertation" (2007, 3). Professional doctorates are far less common than professional master's programs. The most prominent professional doctorate is the EdD; other examples are the doctor of business administration (DBA) and doctor of psychology (PsyD).

Professional doctorates appear to be growing in number and popularity, although reliable system-wide data can be hard to find (for example, Statistics Canada classifies all doctoral graduates together rather than breaking graduates out by degree). But, at least in Canada, they are exceedingly rare in the arts disciplines (outside of clinical psychology). In Canada, the only example we could find at the time of writing was the doctor of social science (DocSocSci) degree offered by Royal Roads University. In contrast, several UK universities offer doctor of social science (DSS or DSSc) degrees, generally emphasizing interdisciplinary study focused on solving contemporary challenges.

The reputation of professional doctorates can be mixed and a sensitive issue, and once again, difficult to pinpoint with hard data. In some areas, the PhD is clearly seen as a more substantive degree, with professional doctorates seen as a less rigorous credential. However, professional doctorates tend to serve a distinct audience of working professionals already in the field who seek to upgrade their credentials, typically while still working. As with research versus professional master's degrees, it is more valuable to consider their distinct purposes rather than trying to make straight comparisons.

The purpose of professional doctorates is fairly clear. Robinson defines the professional doctorate as a "programme of advanced study and research that satisfies university criteria for the award of a doctorate, which develops the capability of individuals to work within their professional context through meeting the specific needs of professional groups internal or external to the university, and which has 'professional doctorate' in its title or description, and does not lead to any other type of award" (2018, 92). Thus, it is an advanced research degree with a professional focus and presumes students have a pre-existing professional background. Students are being prepared to advance their careers in a specific field through the development of research expertise.

In terms of research training, professional doctorates emphasize applied research. Using specific professional cases or topics, these programs typically teach students to design, implement, and communicate research, and to conduct independent research. Students are required to make an original, independent contribution to knowledge that is tied to applied research or professional practice, typically in their own profession. Because this is a research degree, students must be trained in research methodology.

In terms of career development, a professional doctorate allows experienced professionals to engage in applied research relevant to their profession, industry, or community. Professional doctorates often have a different student market—specifically, mid-career professionals who are seeking to advance their knowledge for career advancement and/or career transition.

As these students are often working professionals, most professional doctorates are delivered through blended or other non-traditional modes. This makes them more accessible for non-traditional doctoral students, who may choose to keep working while they study, and who are not available to relocate for the periods of "residency" normally built into PhD programs. Many professional doctoral programs offer considerable structure for the conduct of students' research. Various stages of research are encapsulated in courses, ensuring that students stay on track with their research. These students work with a supervisor, but also have the additional structure of the course format.

As we will discuss, there is considerable alignment between the fundamental purpose and requirements of the professional doctorate and the public good imperatives we identified in chapter 2. The opportunity for leading professionals in public, private, and non-profit sectors to both advance their career and take time to engage in structured reflection about the important challenges in their area of practice holds great potential for furthering the public good. We see professional doctorates—clearly anchored to specific industries and careers—as the most promising area for arts graduate education innovation and expansion.

Arts Graduate Degrees Typology

We have laid out the four main types of graduate degrees, the purposes they serve, and how they compare on the dimensions of research training and career development. And it is clear that there is room for improvement in their clarity and purpose.

This is particularly true for the MA. At present, it is a dog's breakfast. Some MA programs are research focused, but with vague research objectives. Some MA programs are professionally oriented, but with vague professional outcomes. Far too many MA programs allow their murky purposes to result in students being prepared solely for future doctoral study. Arts PhD programs are more coherent, but they remain too focused on training students for academic jobs that do not exist. Professional arts master's degrees are generally the most focused, serving clear purposes and audiences. Professional arts doctorates are also typically well focused, but are rare in Canada.

Explicitly stating the purpose of all four arts graduate degree types helps to provide a focus for programs and for students. We see the following degree purposes:

- Master of Arts: prepare sophisticated generalists with the capacity to conduct basic research.
- Professional master's degree: prepare professional practitioners.
- PhD: prepare research experts for research or research-informed careers.
- Professional doctorate: prepare advanced professional practitioners.

Given the "graduate" designation of all of these and the career needs of students, we do not consider it acceptable for any arts graduate degree to fail to advance research training or to fail to support career development; all arts graduate degrees need to succeed at both. Logically though, academic and professional degrees should differ in emphasis. MA and arts PhD degrees do and should focus more strongly on research training, while professional arts master's and doctorate degrees should be oriented more explicitly around career development. Also logically, master's and doctoral degrees should differ in their level of expertise: master's programs are more basic and foundational, while doctoral programs are more advanced and directed toward making contributions to knowledge. We summarize these distinctions in Table 5.1.

This is not revolutionary. We expect that most readers will largely agree with the typology and descriptions here. But things are not always as clear in practice. Using this typology can help provide clarity to students, programs, and universities. To return to the messy master of arts space, there are a number of emerging professionally oriented degrees holding a master of arts label. Such master of arts degrees signal their professional orientation through the adjective attached to the disciplinary name, such as an MA in "applied politics" rather than politics or political science, or an MA in "public history," rather than history. These programs tend to include an experiential component, like an internship, as well as courses oriented toward developing professional practice. Unlike professional master's degrees, however, their exact career tie can be vague.

TABLE 5.1 **Typology of Graduate Programs by Purpose**

	Master of Arts	Professional Master's	PhD	Professional Doctorate
Purpose	Prepare sophisticated generalists with the capacity to conduct basic research	Prepare professional practitioners	Prepare research experts for research or research-informed careers	Prepare advanced professional practitioners
Research Training	Focus on research preparation and ability to conduct basic research independently or as part of a team	Focus on research literacy	Focus on research contribution and ability to conduct advanced research that advances theory and knowledge in the discipline	Focus on research contribution and ability to conduct advanced research that advances professional practice or some other application
Career Development	Entry level for generalist careers	Tied to specific industry/ profession	A general research career preparation program that trains "stewards of the discipline"	Career advancement or transition, often tied to specific industry/ profession

We certainly applaud such innovations. Our concern is that they run the risk of muddled purposes in trying to serve several audiences and objectives at once. Given their academic degree designation, we would expect (or at least hope) such degrees to continue to meet our revised purpose of an MA, which is to prepare sophisticated generalists with the capacity to conduct basic research. This would then assume that the program has sufficient research training to meet the objective of research preparation, meaning that students are trained to conduct basic research independently or as part of a team. If such research training cannot be provided within the program, its position as a graduate-level academic degree is, in our minds, suspect, and we would encourage the unit to reposition it as a graduate-level professional degree.

What, then, about course-based MAs? Again, we go back to our revised purpose of an MA, which is to prepare sophisticated generalists with the capacity to conduct basic research. It is entirely possible to design a course-based program that includes sufficient training to conduct basic research. Indeed, a well-designed program might provide more rigorous research training than a traditional MA thesis program. However, it is equally possible to imagine a course-based MA with limited or no research training that essentially serves as a fifth year of undergraduate study. Such degrees serve no one, save perhaps the university finance officer.

Again, we are by no means trying to squelch innovation and new ideas. But we are concerned that, for too long, arts graduate education in Canada has expanded in all directions—innovative, perhaps, but lacking direction and clarity. The result is a cacophony that produces both overlap and gaps, leaving it largely up to students to try and figure out what might actually suit their needs, and producing far too much wasted effort and resources while not effectively serving the public good. Returning to the structure laid out in our typology is a first start in making sure that every degree has a clear purpose, and that it is indeed meeting that purpose.

The Degrees We Need: Linking Arts Graduate Education to Canada's Public Good

As outlined in chapter 2, we see considerable potential for arts graduate education to be explicitly and powerfully connected to the public good through thoughtful connection to the wicked problems imperative, the EDID imperative, and the talent imperative. There are important ways that each of the four arts graduate degree types can prepare graduates to engage with the three imperatives while meeting each degree's individual purpose.

The Wicked Problems Imperative

Arts research is essential to addressing wicked problems. This includes utilizing existing arts research in addressing wicked problems and fostering original arts research in the area of wicked problems. By explicitly connecting arts graduate education to the wicked problems imperative, we can increase both the number of individuals able to provide real-world solutions to wicked problems (through theoretical coursework learning that produces new ideas and ways of thinking) and the volume of original research knowledge on wicked problems (through graduate research). What this might mean in the context of reformulated graduate programs varies by program purpose.

All arts graduate programs have the opportunity to engage with the wicked problems imperative through coursework. As MA programs are intended to prepare sophisticated generalists, MA courses can be updated to help students understand ways in which theoretical or methodological tools can be used to offer insights into complex problems. PhD programs are intended to prepare research experts, so their coursework can take this to a higher level, challenging students to employ theoretical or methodological tools to offer novel insights into complex contemporary problems. Professional master's programs are intended to prepare professional practitioners, and their coursework can both familiarize students with research findings that relate to complex problems and push them to translate insights from research into concrete plans of action for professional practice. And as professional doctorate programs are intended to prepare advanced practitioners, their coursework can engage with the wicked problems imperative at a more advanced level by having students draw on their professional experience to articulate complex problems and employ theoretical or methodological tools to offer novel insights into these problems.

With the exception of the professional master's programs, arts graduate programs also have the opportunity to engage with the wicked problems imperative through student research. Some arts graduate students will choose to focus their research on topics that directly engage with wicked problems such as inequality, social polarization, or bioethics. This research will advance theoretical knowledge (in the case of arts PhD research) and applied knowledge (in the case of professional doctorate research). To further address the wicked problems imperative while advancing the degree purpose, programs can focus on the knowledge mobilization of research by graduate students on wicked problems: MA and PhD students can be trained to articulate wicked problems research findings for non-specialist audiences; PhD students can be trained to translate wicked problems research findings for mobilization into practice; and professional doctorate students can be trained to translate wicked problems research findings for application by professional or other audiences.

Of course, many arts graduate students will select research areas that are not clearly related to wicked problems. What can or should arts graduate programs do to prepare these students to address the wicked problems imperative? In addition to the coursework noted above, at a minimum, students should be encouraged and enabled to find the connections between the subject of their research focus and contemporary problems. Reflection on what interested the student in the area of inquiry can be a place to start. Beyond this, it is essential to encourage students to draw explicit connections between the research and the contemporary context, and to support them in identifying interested audiences and facilitating communication of research insights to those audiences.

While all arts graduate students stand to benefit from engaging with the wicked problems imperative, the competencies they develop must connect with the degree's purpose. Let's consider this by thinking through each degree and the wicked problem of climate change adaptation.

- *Master of Arts (e.g., history or sociology)*: Students in an MA program whose research is focused on climate change adaptation should acquire the research and interpersonal skills that will allow them to participate in multidisciplinary research teams that include both science and arts students. They should learn to communicate effectively across disciplinary boundaries and bring insights from research in their disciplinary home to inform the collective undertaking. Upon graduating, they should be able to communicate their research findings to both specialist and non-specialist audiences.
- *Professional master's (e.g., master of climate change, master of sustainability)*: Students in a professional master's program focused on climate change adaptation should learn to draw on relevant social sciences and humanities research in the field to inform plans of action for specific needs or clients.

- *Arts PhD (e.g., philosophy, geography)*: Students in a PhD program whose research is focused on climate change adaptation should become equipped to employ theoretical or methodological insights from their discipline of study to the issue of climate change adaptation. Their research might be part of a multidisciplinary effort involving researchers from the sciences, or it might be independent. Regardless, they should become adept at integrating insights from other disciplines and communicating their research across disciplinary boundaries and to non-specialist/practitioner audiences.
- *Professional doctorate (e.g., doctor of economics, doctor of public policy)*: Students in a professional doctorate program whose professional background is in a field related to (or likely to be affected by) climate change adaptation should learn to use their professional experience to identify research questions of direct interest for professional practice. They might work as part of an interdisciplinary research team, or they might conduct independent research with the objective of providing insights of use to professional practice.

Arts theory and research have tremendous potential to address Canada's public good by increasing student knowledge of theory and research into wicked problems and by supporting student research into wicked problems. Thoughtful program design is necessary to realize this potential.

The Equity, Diversity, Inclusion, and Decolonization (EDID) Imperative

Arts theorizing and research are central to advancing Canada's EDID imperative. In chapter 2, we argued that graduates of our arts graduate programs must be equipped to play a role in leading Canada's transition to become a more equitable, diverse, and inclusive society. This demands that these graduates be equipped with the theoretical tools and perspectives on these questions that are embedded in arts disciplines. By explicitly connecting arts graduate education to the EDID imperative, we can increase both the number of individuals able to provide EDID leadership (through theoretical coursework learning) and the volume of original research knowledge on equity, diversity, inclusion, and decolonization (through graduate research).

While some arts graduate programs have questions of equity, diversity, inclusion, and/or decolonization at their core and others do not, all arts graduate programs have the opportunity to engage with the EDID imperative through coursework. Arts graduate courses can familiarize students with theoretical perspectives and empirical work in their field of study that problematize questions of diversity and inclusion. For professional master's programs, courses can teach students how to integrate EDID best practices into their professional practice, and for professional doctorate programs, coursework can challenge students to reflect critically on their professional experience using theoretical perspectives informed by EDID.

Graduate research provides a further opportunity to engage with the EDID imperative. Regardless of their research topic, all arts research students can be trained to understand practices for EDID-informed research, with PhD and professional doctorate students being expected to employ appropriate techniques for EDID-informed research. (EDID-informed research is, of course, a contemporary research best practice that should be expected of all arts researchers, and not just those studying equity, diversity, inclusion, and/or decolonization!) Professional doctorate students can be trained to translate their research findings to inform inclusive and decolonial professional practice.

It is helpful to think through the meaning of this with concrete examples:

- *Master of arts (e.g., English, international relations)*: MA students must learn to draw on theories of decolonization, intersectionality, and critical theory to inform their understanding of "the canon," research design, and analysis. They must develop a good understanding of the ethical imperatives for research with Indigenous or other marginalized communities.
- *Professional master's (e.g., master of journalism, master of public administration)*: Students in a professional master's program should develop the ability to draw on theories of decolonization and

intersectionality to inform all aspects of their professional practice. They should also acquire relevant subject-matter expertise in areas such as Canada's history of colonialism and racism, or knowledge of Indigenous governance, cultures, and ways of knowing.
- *Arts PhD (e.g., linguistics, anthropology)*: Students in a PhD program should develop a deep understanding of theoretical perspectives, including decolonization, intersectionality, and critical theory. Their methodological approach should employ a sophisticated understanding of the same. For students whose research considers questions related to equity, diversity, inclusion, and/or decolonization, their research should contribute to the theoretical and/or methodological understanding in these areas. They should be prepared to undertake or lead research with marginalized communities.
- *Professional doctorate (e.g., doctor of humanities, doctor of social sciences)*: Students in a professional doctorate program should be able to draw on theories of decolonization, intersectionality, and critical theory to interpret their professional experience, and to identify research questions of direct interest for professional practice. Their research design should be EDID-informed, and if their research considers questions related to equity, diversity, inclusion, and/or decolonization, their findings should be of direct relevance to efforts to promote EDID in their profession or organization. The graduate will be prepared for professional practice as a leader focused on EDID.

Even for those students whose central focus is not on EDID, it is essential that they acquire familiarity with and an understanding of core considerations. This means they should develop an understanding of the theoretical and methodological tools that are employed to understand issues of equity and inclusion in the context of their discipline, and also an understanding of the ethical and methodological imperatives that follow from them. Beyond this, they should be prepared to undertake research or professional practice in the context of a diverse organization.

Arts graduate programs have the potential to lead in advancing Canada's EDID imperative. Indeed, if Canada's arts graduate programs are not going to do so, who will?

The Talent Imperative

In chapter 1, we argued that "universities must prepare students to meet Canada's needs, in practical ways. This requires deliberate attention to the development and refinement of the career competencies and skills that society needs and expects of university graduates." And we identified three literacy categories of skills that are in high demand: human, data, and technological literacy skills.

Human literacy skills—teamwork, communication, connection, motivation, leadership, ethical action, and empathy—are the "home ground" for arts graduate programs. Graduates of these programs must be able to demonstrate their ability to engage in collective and collaborative settings. And so, when we think about what kind of skill acquisition we should see in arts graduate programs, we prioritize these human literacy skills. For all arts graduate degrees, the focus on human literacy skills acquisition must be explicit and integrated into program-level learning outcomes.

As the professional programs are intended to prepare professional practitioners (professional master's programs) and advanced professional practitioners (professional doctorates), graduates must be able to demonstrate advanced levels of competence around these human literacy skills in order to achieve success in their professional practice. Conscious development and demonstration of these skills must form a central element of the curriculum of these programs. Professional doctorate graduates should be expected to demonstrate human literacy skills at a leadership level and be prepared to develop human skills in others, such as in roles as employees and volunteers.

MA programs are intended to prepare sophisticated generalists with the capacity to conduct basic research, so these students must learn to apply human skills, particularly as suited to the context of a research environment. PhD programs are intended to prepare experts for research or research-informed careers, so these students must learn to apply human skills at an advanced level, again particularly as suited to the context of a research environment.

Data literacy skills and technological literacy skills are also important and should be acquired at a level that is appropriate to the subject matter of the degree and/or the research the student is conducting. There is no one right answer here, but programs should identify areas where they can explicitly integrate data literacy skills and/or technological literacy skills into program learning outcomes.

Unlike the above imperatives, we are not going to list illustrative examples here. In most cases, revising arts graduate programs to meet Canada's talent imperative requires little more than deliberate attention to literacy development. Arts graduate programs already develop human literacy skills, and many develop data literacy skills and/or technological literacy skills. Moving literacy development explicitly into program learning outcomes will help programs be more purposeful and effective in their efforts.

Connecting Graduate Degree Purpose with Public Good Imperatives

Earlier in this chapter, we argued for the need for arts graduate degrees to have a clear purpose and presented a typology of degrees and purposes. Connecting arts graduate education with Canada's public good will improve the ability of arts graduate education to achieve these degree purposes (see Table 5.2). Sophisticated generalists with the capacity to conduct basic research (MA graduates), professional practitioners (professional master's graduates), research experts working in research or research-informed careers (arts PhD graduates), and advanced professional practitioners (professional doctorate graduates) are all positioned to be leaders and key actors in advancing Canada's public good. They all will benefit from an understanding of how to use research to address wicked problems, the importance and complexity of equity, diversity, inclusion, and decolonization, and the development of human literacy skills alongside data and technological literacy skills. Engagement with the three public good imperatives will benefit these students' personal career and research contributions. Through these students' impact upon Canada's public good, Canada will benefit as well.

TABLE 5.2 **Addressing the Public Good Imperatives with Arts Graduate Degrees**

	Master of Arts	Professional Master's	Arts PhD	Professional Doctorate
Purpose	• Prepare sophisticated generalists with the capacity to conduct basic research	• Prepare professional practitioners	• Prepare research experts for research or research-informed careers	• Prepare advanced professional practitioners
Wicked Problems Imperative	• Understand ways in which theoretical or methodological tools can be used to offer insight into complex problems • Conduct research as part of a multidisciplinary team • Articulate research findings for non-specialist audiences	• Be familiar with research findings that relate to complex problems • Translate insights from research into concrete plans of action for professional practice	• Employ theoretical or methodological tools to offer novel insights into complex contemporary problems • Conduct research independently or as part of a multidisciplinary team • Articulate research findings for non-specialist audiences • Translate research findings for mobilization into practice	• Draw on professional experience to articulate complex problems • Employ theoretical or methodological tools to offer novel insights into these problems • Conduct applied research independently or as part of a multidisciplinary team • Translate research findings for application by professional or other audiences

TABLE 5.2 *continued*

	Master of Arts	Professional Master's	Arts PhD	Professional Doctorate
EDID Imperative	• Be familiar with theoretical perspectives and empirical work in their field of study that problematize questions of diversity and inclusion • Understand best practices for EDID-informed research	• Be familiar with theoretical perspectives and empirical work in their field of study that problematize questions of diversity and inclusion • Integrate EDID best practices into their professional practice	• Have a deep understanding of theoretical perspectives and empirical work in their field of study that problematize questions of diversity and inclusion • Understand and employ appropriate techniques for EDID-informed research	• Reflect critically on professional experience using theoretical perspectives informed by EDID • Understand and employ appropriate techniques for EDID-informed research • Translate research findings to inform inclusive and decolonial professional practice
Talent Imperative	• Acquire and apply human skills, particularly as suited to the context of a research environment • Acquire and employ data and/or technological skills as appropriate to their research subject matter	• Acquire and apply human skills at an advanced level • Acquire and employ data and/or technological skills as appropriate to the degree's subject matter	• Acquire and apply human skills at an advanced level, particularly as suited to the context of a research environment • Acquire and employ data and/or technological skills as appropriate to their research subject matter	• Acquire and apply human skills at a leadership level, and be prepared to develop human skills in others (e.g., students, employees) • Acquire and employ data and/or technological skills as appropriate to the degree's subject matter

Non-Degree Arts Graduate Education

Our focus in this chapter has been on graduate degrees. But there has been an expansion in recent years in non-degree graduate programming in the form of graduate diplomas and graduate certificates. This field is far less structured, as CMEC does not define graduate certificates and diplomas, and few provinces and no territories have qualifications frameworks that go beyond degree programs specifically for graduate programs (Canadian Information Centre for International Credentials 2022). The exceptions are Alberta and Ontario. Alberta universities can offer six non-degree graduate options: graduate certificates, graduate diplomas, post-master's certificates, post-master's diplomas, postdoctoral certificates, and post-doctoral diplomas (Alberta 2018). In contrast, the Ontario Qualifications guidelines identify nine levels of certificates and diplomas, including a post-diploma certificate, with none of the levels being identified specifically as "graduate" (Ontario 2022). In the absence of provincial frameworks, universities in other provinces establish their own guidelines or develop credentials in the absence of guidelines.

Non-degree graduate programs typically pose limited costs to universities since they are set up on the backs of existing programs and requirements. They may also be seen as revenue generators and as an opportunity to fill empty seats in graduate courses. Broadly speaking, Canadian graduate certificates and diplomas drawing on the arts disciplines come in three general forms:

- *Standalone.* These are typically abbreviated or specialized versions of professional master's degrees. Students are admitted solely to a non-degree program and typically do not aspire to immediate further studies.
- *Laddered.* A student can start by taking a graduate certificate or diploma and then either exit with the non-degree credential or transition into a master's degree.
- *Concurrent.* These are taken by students already enrolled in a master's or doctoral program. These programs-within-programs allow students to develop further specialized credentials through a particular skills or area focus.

It is possible for a single non-degree credential to cover all three of these forms. For example, a graduate certificate in conflict management can be a standalone certificate for students seeking to gain expertise in that area, but also be available for students thinking of laddering into a master's degree in a related field, and also be a concurrent credential for students already enrolled in an MA or PhD program. The non-degree credential space is anticipated to expand over time with the emergence of micro-credentials, which may or may not be offered at the graduate level, depending on provincial- and/or university-specific frameworks.

Non-degree graduate credentials can benefit arts graduate students in a number of ways. Standalone credentials can provide specialized training to students who do not seek full degrees. Laddered credentials can provide access to graduate programs to individuals who do not meet the admissions requirements, allowing them to demonstrate their ability to be successful in future degree-level graduate studies. Concurrent credentials can serve as an off-ramp for graduate students who are unable to complete their degree programs.

There is a significant opportunity for arts programs to use these credentials to do much more to benefit students, the arts, and Canada's public good by organizing around the three imperatives we have laid out. In the end, most existing credentials remain discipline or unit based, running concurrently or on top of existing degrees, and are oriented around content and particular academic areas, whether disciplinary or interdisciplinary. But arts departments could cooperate to offer knowledge and skill development beyond this, by bundling courses together around wicked problems, equity, diversity, inclusion, and decolonization, and/or a particular talent area. There is scope for integration of relevant practitioners as instructors, and for professional development to be incorporated into the credentials' learning outcomes.

To spark your imagination, in Table 5.3, we sketch out the following three possible certificates that could be offered as standalone credentials or as opportunities to ladder into MA programs, or that could be offered concurrently with an MA or PhD program.

- *Professionally oriented graduate certificate in public opinion research.* This could be offered as a standalone for university graduates from

all disciplines or concurrently for arts graduate students in political science, sociology, or other social sciences, who could count some of their graduate courses toward the certificate. Students who took the certificate would be well-placed to find entry-level positions in public opinion research, or in organizations (including government) that frequently work with public opinion data.
- *Graduate diploma in spatial visualization.* This would equip students to use advanced geographic visualization software to display and analyze complex data. With six required courses, but no thesis or other research product, the diploma could be completed in a relatively short period of time or on a part-time basis.
- *Graduate certificate in health policy.* This would bring together expertise from the health sciences and the policy sciences. It would be of interest to health care professionals with an interest in moving into policy-relevant roles in health care administration, as well as students in arts graduate programs in psychology, sociology, and other disciplines whose interests relate to health care policy and administration.

Non-degree graduate credentials present a considerable opportunity for arts units. By having these credentials available as standalone programs, arts units can increase their impact by reaching new markets of students who would never consider a full arts graduate program. By having these credentials available as laddering programs, arts units can foster and build graduate enrollments. And by having these credentials available as concurrent programs, arts units can provide specialized training to interested MA and PhD students—and a graceful off-ramp to those students who need one.

Students and arts units stand to benefit from the development of non-degree graduate credentials that are designed thoughtfully. And so too does Canada's public good.

TABLE 5.3 **Examples of Hypothetical Arts Graduate Non-Degree Certifications**

	Professional Certificates and Diplomas	Specialist Certificates and Diplomas	Interdisciplinary Certificates and Diplomas
Examples	• Graduate certificate in public opinion research	• Graduate diploma in spatial visualization	• Graduate certificate in health policy
Purpose	• Develop career-specific skills	• Develop technical skills	• Develop interdisciplinary understanding of a specific topic
Credential Learning Objectives	• Prepare graduates to work in the public opinion or related industry • Integrate graduates' understanding of public opinion research methodology with professional skills, including communication, teamwork, and marketing	• Prepare graduates to use spatial visualization software and skills in various settings • Prepare graduates for a specialized role using spatial visualization within an organization or as part of a research project • Integrate graduates' advanced technical competencies with professional skills or knowledge in data-oriented settings	• Expose students to an interdisciplinary area of focus, drawing on insights from the health and policy sciences • Equip students to convey a comprehensive understanding of key issues in health policy, and relevant analytical tools for addressing them • Develop professional and research skills that students can apply in their area of study • Offer students graduate-level study that deepens systematic knowledge and fosters professional development
Wicked Problems Imperative	• Apply methodological tools to offer insight into complex problems	• Apply methodological tools to offer insight into complex problems	• Apply theoretical tools to offer novel insight into complex contemporary problems

TABLE 5.3 *continued*

	Professional Certificates and Diplomas	Specialist Certificates and Diplomas	Interdisciplinary Certificates and Diplomas
EDID Imperative	• Utilize theoretical perspectives and empirical work in their field of study that problematize questions of equity, diversity, inclusion, and decolonization • Understand practices for EDID-informed research	• Utilize theoretical perspectives and empirical work in their field of study that problematize questions of equity, diversity, inclusion, and decolonization • Understand practices for EDID-informed research	• Utilize theoretical perspectives and empirical work in their field of study that problematize questions of equity, diversity, inclusion, and decolonization
Talent Imperative	• Build human skills, particularly as suited to the context of a research environment • Build data and technological skills	• Build data and technological skills	• Build human skills, particularly as suited to the context of health policy

Reimagining Credentials

There are a number of ways in which the credential structures of arts graduate education, both degree and non-degree programs, can be reimagined to advance Canada's public good—and at the same time advance the interests of arts graduate students, faculty, and units. But this is just the foundation. In the next chapter, we build our vision of how the content and curriculum of every graduate program can be reimagined and rebuilt to become more efficient, more deliberate, more inclusive, more talent focused, and more student oriented—all in the service of the public good.

6

The EDITS Vision

Picture, if you can, a future state for arts graduate education in Canada. It looks like this. Arts graduate programs are clearly responsive to Canada's public good, occupying an educational sweet spot that brings together the wicked problems, EDID, and talent imperatives. Individuals with Canadian arts graduate degrees are valued and sought-after knowledge workers whose contributions to Canadian society and Canada's economy are recognized and rewarded. Arts graduate students are motivated by the clear connections they see between their studies and the world. Arts faculty members are excited by the renewed focus in their teaching and research programs. Arts deans are sleeping easier, with in-demand programs and newfound respect among their colleagues at deans' council. And arts graduate programs are robust—while enrollments are not necessarily any higher than current levels, program quality is undeniable, and demand has increased as applicants have started to appreciate the value of an arts graduate degree.

Our last chapter laid out a new foundational plan for arts graduate degrees. Now in this chapter, we lay out a vision of how to animate these degrees and link them to the three imperatives of the public good. We also showed in chapter 4 that most arts graduate programs develop and grow more by accident than intentional design. They can be heavy on aspirations and hopes, but are often light on specifics and measurable outcomes. This chapter presents a different approach by laying out an intentional vision to guide all arts graduate education.

Defining the Destination

In our opening chapters, we argued that arts graduate education could help advance Canada's public good by addressing three imperatives: the wicked problems imperative, EDID imperative, and talent imperative. At first glance, the three imperatives seem disconnected from the experience of a student sitting in a library writing a thesis about Beauvoir's early novels. And we can hear our colleagues' scathing critiques of our efforts to turn the PhD into an MBA.

But that is not our purpose. We believe that the student writing about Beauvoir is cultivating rich human literacy. They are situating their work within a cultural and historical context; they are reconsidering their work in light of contemporary conversations and drawing connections; they are finding ways to communicate their understanding of this work to various audiences. Depending on their research question, our student may be considering questions of equity and diversity, drawing upon feminist and intersectional literatures. They may also be considering challenges of and approaches to wicked problems in Beauvoir's time.

We want to ensure that our Beauvoir scholar is able to appreciate and articulate the human literacy they have developed, and to use their advanced communication skills to convey this understanding. We also want to ensure that, along with the opportunity to explore Beauvoir's writing, our student is exposed to professional development opportunities that allow them to identify the competencies that transfer from their arts education, help them transition from their graduate program to rewarding employment, and help them to identify and fill the gaps that they find in making their plans.

We see rich potential for arts graduate education to link directly to Canada's public good imperatives. Arts graduate courses, research, and

TABLE 6.1 **Linking Arts Graduate Education to Canada's Public Good Imperatives**

Imperative	What It Is	Arts Graduate Education Has the Potential to…
Wicked Problems Imperative	• Need for approaches to ill-defined and interwoven society-based problems that lack tidy, lasting solutions	• Advance knowledge of wicked problems and their (untidy) solutions • Increase capacity to develop creative and feasible real-world solutions
EDID Imperative	• Need to address long-standing issues of racism and systemic discrimination • Need to advance decolonization	• Interrogate historical and present practices • Identify opportunities for improved justice, fairness, and equity
Talent Imperative	• Need for advanced knowledge workers with human literacy, data literacy, and/or technological literacy to address the opportunities and challenges that cannot be handled by automation, bots, and artificial intelligence	• Serve as the dominant source of advanced human literacy talent • Develop unique talent capacities through the combination of human literacy with data literacy and/or technological literacy

extracurricular activities have the potential to make lasting meaningful advances. Table 6.1 sketches this out for each of the three imperatives.

But the key word here is "potential." Programs won't realize these results without thoughtful attention, and often some heavy lifting. Alternatively, some might argue "we're already doing all this." Perhaps your program is—but then your program is a rare exception, and the rest of Canada's arts graduate programs need to catch up, so bear with us.

To meet this potential of serving the public good imperatives, arts graduate programs need intentional vision—in their design, their requirements, their content, and their delivery. We've already sketched out the structure of degrees. Now let's look at the vision that should populate those degrees. We call this the EDITS vision.

The EDITS Vision

To serve Canada's public good, and to achieve their potential, arts graduate programs must be efficient, deliberate, inclusive, talent developing, and student focused. And yes, the acronym is EDITS. To edit is to correct, condense, revise, and modify in order to improve. And so, arts graduate programs need EDITS. Next, we lay out the five elements of the EDITS vision, along with checklists of specific aspects that each arts graduate program should have, in order to respond to Canada's public good imperatives. The EDITS framework is intended to apply to programs. For readers interested in adapting it to refine their approach to graduate supervision, Appendix 3 offers some guidance.

Efficient

The concept of efficiency refers to optimal allocation of resources. At the risk of being labeled neoliberal, or simply not a lot of fun, we assert that the resources relevant to graduate education—university funds, faculty members' time, and students' time—have value. And these resources should be allocated in a way that respects that value.

When thinking about program design, efficiency in the use of university resources (most notably the time of faculty) is important. Faculty members' time and energy, collectively and individually, are among a university's top assets. Tiny graduate courses, laborious graduate supervisory and supervisory committee loads, and tedious faculty-run graduate admissions and scholarships processes are all examples of a dubious use of faculty time and energy—and thus a questionable use of university assets.

We're not saying everything is completely wrong. We're not saying that time spent on graduate students is time squandered according to the great balance sheet somewhere in central administration. We're saying that it is often inefficient, in ways that are detrimental for everyone including faculty and students themselves.

While decentralization and discipline-specific education are essential in an arts graduate degree, there are significant opportunities for pan-disciplinary cooperation to increase efficiency in course delivery.

While research is an essential means to achieve learning outcomes for many arts graduate degrees, there are significant opportunities to reconsider "capstone" research products to increase efficiency in graduate supervision. While faculty engagement in graduate administrative processes ensures academic oversight, in most universities there are significant opportunities to streamline procedures.

Degree structures should allow for efficiency not only in program delivery, but also for students, whose time is a valuable resource. Programs should be organized to be completed in the minimum necessary time, acknowledging the opportunity costs of full-time graduate education for students.

Efficiency also requires a better link between programs and funding. Funding packages should be extended to match actual average completion times in the arts, which are different from STEM, especially for the PhD. Achieving this may also mean revising program requirements so that nearly all students can reasonably finish within the funding window they've been given. TA and RA assignments should be more systematic and integrated with students' actual programs—meaning less assigning TAs to courses unrelated to their own interests and barely within their competency. Arts programs should move closer to the STEM lab-based model that integrates RAs' work more closely with their own projects.

Efficiency also goes beyond any individual arts graduate program to consider the larger ecosphere of graduate programming within a university. It allows us to take a hard look at whether the proliferation of graduate programs in arts disciplines is an efficient use of public resources. This includes both between different universities and proliferation within institutions. By aiming for efficiency, universities can foster questions of whether their programs are competing with one another for the same student audiences, and if there are opportunities to reimagine programs to either consolidate or differentiate.

What Does "Efficient" Mean for Program Design?

An efficient program will have all, or at least most, of the following characteristics.

Adequate Resources
The unit(s) are adequately resourced to offer a robust program; they have sufficient capacity to offer courses and supervise. A graduate program that relies on faculty members offering individualized courses off the sides of their desks and in addition to their regular teaching load, on adding a couple of graduate students into upper-year undergraduate courses, and on regularly asking faculty from other units or institutions to supervise is not efficient.

Parsimonious Design
Degree requirements are lean. They only require what is necessary to achieve the degree-level learning outcomes. Funding packages match the actual program. Parsimonious design achieves the following important outcomes:

- *Efficient Use of Faculty Members' Time*: Despite the temptation to think of faculty members' time as elastic, stretching to meet ever-growing demands for teaching, supervision, service, and research, we think of it as finite. An efficiently designed graduate program recognizes that faculty time spent teaching a course with only three students is time not spent on something else. And that the effort involved in teaching three students isn't much less than the effort involved in teaching a dozen students. Likewise, program design in the arts must recognize that graduate supervision does not always contribute to a faculty member's research program in the way it does in most STEM disciplines; most students work on independent projects unrelated to their supervisor's own. This is a crucial point often overlooked in university-wide visions: supervision in the arts is typically a time consumer, not a time saver. Supervisory capacity needs to be treated as a finite and valuable resource.
- *Efficient Use of Students' Time*: In addition to the financial cost of enrolling in a graduate program, students bear the opportunity cost of graduate education: the income they would earn if they were not in school. It follows that program length must be proportional to the value of the credential, linked to the program's learning

outcomes, and funded accordingly. Efficiency in program design supports equity, diversity, and inclusion for students. For potential students from non-traditional backgrounds, the opportunity costs of graduate education are high: they are often less able to afford to take a gamble that the income lost while pursuing five or more years of graduate education might be compensated through higher earnings post-graduation.

Focused Coursework
Individual courses are clearly linked to the degree's learning outcomes.

Integration Between Programs and TA/RA Work
Assistantships are as much as possible linked to students' actual coursework and projects, by design rather than random luck.

Institutional Integration and Coordination
Programs are integrated into their institutional context and achieve efficiencies by coordinating and sharing university resources efficiently. This may involve courses shared across programs or even offered at the faculty level. And programs within a single university do not compete with each other.

Courses and Other Offerings (Like Professional Development) Are Delivered at the Most Effective Level (Department/Unit, Faculty, University)
We think of this as the principle of "anti-subsidiarity"—offerings should be at the most centralized level possible, while still being effective. We believe there is a significant role for arts faculties to play in finding this effective level. University-wide professional development workshops spanning both STEM and arts disciplines may not be very effective, but there isn't a compelling reason why the departments of history, sociology, and political science must each organize their own overlapping professional development workshops. Here, the faculty of arts may be the Goldilocks-style "just right" venue.

Challenging the Idea of Efficient Arts Graduate Programs

We argue that reimagined arts graduate programs should be efficient, and specifically that they should be defined by adequate resources, parsimonious design, focused coursework, and institutional integration and coordination.

Some will fixate on the call for "adequate resources" as the number one challenge to a strong model of arts graduate education. Money may not solve all our problems, but it's a darn good start! Now, there is no doubt that many arts departments and programs have faced resource challenges over the years. Humanities and social science departments in some institutions have seen their faculty complements shrink over time, with graduate student funding limited and diminishing; others have had to settle for stagnant growth or just trying to stay afloat.

As arts faculty, we appreciate this pain. But we will leave it to others to argue with university provosts and provincial governments about adequate university funding. Instead, we make a bold claim here, and one that will undoubtedly upset a few readers: departments should not have graduate programs that the faculty complement size and expertise cannot support. And if this is the case, the solution is not necessarily more resources to catch up, but the discontinuation or curbing of unsustainable programs that are just not affordable.

This may seem unfair to faculty members, who may respond, "But my buddy in computer science has a grad program!" or "I have research money but there are no grad students for me to hire!" And it is. But we are deliberately choosing fairness to students (see our "student focused" discussion later in the chapter) over fairness to faculty relative to their faculty colleagues. As we explained in chapter 4, all too often graduate programs have proliferated to serve faculty interests but not necessarily student interests. We are asking the rude questions that should have been asked long ago: "why do you need a graduate program?" and "is a graduate program the best use of your time and everyone else's?" If you really think a program is warranted, we challenge you to consider how it can be made sustainable and robust beyond the whims of annual budget cycles and short-term faculty needs. These are the questions that senior university administrators have to ask when making difficult resource decisions, so anticipate them. Growth and letting a thousand flowers bloom are not always good.

"Parsimonious design" may also rankle some. Responses here may include: "Everyone should have to learn [insert your discipline's random thing here]!" "Students need to be balanced and learn about nuts *and* soup!" "Students need time to explore and grow in directions they haven't yet thought about!" "We can't stifle creativity to create cookie cutter students!" "If they want an MBA, let them enroll in the business school!" We appreciate these arguments. But we're not arguing for the bare-bones minimum and grad studies lite. We're arguing for careful deliberation and calculation about each step of the program, rather than just following well-worn paths and/or replicating faculty members' own graduate experiences of two decades ago. And we're certainly not against redundancy or overlap, which have clear pedagogical value. But overlap needs to be conscious and planned, not a random by-product.

"Institutional integration and coordination" may also set off some understandable eye-rolling. Universities are decentralized organizations for many good reasons, and the one-size-fits-all approach is definitely not the way to design academic programs. But, we're not arguing for the centralization of everything or for forcing programs into mediocre single-size boxes. If anything, we want to avoid a centralization–decentralization struggle, and instead force a constant question: what level is best equipped to make decisions and to have the resources to do so? The answer varies for different functions and between individual disciplines and programs—and we're good with that.

Deliberate

A deliberate curriculum starts with a clear sense of the purpose of the credential. Faculty members should be able to make a compelling pitch for why their graduate program exists. A degree program should be designed to accomplish something more than simply collecting student tuition and absorbing faculty and student time.

Deliberate curriculum begins with the end in mind. Writing about revitalization of medical school curricula, Krackov and Pohl (2011, 571) write, "the deliberate practice curricular planning model requires students and faculty to focus on purposefully designed outcome-based learning objectives, appropriate content and instructional methods, formative assessment, feedback, reflection, and mentoring at each stage of development as the tools that support learning in a competency-based system." In addition to grounding a student in a discipline or interdisciplinary area of study and preparing them in some way to undertake independent research, curricula should explicitly identify why there is value in this grounding and this preparation. What does the degree prepare graduates to do post-graduation? If the answer is "conduct research," what kind of research? For what audiences? Paid for by whom? If the answer is to contribute to knowledge, what kind of contribution is envisioned? These are hard questions that must be addressed at the beginning of any conversation about curriculum.

This explicit understanding of a program's raison d'etre informs—and ideally directs—curriculum design. For example, if we want our PhD-prepared historians to be able to work in teams to create understanding of historical bases of contemporary issues, then the curriculum needs to give them opportunities to do just that. This might take the form of participating in interdisciplinary research teams (as a form of experiential learning) or doing an internship (work-integrated learning).

In defining the purpose of an arts graduate degree, it is essential to distinguish the degree from undergraduate credentials. Undergraduate arts education prepares flexible generalists: critical thinkers able to communicate effectively, be versatile, and navigate complexity. Graduate education in the arts disciplines should build on these foundations, deepening knowledge in a particular area, but also honing one or two of the key competencies to a level of "mastery."

In chapter 5, we discussed the purposes of various degrees in arts disciplines: the MA, the professional master's, the PhD, and the professional doctorate. Within the broad purpose of each degree there is room for specialization of purpose. For instance, an MA intended to extend students' knowledge of one subfield of a discipline should be structured quite differently from one intended to develop students as researchers. A PhD intended to prepare students to be independent researchers will have different learning objectives than one intended to prepare students to teach a broad range of courses in a discipline. If arts graduate education is to achieve the public good that we envision for it, the purpose of degree programs must be clear. There may be variation across programs, with different purposes articulated, but the purpose must be the first step, even before the identification of learning objectives and then the mapping of curriculum onto them.

If a program substantially recruits international students—and most do—it must also be deliberate about why it does so, beyond vague desires to maintain program size or generate tuition revenue. How does the program benefit students from other countries? Are international students set up for success? Are the learning outcomes and program design appropriate for individuals from other cultures and educational systems?

Graduate students are also typically funded—essentially paid to go to school. As with efficiency above, there is opportunity for much greater integration between programs and funding. The match may not be perfect; the teaching needs of a unit may mean TAs are assigned to courses outside their interests but within their competency, and a good RA assignment outside of a student's main focus may usefully expand their skills and networks. But the default should be that funding is linked and integrated with a student's specific academic program and contributes to their skill development, rather than this being a happy coincidence.

What Does "Deliberate" Mean for Program Design?

A deliberate program will have all, or at least most, of the following characteristics.

Stated Purpose

We advocate that the stated purpose of arts programs must link in some way to the three public goods imperatives (the wicked problems, talent, and EDID imperatives) we set out in chapter 2. Deliberate design means that meeting these imperatives is explicitly and thoughtfully built into the program structure. This explicitness helps students move through and beyond their programs with a sense of purpose. It must be noted that an ethical mission-driven program will prioritize students' needs over faculty research needs and institutional revenue and rankings needs. More on this in a bit.

Clear Learning Outcomes
The provincial quality assurance frameworks that guide the broader curriculum review processes at Canadian universities increasingly demand "degree-level learning outcomes" and the mapping of curriculum onto those outcomes. Many faculty members have gone through the bureaucratic exercise of creating these maps, generally in an effort to avoid changing our curriculum by justifying what we have. We want to suggest a radical proposition: the bureaucrats might actually be onto something here. But to enjoy the benefits of their insight, you have to start with the degree-level outcomes, and then redesign curriculum to meet them. And that means being prepared to change curriculum. Perhaps significantly. Why engage in this challenging task? Because you can't achieve efficiency for students or faculty without doing so.

Parsimonious Design
We discussed this point above with respect to efficiency. Here we will double down on the idea by raising additional ideas:

- *Elimination of the Superfluous*: The beauty of curriculum design driven by program-level learning outcomes is that it allows curriculum designers to distinguish between what's necessary and what's extraneous. For example, a social anthropology PhD requires a deep knowledge of qualitative research methodology, but only requires knowledge of a second language if the linguistic knowledge is necessary for research.
- *Completion Is Possible Within the Allotted Time*: A deliberately designed degree should be possible to finish in the time allotted for the degree. Timeliness should be built into the design and funding packages. Because—we'll say it again—students' and faculty members' time has value, and stretching degrees for additional years isn't a good use of time. And this is particularly true for students from non-traditional backgrounds. Of course, there are exceptions—life happens and circumstances differ—but on balance, timely completion is desirable for all.

Pedagogical Alignment

Deliberate programs match pedagogical approaches to program learning outcomes. If we want graduates of arts graduate programs to be able to work effectively in interdisciplinary teams, then those programs should include working in interdisciplinary teams. If we want an arts graduate program to prepare its graduates to engage meaningfully with the public, then its requirements should include experience engaging meaningfully with the public. Here, we need to think creatively about different kinds of pedagogy, such as courses that don't take place in classrooms and that aren't focused around a long reading list; internships; and research products that don't look like a traditional thesis. Assuming that the program is mission driven, a pedagogically aligned program will almost certainly do the following:

- *Use Research Training and Theoretical Training Purposefully*: The timeworn student lament "when are we ever going to use this?" should not arise in graduate school. If a program or course has particular requirements for research and theoretical training not related to a student's main area of study or project, we must ask why. Vague answers about establishing solid foundations or creating well-rounded students are not enough. Research and theoretical requirements should not be time-consuming detours from the main path. They must clearly link to specific learning outcomes and overall student progress.
- *Integrate Experiential and Work-Integrated Learning to Support Program-Level Outcomes*: We know that we really sound like shills for provincial governments and senior administration at this point, but hear us out. If we want to prepare arts graduate students to meet Canada's public good challenges, we need to consider requiring a little less reading and writing and a little more of the activities that look like what program graduates might be doing out in the community after they graduate. This could mean internships or courses where students take part in an interdisciplinary research mobilization team. To be clear, we don't think that under-resourced graduate programs need to be delivering on all these things; after all, we believe in efficiency.

Rather, our call is on SSHRC to fund interdisciplinary arts training initiatives through programs like the NSERC CREATE program (which provides professional training to new natural science and engineering researchers) and/or the expansion of the SSHRC partnered research training initiative program. Our call is also on arts and graduate studies faculties and universities to provide assistance with internship development and placement. The role for departments and faculty members is simply to be enthusiastic proponents of these kinds of requirements. Departments shouldn't have to create the programs themselves, but they should push for their development and connect students to the ones that do exist, encouraging them to take part.

- *Match Research Products to Program-Level Outcomes*: Graduate degrees in arts disciplines generally require a research product of some kind—normally a major research paper, thesis, or doctoral dissertation. And while coursework-only master's programs are growing, as we've noted, they still inevitably require weighty research papers in each course. There is room for innovation and reimagination. For decades, the form of the doctoral dissertation was fixed: a first draft of a scholarly monograph. Over time, the dissertation form has evolved in some disciplines to include the "three paper" model. But other models are available, as the Canadian Association for Graduate Studies' *Report of the Task Force on the Dissertation* documented (CAGS 2018). What kind of paper, thesis, or dissertation—or other product—should a student produce to demonstrate they have fulfilled the learning objectives of their degree? We urge programs to think carefully about this as they design their degree requirements.

Appropriate Fit for International Students

Programs that admit international students must be designed and appropriate for international students, so that these students are set up for success.

Evidence-Based Refinements

Deliberate design also requires feedback and course correction. It isn't enough just to articulate the purpose of a graduate program ("to prepare graduates to..."); program leaders must then measure their success in doing so. More careful attention to student outcomes—graduation rate, time to completion, and subsequent employment—is essential to fulfill the potential of these degrees. Curriculum design is hard work, and it's often added on top of a full workload for graduate chairs, department chairs, and faculty members in general. But we want to make the case that it is meaningful work, and that graduate curriculum should be reconsidered frequently. Are the program-level learning objectives still appropriate? If so, are they achieving their aims? Where do graduates end up? Are they satisfied with the outcome? Do they have feedback on how well their graduate education prepared them for the work they are now doing? How can the curriculum be updated to reflect this feedback?

Challenging the Idea of Deliberate Arts Graduate Programs

We have argued that reimagined arts graduate programs should be deliberate, and specifically that they should be defined by a stated purpose, clear learning outcomes, parsimonious design, pedagogical alignment, and evidence-based refinements. We have already discussed possible objections to parsimonious design, so let's consider some possible concerns about a deliberate program.

Getting to a "stated purpose" is challenging because it may force difficult conversations. Many graduate programs have a wide but blurred focus in an effort to please everybody in the department, as selecting and expressly emphasizing particular fields or approaches within the discipline could mean winners and losers. The decentralization and democratic nature of academic governance means it is difficult and divisive to make hard choices. Better to just let everyone do their own thing. But putting off hard conversations ultimately serves no one, especially students trying to decide between different programs at different institutions that all offer much the same thing.

The term "learning outcomes" has acquired a reputation as jargon for understandable reasons (especially for anyone who has sat through long discussions of the difference between "learning outcomes" and "learning objectives"). But we strongly believe in the fundamental idea behind learning outcomes: that planning curriculum should start with what students should know and be able to do at the end of a course or program, and then work backwards to identify how to get there. The alternative, too often, is for the instructor to start with a pile of content that they feel obligated to cover and then write up some outcomes at the end based on what's in the pile. This is particularly risky in graduate studies, where the pile can always increase. Working with learning outcomes, or whatever you want to call them, brings discipline and focus. We think that's good.

When it comes to "pedagogical alignment," the issue is that faculty can resist being told "what to teach," often seeing this as an issue of academic freedom. Usher (2020) argues that this is largely unique to Canada and/or North America, while in other systems faculty are much more open to discussing each other's courses and agreeing on common approaches. We'll sidestep taking a full position on this, but we don't think it's overly contentious to suggest that courses and course content in a given program should all fit well together by design, not by osmosis or happy accident. This may mean some give and take from everybody, but so be it.

We admit that "evidence-based refinements" sounds like more jargon. But here are some questions. How many of your graduate students finished on time over the last five years? What are they doing now? Did they find their program satisfactory? What refinements would they suggest? Do the answers vary by subfield or stream? If you don't know the answers to these sorts of questions, perhaps you should start asking them. They might well lead to changes that improve your program.

Inclusive

We argued in chapter 2 that graduate education in arts disciplines holds great potential to help Canada address the profound questions of equity, diversity, inclusion, and decolonization that face us—the EDID imperative. But to do so, graduate programs must be designed with these considerations at their core. This begins with building inclusive and anti-racist practices into admissions processes, designing programs to embody principles of inclusion, and ensuring that curriculum aligns with these principles. It also means finding opportunities to link funding more clearly to actual needs in a way that reduces rather than exacerbates inequities. And it means actually valuing the contributions of international students to enhancing the diversity and quality of programs.

What Does "Inclusive" Mean for Program Design?

An inclusive program will have all, or at least most, of the following characteristics.

Inclusive Environment
Equity, diversity, inclusion, and decolonization are central to the administrative, pedagogical, and engagement practices in an inclusive graduate program. Careful attention must be given to ensuring an inclusive environment within the graduate program, both in the classroom and beyond. This is a challenging undertaking that requires faculty members to reconsider their practices as teachers and supervisors, departments to reconsider everything from their speakers' series to their social events, and students to engage productively with one another. To achieve this, departments will need to do the following:

- *Ensure a Professional Work Setting*: An inclusive program is situated in a professionalized institutional context. Inclusiveness means freedom from harassment, verbal or otherwise. Institutions all have policies—of varying quality—that prohibit harassment and bullying. Where academic leaders can make a difference is in the tone they set and the swift and meaningful actions they take when concerns arise.
- *Invest in Faculty and Staff Training*: Regardless of the diversity of the faculty complement, it is essential to ensure that faculty and program staff are equipped to make inclusive admissions decisions and create an inclusive environment within and beyond the classroom. Anti-bias training for admissions committees is a start, but continuing anti-racism education for faculty, staff, and students is the better standard.

- Foster Welcoming Social Connections: Graduate programs are communities that extend beyond the classroom. Many of the occasions and rituals—often centred around consumption of alcohol—exclude some segment of a diverse faculty and student community. Careful attention must be given to creating new opportunities for social engagement that invite wide participation and serve to bolster inclusion.

Diverse Community

The days of social science and humanities programs and disciplines being staffed entirely by white, cisgender male, able-bodied, heterosexual-presenting individuals are long behind us, and this should be reflected in the faculty complement, the staff complement, the graduate student body, and, over time, the program alumni. Achieving a diverse community requires careful attention to systemic discrimination and racism in hiring and admissions processes. Specifically, arts departments will need to adopt the following:

- *Faculty Complement Plans That Prioritize Faculty Diversity*: An inclusive program means building and maintaining a diverse faculty complement. Changes to the composition of the faculty complement can be slow, particularly when budgetary constraints limit hiring and some faculty choose not to retire. But to the extent that change is possible, diversity in the faculty complement needs to be a priority. And where this change isn't feasible in the short to medium term, it's important to think carefully about ways to signal to students that they belong and are the future of the discipline, such as by inviting a diverse range of guest speakers or helping students to forge connections beyond the unit.
- *Flexible Practices That Allow Programs to Draw On Expertise from Outside the Faculty Complement, as Required*: Indigenous students undertaking research degrees have called on institutions to create space for Elders or Knowledge Keepers to sit on supervisory and examining committees (Braith et al. 2020). This opportunity should be available to Indigenous students (as is already the case at many Canadian universities), and programs should

consider whether this could be a model for students from other equity-deserving groups.
- *Inclusive Admissions Processes*: An inclusive program means creating a diverse student body through inclusive admissions processes. As Posselt (2016) demonstrated in her landmark book *Inside Graduate Admissions: Merit, Diversity, and Faculty Gatekeeping*, selective admissions processes tend to favour students who remind faculty of themselves. And so, patterns of exclusion continue within disciplines. To fulfill the public good imperatives, the graduates of Canada's arts programs need to be as diverse as the population will be twenty years later. At a minimum, admissions processes should not replicate the composition of the faculty complement. Ideally, they should be undertaken with a view to addressing the EDID imperative, and to ensuring that BIPOC students are offered the opportunity to be engaged in the public good imperatives. This will require a fundamental rethinking of what "excellence" or "likelihood for success" looks like, as many of those concepts are really markers of privilege.

Anti-Racist Curriculum

An inclusive program offers an inclusive, anti-racist curriculum. Inclusion demands a reconsideration of curriculum—what questions are considered important, what scholarship is required reading, and how the discipline is situated. In many of the arts disciplines, curriculum is currently being contested and questioned with these considerations in mind. An inclusive program will find space for these conversations and for previously marginalized voices and perspectives. As Smith notes, "a conscious focus on race, Indigeneity, and diversity is especially relevant to the wide-ranging epistemological, ontological, conceptual, and methodological questions that necessarily challenge all of the social science disciplines in a settler colonial state. The social sciences are increasingly asked to recognize their own role, however unconscious, in the politics of racialization and colonialism" (2017, 242–43).

Inclusive Assessment
Assessment practices in the inclusive program, including course assignments and program requirements, should not exclude or disadvantage some students. Universities (and by extension, programs and faculty members) are typically willing to provide accommodations for students based on disability, neurodiversity, religion, and other grounds. Inclusive assessment goes beyond accommodation to ensure that evaluation is clear and fair to students of different backgrounds (for example, by avoiding questions that implicitly assume familiarity with Canadian history, systems, or culture, except when these are the subjects of study). It can also include allowing choice in the methods by which students demonstrate their learning (for example, a paper or a presentation), provided that the choices allow the instructor to fully assess the learning outcome. In the context of research-based degrees, this may extend to the thesis itself, both in its form and in how it is examined.

Valuing Contributions of International Students
The presence of international students should be valued as enhancing the quality and diverse ideas of a program, and in an active rather than passive way. Programs should be designed to solicit and make best use of the contributions of international students.

Inclusive Funding Models
Standard one-size-fits-all funding models based solely on grades or other measures of "merit" should be supplemented with additional funding targeted to specific equity-seeking groups and/or individual needs and circumstances. Ideally, scholarships should increase automatically based on cost of living and/or increases in TA/RA collective agreements.

Non-Traditional Student Focus
Program leaders must stop assuming that students are from homogeneous backgrounds, are at particular life or career stages, and have particular financial, social, and other resources. To do so, programs must do the following:

- *Prioritize and Build Mental Health*: There is universal value to prioritizing students' mental health, but the value is arguably greater for non-traditional students, or those from equity-seeking groups. In addition to the academic and other pressures that create mental health challenges for all students, non-traditional students face challenges stemming from a sense that they do not belong, that they are in an unfamiliar culture, and/or that they are not welcome. This can have significant negative mental health consequences. Program culture and design must prioritize positive mental health.
- *Equip Students to Articulate Competencies*: For some "non-traditional" students, the absence of a clear connection to a career is a barrier to pursuing graduate education in arts disciplines. This is a complex challenge, but one element of a solution involves ensuring that students are able to articulate the competencies they have developed in an arts graduate program.
- *Value Students' Time*: Our above emphasis on efficiency—keeping arts graduate degree lengths only as long as they need to be and ensuring that students can complete their degree in the allotted time—has even greater importance for non-traditional students, who often face the highest opportunity costs of undertaking full-time education. Such students are the most likely to be balancing their studies with paid employment and/or caregiver responsibilities, and time spent in an arts graduate program is time the student could have been investing in those other priorities. For such students, opportunity costs may weigh especially heavily in decision making, and so the benefit of efficient program delivery will be greater.

Challenging the Idea of Inclusive Arts Graduate Programs

We argue that reimagined arts graduate programs should be inclusive, and specifically that they should be defined by an inclusive environment, diverse community, anti-racist curriculum, and a non-traditional student focus. We anticipate criticisms from two directions here: one, that we're going too far, and the other, that we're not going far enough. Let's go through this point by point.

When it comes to "inclusive environment," Canadian universities have come a long way from outright barring or limiting the admission of people based on their race, ethnicity, gender, disability, and more. Some will say we now have a meritocracy that does not "see" race or gender and that treats everyone equally. We disagree. An inclusive environment is not simply one that "treats everyone the same." It's one that also recognizes differences in backgrounds, assumptions, ways of thinking, and more—differences that inevitably shape how we think and work. Inclusiveness goes beyond personal respectfulness. It's about questioning curriculum, program requirements, funding mechanisms, and work processes. We believe there is still plenty of progress to be made here.

In terms of ensuring a "diverse community," graduate programs can be particularly vulnerable to overlooking the need for diverse people and perspectives because of their advanced focus on "excellence," not to mention academia's long-standing tolerance for some types of eccentric personalities and non-conformists. It's easy to feel that "it's all about who does the best work." Not everyone has the ability to succeed at this level, after all, and so it can be easy to overlook who is absent and the possible discriminatory patterns that lurk behind a simple focus on "merit." Furthermore, the demographic composition of Canada continues to change, with ever more diversity in race, gender, (dis)abilities, and other identities that challenge the historic generic/default academic: a white man. It follows from this that: (a) universities must respond to these changing demographics by creating positive experiences and intellectual space for the very diverse generation that is walking through our doors; and (b) arts graduate programs have a particular role to play in ensuring that Canada has the talent it needs to maintain social cohesion within a diverse population. Representation matters here. Considerable evidence shows us that students look for people and role models that look like themselves, and that seeing this contributes to student success (Llamas, Nguyen, and Tran 2021). Even if our other points aren't convincing, self-interest should be. Simply put, there are basic demographic realities that arts graduate programs must respond to if the goal is to recruit today's generation of students and stay in operation.

In bringing attention to the need for "anti-racist curriculum," we are calling not only for inclusive programs but ones that expressly revisit and challenge past (and present) assumptions and practices around race and colonialism. Some colleagues might reject this call, arguing that integrating anti-racism and decolonization into curriculum challenges their academic freedom to determine what they teach and how they teach it. This is an important consideration: to have these requirements imposed on unwilling faculty does raise concerns about academic freedom. Our hope here is that colleagues are convinced by our argument that EDID is a public good imperative and feel motivated to move forward on this front. Even if they agree with some of our above points, some colleagues may believe this call for anti-racist curriculum is overkill, arguing that it's better to just move on and focus on an optimistic future. We strongly disagree, especially given our arts focus! Understanding human society and behaviour means confronting and understanding past as well as present conditions. This may, and should, provoke difficult conversations and disagreements. But surely that is the purpose of the arts.

Working toward "inclusive assessment" is a particular point that can raise a number of concerns. Does this mean watering down standards? Will it create more work for instructors, who now need to grade papers, podcasts, graphic novels, and interpretive dances? The big thing to keep in mind is this: the goal is to assess the student's learning, so what would count as legitimate evidence of the learning outcome(s)? It is possible to use clear communication of assessment expectations and grading criteria to both improve learning and make the grading process easier for instructors. And frankly, some of the resulting assignments may be more enjoyable for instructors to grade.

We call for "explicit mental health strategies," and again, if you feel that "grad school without stress isn't grad school" and students just need to toughen up and quit crying, this may not be the book for you. For everyone else, we do recognize that while universities, programs, and faculty are increasingly recognizing the importance of mental health, it can be challenging to balance this with academic expectations and standards. How flexible can deadlines be? Do faculty have to make extra efforts to accommodate different students' needs? Should they be expected to do care work for students (and how does this break down by gender and other patterns)? But these questions show precisely why mental health strategies need to be explicitly incorporated into program design and expectations, anticipating and accommodating people from the start, rather than being brought in at the end to deal with "stragglers."

We anticipate that our call for a non-traditional student focus will lead some to say we advocate "lowering standards" and/or that some will say a "non-traditional" focus is fine—for other lower-prestige institutions but not their own elite programs. To be clear, we have no interest in lowering standards or the pursuit of excellence; instead, we believe in broadening the outlook and how we understand quality and excellence. And we believe it is the most elite and traditionally prestigious programs that should lead the way, demonstrating their adaptability and willingness to embrace change, new types of students, and new frontiers of knowledge. Knowing universities as we do, we are confident that if the top institutions set the pace, others will follow. Arts departments in Canada's U15 universities: we are talking to you!

On the flipside, we acknowledge our own privileged positions as white, Canadian-born, and long-time faculty members who have had beneficial careers in the current system. We recognize that our own perspectives and lived experiences shape and limit what we personally bring to this discussion. Nevertheless, we have written this book precisely as insiders who have held power, and who have seen the system's deficiencies—as well as its possibilities. We want to use our privileged positions and backgrounds to illuminate those possibilities and the concrete steps to get there.

Talent Developing

For decades, if not centuries, devotees of the arts have argued that the arts train students in human literacy. And while this can be true, it is not necessarily so. Arts program leaders need to accept that, for the program to be effective, skill development must be an explicit and conscious part of that program's design.

This responds directly to one of the three public good imperatives—the talent imperative. The need for arts disciplines to pay attention to talent development is pressing, and arts graduate programs have the opportunity to step up. As we argued in chapter 2, graduate education in the arts disciplines is uniquely well suited to developing advanced competencies relating to human, data, and technological literacy. We'd go so far as to say that the primary purpose of arts graduate programs should be the development of advanced human, data, and technological literacy. Disciplinary knowledge should be secondary.

Don't panic, colleagues. We're not suggesting that we strip out theory or disciplinary knowledge in favour of job training. But we are suggesting a reprioritization.

The default of university teaching at all levels is typically content: "students need to know about this"—this work of literature, this historical period, this electoral system. And after all, students are inevitably interested in disciplinary content; it's why they signed up for a history degree, not philosophy or economics. But content knowledge itself should not be the primary focus. Rather, how can disciplinary content drive and animate the acquisition of skills and capabilities? For example, rather than thinking about graduates with an MA in history as having robust knowledge of one period of history in a particular geographic setting—oh, and secondarily as being clear communicators—think about them as possessing, at an advanced level, an understanding of ethics, interpersonal dynamics, and political and social forces, and as having the capacity to communicate orally and in writing, all developed while gaining a deep understanding of a particular period of history. Content is the means more than the end.

Graduates must exit their program able to both articulate and demonstrate that they are proficient practitioners of at least one of the key literacies (human, data, technological). Ideally, they will become proficient in more than one. The Conference Board of Canada writes, "when individuals are developing and learning, it is important to nurture synergistic skills as a group. Teaching skills in combinations will also help build the skill sets demanded by employers" (FSC-CCF 2022, 12). We agree. Similarly, we make the bold claim that TA and RA work should directly lead, as much as possible, to the development and enhancement of skills, and not just be used for student income and to help the rest of the institution chug along.

What Does "Talent Developing" Mean for Program Design?

A talent-developing program will have all, or at least most, of the following characteristics.

Explicit Literacy Focus

A talent-developing program prioritizes development of students' competencies in one or more of the three literacy areas. Rather than thinking of skill development as secondary or a by-product of graduate education, curriculum should prioritize it. Again, content should be used to drive skill development: we need to move from "learned a lot about mid-century literature, and communicated it clearly" to "demonstrated the ability to communicate clearly in conveying research findings about mid-century literature." Many of the skills acquired during graduate education are only picked up incidentally, as needed. This often places the onus on the student to both identify what skills they require and acquire them. What if skill acquisition was built into the program? An explicit literacy focus requires that literacy development is included in the program's learning outcomes—and that faculty deliver on that promise.

Curricular Talent Development

Courses serve as the foundation of graduate programs, and an explicit literacy focus requires explicit talent development within courses. This means programs need to:

- *Include Literacy Development in All Course-Level Learning Outcomes*: If graduate programs are going to develop literacies, they must be explicitly named, particularly in course outlines—the meta-documents that best help students understand the competencies they are acquiring.
- *Devote Class Time to Literacy Development*: Courses must then follow through and deliver these outcomes. Content can and will take up the bulk of class time, but it must serve as a means to developing literacies, and specific time needs to be set aside for the latter. Skills should not be a random by-product.

- Equip Students to Recognize and Articulate the Literacies They Are Developing and Their Connection to the Broader World: This is achieved by identifying these literacies explicitly, and linking work done within and beyond courses to the competencies. Encouraging students to create and maintain a portfolio of items demonstrating their development of these competencies is a good practice.

Extracurricular Talent Development

A graduate program is more than a set of courses, and there is considerable opportunity for programs to provide students with opportunities to develop literacy areas outside the classroom. This requires programs to:

- *Explicitly Treat Teaching and Research Assistantships as Talent Development*: Many arts graduate students also work as TAs and RAs. But much of this work is not systematized to expressly develop their talents. This is changing somewhat for RAs, given the increasing importance of training for Tri-Council and other grant programs. But TAing remains a randomized world, dependent largely on the inclinations and needs of individual instructors who understandably view TAs primarily as short-term help, with a primary focus on undergraduates. There's a missed opportunity here to be more systematic about teaching assistantships, particularly as opportunities for systematic talent development, not just for helping professors reduce their piles of grading while hopefully picking up some skills along the way.
- *Offer Opportunities for Students to Develop and Demonstrate Skill Development in Non-Academic Settings*: Whether through work-integrated learning like internships or experiential learning built into program requirements, graduate students benefit from opportunities to engage outside the academy.
- *Draw Upon University-Level Resources*: Units shouldn't be going it alone when it comes to literacy development. University resources can be used to provide students with opportunities for professional development, alumni connections, network development, and work-integrated learning. Some professional development can be offered within a graduate program, targeted to the particular

needs and aspirations of the students. But more generic skill development is best offered at a faculty or institutional scale, and program leaders should find ways to direct students to these resources and ensure they benefit from them.

Attention to International Students' Needs
Many international students have explicitly chosen a Canadian graduate education to enhance their talents and employability, whether in Canada or back home. Programs should recognize and serve this, including specifically assisting students to adapt to the context of the Canadian employment market while also being conscious of the context of the employment market in the student's home country.

Evidence-Based Refinements
A talent program must be adaptive and responsive. It should be attentive to the evolution of Canada's public good needs and adapt accordingly. If the above things aren't working, they should be revisited and rethought until they do.

Challenging the Idea of Talent-Developing Arts Graduate Programs

We have argued that reimagined arts graduate programs should be talent developing, and specifically that they should be defined by an explicit literacy focus, curricular talent development, extracurricular talent development, and evidence-based refinements. Here are the critiques we expect.

We can hear our colleagues, particularly in the humanities, sigh as they read our pitch for an "explicit literacy focus." Our argument, they might say, is tied up in "an underlying tendency to [think] about the role of the university in more narrowly vocational terms as an institution whose primary role is to ensure that graduates secure well-paying jobs" (Keen 2014, 76). This very idea will irritate those who want the university to remain "pure" from such mundane issues as students' employment outcomes. But, as Keen warns, "special pleading for some rarified position sheltered from the corrupting influence of the world will not ultimately help us to develop an adequate response to the crisis in the humanities today" (2014, 79).

We want arts graduate students to find a meaningful and well-compensated place in the world. We want them to contribute and to be appropriately rewarded for their contributions. And we believe our disciplines offer valuable education for meeting those public good challenges. And so, we want to find a way to help our students see the value in our disciplines, and to arm them to deploy this value beyond the academy.

Our critics who say we are trying to turn graduate arts academic programs into vocational programs need to pause for a moment and look at existing programs. As we showed in chapter 5, arts graduate degrees are already vocational. The MA is designed primarily to meet the needs of students moving on to the PhD (or alternatively to act as a fifth—or sixth, or seventh—year of undergraduate study to give them a leg up in the non-academic job market). And the PhD is blatantly designed as a vocational degree—to prepare the next generation of university professors. Our "utilitarian" call is to broaden the vocational scope so that we are preparing students not only for the small (and shrinking) number of tenure-track jobs but also for alternative careers where they can make meaningful contributions.

If we are successful, we will profoundly challenge universities' ability to rely on an endless cheap pool of PhDs eager to teach. The "adjunct track" will be vastly less appealing than the meaningful jobs outside the academy. And, as our friends in the economics departments will tell us, if the supply of underemployed PhDs willing to teach is reduced, then employers will be forced to pay more for their labour.

We suggest there is a need for "curricular talent development." At this point, we realize that we've probably either convinced you or will never convince you that graduate programs need to focus explicitly and deliberately on building specific student skills. This needs to be the main purpose, not just a happy by-product if you cover enough content. But we will repeat our argument that if arts graduate programs do not do this in a systematic way, they will steadily become more irrelevant and marginalized in the university. They will become, even more than they are currently, a place for wealthy elite students who can afford "the life of the mind" without worrying about future employment prospects, and/or a trap for students of lesser means who don't realize until too late that a degree in itself does not necessarily lead to opportunities.

When it comes to "extracurricular talent development," we do realize that extracurricular is typically a term reserved for undergraduate study or high school, where there is a strong divide between the classroom and other activities such as clubs and athletics. Graduate school is a different, more immersive experience. Most graduate programs promote an intellectual community, where classes, visiting speakers, TA and RA work, and hallway conversations all overlap and reinforce each other. So, we're not asking for much new here. We are asking for a more organized and explicit approach that ensures students are getting the maximum benefit out of this community. For example, why not ask graduate students to take the lead in organizing a speaker series?

In terms of "evidence-based refinements," we're not saying everything is measurable. Education and teaching will always have an ephemeral element (okay, we'll say it: "magic") that can't be captured on a spreadsheet. But we do firmly believe there is a lot that can be assessed and tracked much better than it is now. We need to take what can be measured and weighed, and then use it to make things even better. To keep the magic going.

Student Focused

It shouldn't be radical to say that a graduate program should be student focused. But, as we discussed in chapter 4, there are sets of mutually reinforcing incentive structures that result in graduate programs that prioritize the needs of the institution and/or the faculty, with students' interests ultimately being a secondary or even tertiary consideration.

A student-focused approach prioritizes student learning and experience and places emphasis on preparing students for post-graduation employment. Much of what we have discussed with the other EDITS descriptors already contributes to a student-focused program. But "student focused" goes beyond this: the raison d'être of the program is to prepare students, full stop. The program does not exist to ensure an adequate supply of teaching assistants, to provide faculty with the "opportunity to supervise," or to keep the rest of the institution financially afloat. While these may be collateral benefits, they cannot be the drivers.

Student focused does not necessarily mean student driven, in the sense of merely responding to whatever students say and demand. There is still an essential role to lead and teach students to expand their horizons. For example, the majority of PhD students embark on their degree in the hope that they will secure a tenure-track job, despite the long-standing realities of academic hiring in the arts. This does not mean that PhD programs should cater to that aspiration. Instead, a truly student-focused approach insists that students equip themselves for subsequent employment outside the academy, as this will be the reality for roughly 67–90 percent of them.

Most of all, a student-focused program is realistic about the costs and benefits of the program, financial and otherwise. Tuition is set based on what students can realistically reap from the investment. Funding may not be lucrative, but it should be in line with program requirements and integrated with program progress as much as possible. Prospective students should be given as much information as possible, so they can make an informed choice about whether a program is truly for them. This is particularly the case for international students, whose tuition costs are usually considerably higher.

What Does "Student Focused" Mean for Program Design?

A student-focused program will have all, or at least most, of the following characteristics.

Explicit Prioritization of Students' Needs

Student needs must take clear priority over faculty research needs and institutional revenue and rankings needs. This may be a tough hurdle. It asks programs and the departments that house them to ask questions about how many students they are admitting and why. If the answer has to do with a need for revenue—met especially through recruiting more international students—or enabling faculty members' research, or meeting teaching assistance needs—or worst of all, supplying a pool of available sessional instructors—then there's a problem. The system is serving the institution, not the students.

Diverse Career Preparation

A student-focused program prepares students for diverse career trajectories. To reiterate, most arts PhD programs, and even many arts MA programs, are already vocationally oriented: they prepare students to become faculty members. A student-focused approach broadens the focus and insists that students need to prepare themselves for more than one possible career trajectory. To achieve this, programs must:

- *Integrate Some Career Orientation and Planning into Their Curriculum*: This will support students in making decisions for their future while still in school.
- *Draw Upon University-Level Resources to Provide Students with Opportunities*: Providing students with opportunities for professional development, alumni connection, network development, and work-integrated learning will better support them in being prepared for their careers post-graduation.
- *Equip Students to Articulate the Literacies They Have Mastered*: Students should develop and be able to articulate an individualized sense of their purpose in undertaking the degree, how it might contribute to Canada's public good, and what literacies they have developed in support of this.

Explicit Mental Health Strategies

A student-focused graduate program must be designed and administered with students' well-being in mind. Program milestones must be achievable. Faculty should be responsive to students' concerns and unique situations. Supervisors should be trained and appropriately mentored to enable them to provide support and meaningful feedback. The program must value students' time and allow for efficient completion.

Transparency of Costs and Benefits

Going to grad school shouldn't be a shot in the dark. Programs should provide as much information as possible about financial and other costs, such as time demands, and about the likely short- and long-term benefits through funding and future earnings. The availability of this information will vary, but when it is there, programs should be transparent about it.

Evidence-Based Refinement
A student-focused program is reformed frequently based upon feedback from both graduates and discontinued students.

Challenging the Idea of Student-Focused Arts Graduate Programs

We have argued that reimagined arts graduate programs should be student focused, and specifically that they should be defined by an explicit prioritization of students' needs, attention to diverse career preparation, and evidence-based refinements. Let's get into our final set of possible objections.

For "explicit prioritization of students' needs," we anticipate an obvious backlash: that students have been the focus all along, and who are we to suggest otherwise? But as we have shown, graduate education has developed and proliferated for a lot of different reasons, such as universities' quest to climb the rankings through research intensity, the need for faculty research assistants, and the money that students bring in through tuition and government grants. Frankly, often students and their needs are not the prime focus.

We concede that this can raise reasonable questions about who defines and frames "students' needs." Some may argue we are being too narrow and paternalistic in saying now what's best for students. After all, students continue to apply to arts graduate programs in their current form; students must be reasonably happy with the status quo. Fair enough, but we strongly feel that the current system is not serving students' needs, and students, particularly at the end of their program (or as they drop out), are realizing and saying this. The system badly needs a reset to ensure it truly is "student focused."

We suggest that programs should provide "diverse career preparation." Arts graduate education, especially the PhD, is inevitably focused on academic careers because that is the long-standing and most obvious option for graduates, and sometimes seemingly the only one. "Diverse careers" may seem fuzzy and overly optimistic, and if you are thinking that the world isn't specifically clamoring for more anthropology PhDs or philosophy MAs, you're not necessarily wrong. But our focus isn't disciplinary or on degree titles, because those are generally not what employers outside academia hire based on anyway. Rather, our focus is on the skills and competencies that students develop during their degree, and we are confident that employers do need these. Report after report has identified critical skills shortages around precisely the kinds of literacies and competencies that arts graduate programs hone (see, for example, RBC 2018 and FSC-CCF 2022). And yet we also find evidence that graduates of arts graduate programs struggle as they enter the labour force (Council of Canadian Academies 2021). Right now, the talent and the opportunities aren't finding one another. Our hope is that by placing a higher priority on developing and articulating these skills, arts graduate programs can help with the mismatch. We know that, for PhDs in general, employment outcomes tend to be quite good, but with an extended period of transition from education to employment. This is a product of the implicit rather than explicit skill development that occurs in most doctoral programs. We need to move to a system that makes these explicit, rather than seemingly developed and deployed by accident.

In terms of the need for "evidence-based refinements," we have spoken about this at length for the other EDITS categories, so see the previous sections.

Bringing EDITS Together

While we have explained each idea individually, the five EDITS characteristics overlap with and reinforce one another. For example, a program designed to be efficient places value on years of a student's life; in that respect, it is also student focused and inclusive. Due to the overlapping and reinforcing nature of EDITS, the characteristics are less overwhelming and more aspirational when considered as a whole (see Table 6.2).

Moving Forward

EDITS is the core of our vision to transform arts graduate education for the public good. It counteracts the drift and warped incentives that have shaped the present system. EDITS calls on us to be intentional in our planning and design of graduate programs. And it forces us to consider why we often do things simply because that's the way they've always been done.

TABLE 6.2 **EDITS Characteristics**

Efficient	Deliberate	Inclusive	Talent Developing	Student Focused
• Adequate resources	• Stated purpose	• Inclusive environment	• Explicit literacy focus	• Explicit prioritization of students' needs
• Parsimonious design	• Clear learning outcomes	• Diverse community	• Curricular talent development	• Diverse career preparation
• Focused coursework	• Parsimonious design	• Anti-racist curriculum	• Extracurricular talent development	• Evidence-based refinements
• Institutional integration and coordination	• Pedagogical alignment	• Inclusive assessment	• Evidence-based refinements	
	• Evidence-based refinements	• Explicit mental health strategies		
		• Non-traditional student focus		

Some will simply say that we are utilitarians determined to squeeze out the essence of learning and inquiry in order to produce workers for the capitalist economy. We disagree. In fact, one of our overriding reasons for writing this book is precisely to save arts education from being crushed under the relentless march toward supposedly "practical" disciplines. We strongly believe that our ideas will preserve and strengthen the place of arts in the modern university, upholding its basic raison d'être—make reflective, curiosity-based inquiry about the human condition. So please keep reading.

But one final question we anticipate is: why are you talking about graduate education at all? Why not just "fix" the underlying foundation—arts undergraduate education? We have two responses to this.

Our first response is that we're really addressing two separate problems—the need for change in arts graduate education, but also Canada's public good challenges. The latter involve big questions and "wicked problems" of the country, and the three imperatives of wicked problems, EDID, and talent. These specifically require the sophistication and advanced skills that are honed in post-baccalaureate education. Many of our ideas also apply to undergraduate arts programs, and we invite colleagues to adapt these ideas to the undergraduate context. But our focus is deliberately on the advanced level, to address advanced problems.

Our second response is that there's no shortage of discussion already on how to "fix" undergraduate education, in the arts and beyond. But hardly anyone is talking about arts graduate education. Perhaps reformers assume the issues and solutions are the same; alternatively, or additionally, arts graduate education gets addressed as part of the larger focus on STEM research and "innovation."

But it doesn't fully fit with either paradigm; in fact, some of the challenges are precisely because arts graduate education is getting stretched between its "arts" and "graduate education" elements. We're calling for a new and almost unprecedented focus squarely on a sector that has long been overlooked, and yet in our view contains the most opportunity for gain. We strongly believe that the best advances can be made in reforming arts graduate programs to better align them with Canada's wicked problems, EDID, and talent imperatives. If this helps advance change in undergraduate education as well as in the rest of the graduate education world, all the better.

So, let's move forward. In the next chapter, we discuss what it would mean to make EDITS a reality.

Reimagining Arts Graduate Education Through EDITS

We've laid out the broad EDITS vision. In this chapter, we begin to work through how it can be implemented. Critically, this must be a collective process. Canadian universities are based upon a model of collegial governance, including collegial determination of curriculum. The ideal reimagined arts graduate programs will both meet the EDITS characteristics (efficient, deliberate, inclusive, talent developing, student focused) and capture the imaginations and enthusiasm of the faculty members who will deliver on the programs' promises. Faculty connection and engagement with arts graduate education is necessary for these programs' success.

There is no one-size-fits-all model here. Academic departments and units are each unique. Disciplinary and interdisciplinary variations are, of course, important. But perhaps even more important here are the larger institutional context and the permanent faculty who animate the programs. For example:

- University-level resources and programs for graduate students (co-operative or work-integrated learning; professional development; career services) will vary, including the extent to which units are able to coordinate with them.
- A unit may have access to university-level resources and programs for faculty members (supervisor training; teaching and learning supports; curriculum design supports)—or not.
- Within the same university, arts departments' faculty complements may vary in size, composition (tenured versus tenure track), diversity (sub-disciplines; sociodemographic), and other factors.
- Within the same discipline, a department with over fifty tenure-stream faculty in a large, research-intensive U15 university will have different resources and capacities than a department with fewer than ten tenure-stream faculty in a smaller comprehensive university.

A successful reimagined arts graduate curriculum must take all of these factors into account. A cookie-cutter approach to curriculum that fails to consider context will create limited results. So, in this chapter, we get into the work of reimagining within the EDITS framework, while keeping institutional realities in mind.

EDITS is also not an all-or-nothing process. Change probably won't occur overnight. Thus, we present the EDITS framework as a continuum ranging from unsatisfactory to excellent, with the goal being for programs to improve within the confines of their circumstances. We present a rubric to guide this continuum and work through some examples of how modest changes can make a difference.

The EDITS model leaves considerable room for innovation and creativity. The challenge for many faculty members is envisaging what such a reimagined program would mean in practice and how it might work in their particular context. The arts graduate program status quo persists in part because it is hard to imagine an inspiring alternative. In this chapter, we aspire to disrupt this curricular inertia by challenging faculty members, university leaders, and graduate students to see easy, achievable improvements within their own contexts. For others, this chapter will provide an improved understanding of what EDITS can mean in practice.

The EDITS Rubric

The EDITS criteria in chapter 6 present an ambitious endpoint. One challenge with ambitious endpoints is that they can seem... overwhelming.

For this reason, it is important to view the EDITS model as a continuum ranging from unsatisfactory to excellent, and to set a goal of moving arts graduate programs up the continuum. Some units may have the resources (leadership, change culture, available time) to aim for excellence across all categories. Other units might be better positioned to simply work to move their program from unsatisfactory to satisfactory, or from satisfactory to good. In some cases, there may be immediate momentum for change on one criterion (e.g., inclusive), but limited support for making change on other criteria, at least for the moment.

What might it mean for your MA program to move from satisfactory to good with respect to talent developing? How could your PhD program move from unsatisfactory to satisfactory with respect to efficiency? To answer such questions, we have operationalized the EDITS descriptions from chapter 6 into a rubric (see Table 7.1). The rubric can be used to assess existing programs and then identify areas for change. It can also be used to help design new programs. Note that the goal is to have no items in the "unsatisfactory" column (shaded grey).

Assessing an existing program will allow you to identify opportunities to make relatively small changes to improve your program. To illustrate this, we will focus on each of the EDITS categories individually with hypothetical examples. Note: In the tables accompanying the examples, the ✗ indicates that the description does not apply to the program in question, while the ✓ indicates it does apply. As the descriptors in the "Unsatisfactory" column are negative, programs should aspire to have no ✓s in that column. As the descriptors in the other columns are positive, programs should aspire to have many ✓s in these columns.

TABLE 7.1 **The EDITS Program Rubric**

Note: for simplicity, the rubric speaks to the "offering unit" because not all programs are offered by "departments." The rubric refers to a single unit offering a program; in reality, programs are sometimes offered by multiple units in collaboration.

	Unsatisfactory	Satisfactory	Good Meets all satisfactory criteria, plus:	Excellent Meets all good criteria, plus:
Efficient	☐ Offering unit relies on contingent faculty to support program delivery, including supervision ☐ Program length is disconnected from program purpose ☐ Courses are not explicitly tied to program-level learning outcomes ☐ Most or all courses are cross-listed with undergraduate courses ☐ Students in other programs are prohibited from enrolling in program classes	☐ Offering unit has sufficient permanent faculty to support program delivery, including supervision ☐ Program length is as short as possible relative to program purpose ☐ All courses are explicitly tied to the program-level learning outcomes ☐ Most courses are program specific (i.e., are not cross-listed with undergraduate courses) ☐ Courses are available to students in other programs and may be cross-listed with other programs, and/or arrangements are in place with other institutions for reciprocal course enrollment	☐ Offering unit has a multi-year admissions plan that accounts for anticipated changes in faculty complement (sabbaticals, retirements, etc.) ☐ All courses have a minimum number of students ☐ Program is comprised primarily of core required classes, and electives are limited ☐ Where possible and appropriate, program requires students to participate in faculty- or university-level offerings (e.g., professional development) rather than program-specific offerings ☐ Individualized supervision is required only where necessary to achieve program-level learning outcomes	☐ Program size is below offering unit's maximum capacity to allow for unanticipated changes in faculty complement ☐ Faculty supervisions are limited to areas of faculty expertise ☐ Elective courses outside program are encouraged, provided there is a clear link to program-level learning outcomes ☐ Program is clearly differentiated from other programs at the university and from similar offerings at other universities

TABLE 7.1 *continued*

	Unsatisfactory	Satisfactory	Good Meets all satisfactory criteria, plus:	Excellent Meets all good criteria, plus:
Deliberate	☐ Program's purpose is unspecified ☐ Program's learning outcomes are unspecified or vague ☐ Connection between program requirements and program learning outcomes is unclear ☐ Degree completion guidelines are unstated or unrealistic ☐ Pedagogical approaches are disconnected from program learning outcomes ☐ Offering unit has no plans or measures to evaluate program success	☐ Purpose of program is clearly stated ☐ Program has explicit, clearly stated learning outcomes ☐ All program requirements are explicitly tied to program learning outcomes ☐ Program has explicit and realistic degree completion guidelines ☐ Program explicitly matches pedagogical approaches to program learning outcomes ☐ Offering unit has a clear evaluation plan to use student outcomes to assess program success and inform curriculum refinement	☐ Program is explicitly linked to one or more of Canada's public good imperatives ☐ Program learning outcomes are directly tied to program's purpose ☐ Program requirements are truly necessary for program learning outcomes ☐ Program has explicit pathways for students to realistically complete the degree in a specified timeframe ☐ Program uses research training purposively, with research products matched to program-level learning outcomes ☐ Offering unit consults with current and former students, including students who discontinued studies, to obtain feedback on how well their graduate education prepared them for work they are doing	☐ Program's structure is thoroughly connected to one or more of Canada's public good imperatives ☐ Program learning outcomes are thoughtfully coordinated with course-level learning outcomes ☐ Program electives are limited and explicitly tied to program learning outcomes ☐ Program website provides clear information about degree completion timelines over the past five years ☐ Program integrates experiential and/or work-integrated learning to support program-level learning outcomes ☐ Offering unit openly shares student outcomes and feedback data and how it is continuing to refine curricula

TABLE 7.1 *continued*

	Unsatisfactory	Satisfactory	Good Meets all satisfactory criteria, plus:	Excellent Meets all good criteria, plus:
Inclusive	☐ Program does not have admissions goals ☐ Program does not have harassment policies ☐ Program's social and extracurricular events centre on alcohol ☐ No awareness of areas of non-diversity ☐ Course instructors are unaware of how representative their course materials are ☐ Program assessment practices exclude or disadvantage some students ☐ Program design, including workloads and structure, is uncoordinated and haphazard	☐ Program's admissions goals include attention to student diversity ☐ Program actively works to create a clear welcoming tone with zero tolerance for harassment in classes, at events, and in other spaces ☐ Program proactively avoids social and extracurricular events that exclude identifiable groups ☐ Program balances areas of non-diversity with appropriately compensated external expertise ☐ Course instructors have assessed their course materials with an eye to representation and the centring of diverse voices ☐ Course instructors have assessed their course assessments with an eye to inclusion of students with diverse abilities and from diverse backgrounds ☐ Program design, including workloads and structure, prioritizes student well-being and mental health	☐ All faculty and staff involved in admissions decisions have completed anti-bias training ☐ Admissions requirements and processes are designed to promote diversity ☐ Offering unit ensures inclusion and diversity in invited speakers and guests ☐ Offering unit's faculty and staff complement plans include diversity as a key criterion ☐ Course instructors include consideration of decolonization and anti-racism among course learning outcomes ☐ Course instructors communicate assessment expectations and grading criteria clearly and in advance ☐ Offering unit's culture prioritizes student well-being and mental health	☐ All faculty, instructors, and staff have completed anti-racism training ☐ Offering unit undertakes ongoing efforts to promote inclusion as a shared commitment ☐ Offering unit offers innovative and inclusive events ☐ Offering unit's faculty and staff complement plans prioritize diversity ☐ Program-level learning outcomes include consideration of decolonization and anti-racism ☐ Course instructors allow students to choose among a number of assessment options ☐ Faculty, university, and/or offering unit provide students with tools to build their well-being and mental health

TABLE 7.1 *continued*

	Unsatisfactory	Satisfactory	Good Meets all satisfactory criteria, plus:	Excellent Meets all good criteria, plus:
Talent developing	☐ Program-level learning outcomes are limited to content/ knowledge learning ☐ Course-level learning outcomes are limited to content/ knowledge learning ☐ Faculty members view TAships and RAships primarily as teaching/ research support ☐ Talent development learning outcomes are not formally evaluated	☐ Program-level learning outcomes explicitly include numerous human literacy skills ☐ All courses include literacy development among course-level learning outcomes ☐ Faculty members view TAships and RAships primarily as talent development rather than teaching/ research support ☐ Offering unit uses summative evaluation to assess students' achievement of talent development learning outcomes ☐ Faculty, university, and/or offering unit provide students with tools to explicitly recognize and articulate their literacy skills	☐ Program-level learning outcomes explicitly include numerous human literacy skills and some data literacy and/or technological literacy skills ☐ Faculty members devote class time to literacy development ☐ Faculty, university, and/or offering unit provide students with skills training programs to support their TA and RA work ☐ Offering unit regularly considers information on Canada's talent needs to inform its curriculum refinements	☐ Program-level learning outcomes explicitly include numerous human literacy skills and numerous data literacy and/or technological literacy skills ☐ Faculty, university, and/or offering unit provide students with tools to connect their TA and RA work to their literacy skills ☐ Offering unit regularly consults with dominant industries that employ its graduates to understand emerging talent needs to inform its curriculum refinements

TABLE 7.1 *continued*

	Unsatisfactory	Satisfactory	Good Meets all satisfactory criteria, plus:	Excellent Meets all good criteria, plus:
Student Focused	☐ Connection between program's purpose and student needs is unclear ☐ Program is not positioned as tied to career preparation of any sort or is limited to academic career preparation ☐ Program milestones cannot realistically be achieved in a reasonable timeframe ☐ Offering unit does not consult with current and former students to obtain feedback on the program	☐ Program's stated purpose clearly prioritizes student needs over other considerations ☐ Program explicitly promises to prepare students for diverse careers ☐ Program milestones are achievable in a reasonable timeframe ☐ Offering unit consults with current and former students, including students who discontinued studies, to obtain feedback on the program, and uses this information to refine its program	☐ Program admissions are based on and limited by offering unit's capacity to meet students' needs over the entirety of their degree ☐ Faculty, university, and/or offering unit provide students with tools for explicitly tying their literacy skills to diverse careers ☐ Faculty members are responsive to students' concerns and unique situations ☐ Offering unit consults published literature for best practices in graduate programming and uses this information to refine its program	☐ Student TA and RA assignments prioritize student training over other considerations ☐ Faculty, university, and/or offering unit provide students with opportunities for work-integrated learning, network development, and alumni connection ☐ Supervisors are trained and appropriately mentored to provide student support and meaningful feedback ☐ University and/or faculty provide support for regular program reviews

Efficient

Imagine your graduate committee assesses one of your existing graduate programs and comes up with the following scoring (Table 7.2).

TABLE 7.2 **"Efficient" Assessment Example**

	Unsatisfactory	Satisfactory	Good Meets all satisfactory criteria, plus:	Excellent Meets all good criteria, plus:
Capacity	✗ Offering unit relies on contingent faculty to support program delivery, including supervision	✓ Offering unit has sufficient permanent faculty to support program delivery, including supervision	✗ Offering unit has a multi-year admissions plan that accounts for anticipated changes in faculty complement (sabbaticals, retirements, etc.) ✓ All courses have a minimum number of students ✓ Individualized supervision is required only where necessary to achieve program-level learning outcomes	✗ Program size is below offering unit's maximum capacity to allow for unanticipated changes in faculty complement ✓ Faculty supervisions are limited to areas of faculty expertise
Program Length	✗ Program length is disconnected from program purpose	✓ Program length is as short as possible relative to program purpose		
Course Purpose	✓ Courses are not explicitly tied to program-level learning outcomes	✗ All courses are explicitly tied to program-level learning outcomes		
Course Focus	✗ Most or all courses are cross-listed with undergraduate courses	✓ Most courses are program-specific (i.e., are not cross-listed with undergraduate courses)	✓ Program is comprised primarily of core required courses, and electives are limited	✓ Elective courses outside program are encouraged, provided there is a clear link to program-level learning outcomes
University Connection	✗ Students in other programs are prohibited from enrolling in program courses	✓ Courses are available to students in other programs and may be cross-listed with other programs, and/or arrangements are in place with other institutions for reciprocal course enrollment	✓ Where possible and appropriate, program requires students to participate in faculty- or university-level offerings (e.g., professional development) rather than program-specific offerings	✓ Program is clearly differentiated from all other programs at the university and from similar offerings at other universities

From this, the graduate committee sees a number of areas for program improvement that would move your program from the lower end of the continuum to the higher end, including:

- Multi-year admissions planning that allows for unanticipated changes in the faculty complement.
- Explicitly tying individual courses to program learning outcomes.

These are not large-scale changes that would require significant new resources, but they would require your unit to pay attention to processes and be mindful and explicit about how the program courses support the program learning outcomes.

Deliberate

Continuing its assessment, your graduate committee considers the same graduate program using the deliberate criteria and discovers the following (Table 7.3).

TABLE 7.3 **"Deliberate" Assessment Example**

	Unsatisfactory	Satisfactory	Good Meets all satisfactory criteria, plus:	Excellent Meets all good criteria, plus:
Purpose	✓ Program's purpose is unspecified ✗ Program's learning outcomes are unspecified or vague	✗ Purpose of program is clearly stated ✓ Program has explicit, clearly stated learning outcomes	✗ Program is explicitly linked to one or more of Canada's public good imperatives ✗ Program learning outcomes are directly tied to program's purpose	✗ Program's structure is thoroughly connected to one or more of Canada's public good imperatives
Require- ments	✗ Connection between program requirements and program learning outcomes is unclear	✓ All program requirements are explicitly tied to program learning outcomes	✓ Program requirements are truly necessary for program learning outcomes	✗ Program learning outcomes are thoughtfully coordinated with course-level learning outcomes ✓ Program electives are limited and explicitly tied to program learning outcomes
Timelines	✗ Degree completion guidelines are unstated or unrealistic	✓ Program has explicit and realistic degree completion guidelines	✗ Program has explicit pathways for students to realistically complete the degree in a specified timeframe	✗ Program website provides clear information about degree completion timelines over the past five years
Pedagogy	✗ Pedagogical approaches are disconnected from program learning outcomes	✓ Program explicitly matches pedagogical approaches to program learning outcomes	✓ Program uses research training purposively, with research products matched to program-level learning outcomes	✗ Program integrates experiential and/or work-integrated learning to support program-level learning outcomes
Evidence based	✓ Offering unit has no plans or measures to evaluate program success	✗ Offering unit has a clear evaluation plan to use student outcomes to assess program success and inform curriculum refinement	✗ Offering unit consults with current and former students, including students who discontinued studies, to obtain feedback on how well their graduate education prepared them for work they are doing	✗ Offering unit openly shares student outcomes and feedback data and how it is continuing to refine curricula

Again, there are many "low-hanging fruit" opportunities to make meaningful improvements in the program. Specifically, your graduate committee could:

- Work with department colleagues to clarify the program's purpose
- Ask faculty teaching in the program to coordinate course learning outcomes with program-level learning outcomes
- Create a one-page overview listing pathways for degree completion in the expected timeframe, sharing this with all graduate students and supervisors
- Add information about average degree completion times to the program website
- Establish an evaluation framework

If your committee wanted to take things further, they could also start discussions about work-integrated learning and/or work with the faculty of graduate studies to establish a more fulsome evaluation project. Those would be more work, however, and our point here is not to scare faculty and units off with intimidating levels of change, but to suggest possibilities. So, these are just options to consider.

Inclusive

Your graduate committee continues to assess its current program, this time with an eye to the inclusive criteria. While your committee had assumed your current program would shine in this category, given its faculty members' commitment to EDID, the committee is surprised to see that individual-level commitments have not fully rippled into the graduate program (Table 7.4).

TABLE 7.4 "Inclusive" Assessment Example

	Unsatisfactory	Satisfactory	Good Meets all satisfactory criteria, plus:	Excellent Meets all good criteria, plus:
Admissions	✓ Program does not have admissions goals	✗ Program's admissions goals include attention to student diversity	✗ All faculty and staff involved in admissions decisions have completed anti-bias training ✗ Admissions requirements and processes are designed to promote diversity	✗ All faculty, instructors, and staff have completed anti-racism training
Culture	✓ Program does not have harassment policies	✗ Program actively works to create a clear welcoming tone with zero tolerance for harassment in classes, at events, and in other spaces		✗ Offering unit undertakes ongoing efforts to promote inclusion as a shared commitment
Events and Extra-curriculars	✓ Program's social and extracurricular events centre on alcohol	✗ Program proactively avoids social and extra-curricular events that exclude identifiable groups	✗ Offering unit ensures inclusion and diversity in invited speakers and guests	✗ Offering unit offers innovative and inclusive events
Faculty and Staff Complement	✗ No awareness of areas of non-diversity	✗ Program balances areas of non-diversity with appropriately compensated external expertise	✓ Offering unit's faculty and staff complement plans include diversity as a key criterion	✗ Offering unit's faculty and staff complement plans prioritize diversity
Course Materials	✓ Course instructors are unaware of how representative their course materials are	✗ Course instructors have assessed their course materials with an eye to represen-tation and the centring of diverse voices	✗ Course instructors include consideration of decolonization and anti-racism among course learning outcomes	✗ Program-level learning outcomes include consideration of decolonization and anti-racism
Assessment	✓ Program assessment practices exclude or disadvantage some students	✗ Course instructors have assessed their course assessments with an eye to inclusion of students with diverse abilities and from diverse backgrounds	✗ Course instructors communicate assessment expectations and grading criteria clearly and in advance	✗ Course instructors allow students to choose among a number of assessment options
Well-Being	✓ Program design, including workloads and structure, is uncoordinated and haphazard	✗ Program design, including workloads and structure, prioritizes student well-being and mental health	✗ Offering unit's culture prioritizes student well-being and mental health	✗ Faculty, university, and/or offering unit provide students with tools to build their well-being and mental health

To address these unsatisfactory areas, the graduate committee could:

- Set diversity-based admissions targets
- Complete university-offered programs for anti-bias training in preparation for making admissions decisions
- Ask the university teaching and learning centre to provide unit-specific workshops on how to reassess course materials through an anti-racist lens and how to create inclusive assessments
- Encourage faculty teaching in the program to clearly communicate course deadlines and workloads

Could they do more? Of course. If the department has an EDID committee, the graduate committee could request its assistance with improving inclusion in the graduate programs. If the university offers anti-racist training, the graduate committee could work with the department chair to promote this within the department. But those might be steps to take at a later stage. For now, the point is to keep taking steps to improve.

Talent Developing

Your graduate committee feels it should do relatively well in the talent-developing category—after all, the program website claims your program advances critical thinking skills, communication skills, and data analysis abilities! After its assessment against the rubric, here are what the results suggest (Table 7.5).

TABLE 7.5 **"Talent Developing" Assessment Example**

	Unsatisfactory	Satisfactory	Good Meets all satisfactory criteria, plus:	Excellent Meets all good criteria, plus:
Program learning outcomes	✗ Program-level learning outcomes are limited to content/knowledge learning	✓ Program-level learning outcomes explicitly include numerous human literacy skills	✓ Program-level learning outcomes explicitly include numerous human literacy skills and some data literacy and/or technological literacy skills	✗ Program-level learning outcomes explicitly include numerous human literacy skills and numerous data literacy and/or technological literacy skills
Course learning outcomes	✓ Course-level learning outcomes are limited to content/knowledge learning	✗ All courses include literacy development among course-level learning outcomes	✗ Faculty members devote class time to literacy development	✗ Faculty, university, and/or offering unit provide students with tools to connect their TA and RA work to their literacy skills
Assistants	✓ Faculty members view TAships and RAships primarily as teaching/research support	✗ Faculty members view TAships and RAships primarily as talent development rather than teaching/research support	✗ Faculty, university, and/or offering unit provide students with skills training programs to support their TA and RA work	
Evaluation	✗ Talent development learning outcomes are not formally evaluated	✓ Offering unit uses summative evaluation to assess students' achievement of talent development learning outcomes		
Connection External world	✓ Program is not proof tested against the real world	✗ Faculty, university, and/or offering unit provide students with tools to explicitly recognize and articulate their literacy skills	✗ Offering unit regularly considers information on Canada's talent needs to inform its curriculum refinements	✗ Offering unit regularly consults with dominant industries that employ its graduates to understand emerging talent needs to inform its curriculum refinements

Your graduate committee notes the disconnection between program and course learning outcomes as an area for attention. As a first step, the committee decides to invite the university's teaching and learning centre to offer a workshop for instructors on embedding skill development in graduate courses.

An additional area for improvement is seen with teaching and research assistants. As a first step, the graduate committee decides to reach out to the university's teaching and learning centre to identify what supports exist for TAs and RAs.

Of course, this will not address the issue of lack of feedback from external sources. This would require a more ambitious plan of action. As a first step, the committee could investigate what resources exist elsewhere in the university—in the arts dean's office and in the faculty of graduate studies—to support a graduate program in gathering such information and forging relationships with external stakeholders.

Student Focused

Your graduate committee is relieved—nay, excited—to reach the S in EDITS: student focused. In this category, the committee identifies a number of areas that need attention (Table 7.6).

The graduate committee decides that the first step is to complete a task identified earlier: work with department colleagues to clarify the program's purpose.

TABLE 7.6 **"Student Focused" Assessment Example**

	Unsatisfactory	Satisfactory	Good Meets all satisfactory criteria, plus:	Excellent Meets all good criteria, plus:
Student needs	✓ Connection between program's purpose and student needs is unclear	✗ Program's stated purpose clearly prioritizes student needs over other considerations	✗ Program admissions are based on and limited by offering unit's capacity to meet students' needs over the entirety of their degree	✗ Student TA and RA assignments prioritize student training over other considerations
Career connection	✓ Program is not positioned as tied to career preparation of any sort or is limited to academic career preparation	✗ Program explicitly promises to prepare students for diverse careers	✗ Faculty, university, and/or offering unit provide students with tools for explicitly tying their literacy skills to diverse careers	✗ Faculty, university, and/or offering unit provide students with opportunities for work-integrated learning, network development, and alumni connection
Milestones and support	✗ Program milestones cannot realistically be achieved in a reasonable timeframe	✓ Program milestones are achievable in a reasonable timeframe	✓ Faculty members are responsive to students' concerns and unique situations	✗ Supervisors are trained and appropriately mentored to provide student support and meaningful feedback
Student consultation	✓ Offering unit does not consult with current and former students to obtain feedback on the program	✗ Offering unit consults with current and former students, including students who discontinued studies, to obtain feedback on the program, and uses this information to refine its program	✗ Offering unit consults published literature for best practices in graduate programming and uses this information to refine its program	✓ University and/or faculty provide support for regular program reviews

Forward Is Forward

The point of the rubric is to encourage faculty involved in graduate programs to be mindful of those programs. What small steps could be taken to improve existing programs? What larger steps would result in further improvement? And—importantly—what is feasible given the resources available?

We love the idea of across-the-board excellent programs. At the same time, we are realists and understand that academic cultures can be change resistant. For this reason, we embrace improvement of any magnitude. Forward is forward. Excellence should not be the enemy of better than before.

That being said, it can be helpful to imagine excellent programs. We provide some hypothetical examples in the next chapter to spur your imagination.

Imagining Excellent Arts Graduate Programs

If we could start with a blank slate, what could excellent arts graduate education look like? The EDITS model leaves considerable room for innovation and creativity. The challenge for many faculty members is envisaging what such a reimagined program would mean in practice, and how it might work in their particular context. We suspect that the status quo persists for arts graduate programs in part because it is hard to imagine an inspiring but attainable alternative. So, in this chapter we present both real-world promising practices and hypothetical reimagined arts graduate programs in order to disrupt this curricular inertia and challenge readers to see new options.

In the imaginary programs that follow, we are deliberately nonspecific in hopes that they will inspire your creative thinking for possibilities in your own discipline or unit. Thus, when you see "[discipline]" or "[disciplinary]," imagine your own field of study. We want these examples to prompt reimagination of an English program as well as an economics program, an anthropology program, a history program, and so on. There will naturally be limits to how far this stretching can occur, but where there are points of disciplinary incongruence, please ask yourself if these are true barriers or simply challenges to how things are traditionally done.

We also want to stress that these hypothetical visions for a reimagined arts graduate education are meant to inspire thinking and adaptation, not straight copying. We do not think that your unit's programs need to adopt all or even any of the structures we outline. But as you read through the examples, please consider options that could fit your context—especially options that would also satisfy the "excellent" scoring criteria on the EDITS rubric (see Appendix 2). Note that because the excellent criteria include all of the "satisfactory" and "good" criteria, the lists are long. The excellent category is deliberately aspirational. Excellence is a tough bar!

And while we're talking about blank slates, we want to suggest that there may be merit in leaving the slate blank—that is to say, not introducing new programs despite institutional pressures and faculty appetites to do so, and instead focusing on improving existing programs. Elsewhere in this book, we've talked about the proliferation of graduate programs in the arts disciplines. It's easy to get caught up in the excitement of starting from scratch and developing a new arts graduate program from the ground up. But listen carefully to the reasons being offered: if the program is being developed "to give faculty the opportunity to supervise" and students are not mentioned, it's a red flag! There can also be a temptation to favour optimistic scenarios ("this new program will work beautifully and solve all our problems"). The EDITS framework is a useful tool to assess both new and existing programs. But introducing new programs is rarely the solution for problems in existing ones.

Promising Practices

Before we dive into some "reimagined" programs, we will start by offering a non-exhaustive list of real-world promising practices that might be employed as components of an arts graduate program designed to meet the public good imperatives.

The Wicked Problems Imperative

Arts graduate programs can connect with the wicked problems imperative by fostering connections with communities outside academia. There are many incentives embedded in graduate education, and in scholarship more generally, to orient students' research toward traditional scholarship—intended for a scholarly audience, with no immediate impact beyond the scholarly conversation. However, there are examples that go beyond this to encourage community-engaged scholarship.

One example of this is the University of British Columbia's Public Scholars Initiative (UBC n.d.-c). This initiative supports a cohort of PhD students to enable them to "expand or strengthen their dissertation research through partnerships with those outside the academy (or in alternative roles in the academy), working on projects of mutual interest that contribute purposefully to the public good" (Porter 2021, 30). In the words of the program's founder, "students are supported to create change as well as knowledge, to 'liquefy' the traditional borders of their disciplines and research methodologies, to employ different epistemologies, and to otherwise view and perform their work from different perspectives" (Porter 2021, 30). After five years, there was evidence that the program was highly valued by scholars seeking to "make a difference" through their research, and that it met the needs of students whose ambitions and professional orientations were not aligned with the traditional academic path. The research produced has been nuanced and innovative (Porter 2021, 32–34).

Another example of a doctoral initiative to encourage community-engaged scholarship was the University of Texas' Intellectual Entrepreneurship Program, which had the objective of "creating citizen-scholars to work on community challenges" (Cassuto and Weisbuch 2021, 53). Despite its considerable success, the program was closed following a change in leadership at the graduate school, but its model provides inspiration as a promising practice. The program included cross-disciplinary courses, connections to community groups, and advice for students, who were encouraged to "take responsible ownership of their education, learn to think across disciplinary boundaries as well as across the boundary of academia itself, and gain experience in collaborative work" (as cited in Cassuto and Weisbuch 2021, 54).

Community-engaged scholarship opens up the opportunity for collaborative research projects at the graduate level. Again, the University of British Columbia provides an innovative example with its collaborative PhD option: "'Collaborative Ph.D.s' involve students working with different supervisors, in different departments/programs and disciplines, to address a common complex, real world problem. The dissertation would involve sole- or multi-authored components, with at least some elements solely authored (as is appropriate for a given discipline), but at least one component would be co-authored by students from diverse disciplinary locations" (UBC n.d.-b). This conception of the collaborative PhD connects directly with the wicked problems imperative.

The EDID Imperative

Addressing the EDID imperative requires action at all stages of the graduate program, from student recruitment through graduation.

Recruitment

Given that individuals from under-represented groups may not consider graduate school, initiatives designed to provide an introduction to the research environment may be valuable. McMaster University pioneered a program open to Indigenous students from across Turtle Island (Canada) to participate in a funded Indigenous Undergraduate Summer Research Scholars program (now renamed IndiNerds) designed to give them a taste of graduate student life (McMaster n.d.).

Admissions

To ensure that diversity is a key consideration in graduate admissions, programs can ensure that committee members complete training in recognizing and combatting unconscious bias. In addition, programs can ensure that conversations take place to define criteria and process. Moreno (2021) argues that "equity and inclusion within graduate admissions are strengthened when faculty consensus on criteria and review methods are defined prior to the start of graduate application review."

Program Delivery
Most arts graduate programs are built on the expectation, either explicit or implicit, that students will be located at the university offering the program for part or all of the time they are enrolled. This, combined with expectations that students will not complete all their degrees at one institution, can pose a barrier to Indigenous students and students from other equity-deserving groups who are rooted in community and unable to physically relocate. Development of blended (or low-residency) graduate programs has the potential to increase diversity in graduate programs. While many arts faculty members might have previously struggled to imagine delivering a graduate program this way, the experience of distance delivery during the COVID-19 pandemic may have increased openness to this idea.

Research Products
The traditional form of and approach to the doctoral dissertation can be alienating to Indigenous students and others working outside the mainstream (Czuy and Hogarth 2019). Supporting and encouraging non-traditional dissertation forms (CAGS 2018) can signal an important openness to innovation to BIPOC students.

The Talent Imperative

In chapter 4, we argued that human literacy should be the "home ground" for arts graduate education. Several of the associated competencies—the ability to work in complex and diverse teams, to make connections, and to lead and motivate—are not readily developed sitting alone in a library.

Experiential and Work-Integrated Learning
In the form of internships or co-op placements, this type of learning is an important means of supporting students to develop their human skills, while also drawing connections between their area of study and the challenges facing the organization hosting them. These can be embedded as program requirements or options (usually as a co-op within an MA or PhD program), or sponsored and organized by an external organization. Mitacs plays a significant role in this regard, and has substantially

increased the opportunities for graduate students in arts disciplines to participate in its research internships.

Beyond their positive impact on students' skill development, internships assist with students' transition to the labour force. A 2015 study found that most non-STEM, or BHASE, graduate students who participated in work-integrated learning were very likely (67 percent of master's and 74 percent of doctoral graduates) to state that the experience helped them find a job after graduation (Statistics Canada 2021); BHASE refers to the non-STEM fields of business, humanities, health, arts, social science, education, legal studies, trades, services, natural resources and conservation, and we would anticipate that the rate would be lower for social science and humanities students alone. While it is a promising practice, there is considerable room to increase arts graduate students' participation in work-integrated learning. Statistics Canada (2021) reports that in 2015, 41 percent of BHASE master's graduates and 25 percent of BHASE doctoral graduates participated in work-integrated learning.

Graduate students' skill development objectives and trajectories will necessarily be highly individualized. An increasingly common mechanism for formalizing and documenting graduate students' professional and skill development is independent development plans, which set out short- and long-term objectives for skill development and help students to document their skill acquisition. This formalization of professional development can both accelerate and sharpen its effectiveness.

Summary

These promising practices in arts graduate education suggest specific ways that programs can connect with Canada's public good. But what might entire programs directed at Canada's public good through attention to the wicked problems, EDID, and talent imperatives look like? To answer this question, we present hypothetical complete programs as a thought exercise to help readers envision what is possible for their real-world programs. For each example, we go through the EDITS framework category by category, speaking to each criterion.

Reimagining the Master of Arts

Our first hypothetical program is a disciplinary master of arts program.

Efficient

Assuming full-time study, this master of arts program is designed to be completed in a period of ten to sixteen months. The program has a clear thematic niche, "identities and society," that is unique from other master's programs at the university and from programs at the university's main competitors. The program is lean in design, with three required courses in the fall term and one required course and two elective courses in the winter term, followed by a faculty-supervised major research project (MRP) to be completed over the spring and summer terms. Students are also required to complete professional training modules offered by the faculty of graduate studies.

All of the required courses are exclusive to master's students, with graduate students from other units' programs allowed to register with approval from the graduate chair. Because all students must take each of the required courses, there is a guaranteed minimum class size, making the courses fiscally sustainable for the unit. For elective courses, students may take one of a small number of program-specific courses offered that year, a cross-listed undergraduate or doctoral course, or an approved course from another unit. All courses are clearly and explicitly tied to the program-level learning outcomes. Indeed, the required courses include assignments that set students up for their upcoming MRP, allowing motivated students to complete large parts of their MRP through their coursework.

As the program learning outcomes focus on research literacy—the ability to conduct basic research, and the ability to apply a theoretical model—the unit has specified that the MRP's purpose is to demonstrate competency rather than make an original contribution to knowledge. The unit has also identified that focused, succinct communication is a desired learning outcome. For this reason, the MRP requires the use of secondary data and/or documentary sources, with no original data collection, and is limited to 10,000 words, with the student encouraged to aim for

8,000 words. Students present their MRP at an end-of-summer master's symposium, which is attended by faculty, students, and alumni.

To ensure both supervisory excellence and program sustainability, the program size is deliberately held at a minimum of 20 percent below the faculty complement size, and student admissions are limited to applicants who are interested in working in areas in which the permanent faculty have expertise. Individual faculty supervision assignments are limited to two per year. Program size is determined by the total number of students in the program, rather than annually, to prevent a backlog of incomplete students occupying a particular faculty member's supervisory capacity.

Deliberate

The program has a bold and clearly stated purpose:

> Through the study and application of [disciplinary] theory and research, this program grounds students in how identity contributes to contemporary social issues. This understanding prepares students to work across diverse sectors to design solutions to contemporary societal challenges with empathy and creativity.

This purpose is woven through the program structure: all courses engage with the theme of identity and society, and each student's MRP applies this lens to their research.

The program has six overarching learning outcomes that are connected to the program requirements, and this connection is mapped clearly for students on the program website (see Table 8.1).

In designing the program, faculty members have explicitly linked their course-level learning outcomes to the program-level learning outcomes. Working with experts from the campus teaching and learning centre, the faculty members have also mindfully aligned their pedagogies with the program learning outcomes. For example, faculty members have opted to move away from the discipline's propensity toward the exclusive use of long research papers to embrace oral presentation skills and data visualization. Team-based assignments are used as frequently

TABLE 8.1 **Hypothetical Master of Arts Learning Outcomes and Program Requirements**

Learning Outcome	Program Requirements
Trace and defend the evolution of [disciplinary] theories and research on identity and society.	• ARTS 801 (required, fall term) • ARTS 804 (required, winter term) • One or both approved electives
Critically evaluate how issues of racism and colonization are addressed in dominant [disciplinary] theories and research on identity and society.	• ARTS 802 (required, fall term) • One or both approved electives
Communicate effectively in multiple formats for a variety of audiences.	• Assignments in required and elective courses • Faculty of Graduate Studies Professional Development series (required) • Master's student research symposium (required, summer term)
Work successfully in diverse teams and independently.	• Experiential learning project in ARTS 804 • Assignments in required and elective courses
Assess data sources critically.	• ARTS 803 (required, fall term)
Formulate and defend an evidence-based and theoretically grounded argument about how identity connects to a contemporary social issue.	• Major research project (required, spring/summer term)

as individual assignments, including an innovative team-based community-engaged research project in the winter term.

For the MRP, the program provides students with clear guidelines and expectations. Students understand that they are expected to use the research to demonstrate their mastery of the subject through an applied analysis (but not a new contribution to knowledge). The final research products—a research report (the MRP) and an oral presentation at the master's symposium—allow students to demonstrate their human literacy skills, while the research project itself allows students to demonstrate their data literacy skills.

The program website advertises the program as requiring eight to sixteen months of full-time study, and the site is annually updated to provide a rolling five-year average of completion times. The website provides the following recommended milestones for students and supervisors:

- Fall term: completion of three required courses, monthly progress check-in with supervisor, selection of MRP topic, monthly meeting with MRP cohort.
- Winter term: completion of one required course and two elective courses, monthly progress check-in with supervisor, selection of MRP data sources, completion of MRP outline, monthly meeting with MRP cohort.
- Spring term: twice monthly progress check-in with supervisor, weekly meeting with MRP cohort, completion of at least half of MRP draft.
- Summer term: twice monthly progress check-in with supervisor, weekly meeting with MRP cohort, completion of MRP, master's symposium presentation, application for graduation.

To ensure that all faculty have the necessary supervisory skills to support students to reach these milestones, the unit has brought in the faculty of graduate studies to provide supervisory training. To provide students with peer support in reaching these milestones, the program establishes MRP cohorts of four to six students who meet regularly to discuss their MRP progress while building student bonds. And to protect student well-being, the program has carefully allocated workloads across and within the terms.

The department surveys its current and former students (be they alumni or discontinued students) annually to track student outcomes over time. By asking students about program satisfaction and areas for improvement, the department is able to use student outcomes to inform curriculum refinement. To model transparency for students, the summary data and the department's intentions to use the information for continual curriculum improvement are shared on the program website.

Inclusive

The program is committed to inclusion. The department's faculty and staff have participated in an anti-racism workshop with the university's equity office, and have subsequently spent some time considering what this means in the context of their graduate program. Faculty have also been provided with additional training on how to evaluate the diversity of their course content and how to use inclusive assessment in their courses. The program-level learning outcome, "critically evaluate how issues of racism and colonization are addressed in dominant [disciplinary] theories and research on identity and society," is a central focus of one of the required courses. In addition, several individual instructors include course-level learning outcomes relating to issues of racism and colonization. Instructors are invited to submit their reading lists to a subcommittee of the graduate committee that offers constructive advice on ensuring that they are inclusive. The overall result has been an updating of admissions processes and significant changes in course content and assessment practices.

In considering issues of equity, diversity, and inclusion, the limited diversity of the faculty complement was quickly apparent. The current composition of the department is divided fairly evenly between faculty who identify as men and those who identify as women, but there is only one BIPOC colleague and no self-identified LGBTQIA+, disabled, or neurodivergent colleagues. The department has crafted a faculty complement plan that prioritizes hiring a second BIPOC faculty colleague as a first step. The department chair is petitioning the dean to grant the department a faculty hire to start to address the lack of faculty diversity. In the meantime, faculty are actively seeking opportunities to bring diverse speakers into their classes, and the department is using some of its limited funds to provide honoraria to facilitate this.

The department is also actively working to create a welcoming tone for all of its students. It has established a joint faculty-student working group that serves as a feedback mechanism so that concerns are heard. There is a clear zero tolerance policy for harassment, and faculty and staff are trained to pay attention to student well-being and mental health. The department also encourages students to participate in the university's graduate student wellness program.

The result is a lively and positive departmental culture. Events are planned to be accessible to student who are parents and students who are working while completing their program. The faculty pay careful attention to the diversity of invited speakers and guests, and the department hosts at least one talk per year specific to issues of inclusion in [discipline]. Students know that their well-being matters to the department and that their uniquenesses are celebrated.

Talent Developing

Talent development is an explicit goal of the program. Indeed, two of the six program-level learning outcomes are specific to human literacy ("communicate effectively in multiple formats for a variety of audiences"; "work successfully in diverse teams and independently") and one relates to data literacy ("assess data sources critically"). All of the courses include literacy development among the course-level learning outcomes. In the course sessions, faculty members take time to explicitly teach students these skills, and students demonstrate their mastery through course assignments. Each year, the university's career office provides students with a popular workshop on how to identify their career competencies and explain them to future employers.

One innovation the department has adopted is using TA work as an opportunity to develop student talents. TAs are provided with paid time to participate in the faculty of graduate studies' "TA Success" training program. The department then follows this up with a TA discussion in which faculty and TAs identify opportunities to use TA work to develop human literacy skills specific to empathy, communication, and ethics.

The department has also seized the opportunity to use evidence to inform how it approaches skill development. With its student survey (noted earlier), the department can identify the sectors in which its graduates are working. Every few years, the department hires an RA to complete a research project that synthesizes current information on Canada's talent needs and supplements this analysis with interviews with select employers about their workplace skills needs. The department then uses this information to assess if its curriculum is continuing to meet the career needs of its graduates.

Student Focused

It is clear to everyone that the "identities and society" themed MA program prioritizes student needs. Its stated purpose focuses on student career preparation. The program lays out achievable milestones and provides students with support to achieve them. The department connects students with university programs to help them identify and articulate their career competencies.

Student support is part of the departmental culture. From the supervisory training to the mental health and wellness training, faculty and staff are trained to be responsive to student needs. Their ability to do so is protected by careful attention to enrollment management, with admissions being limited to numbers below full capacity.

The department is also committed to evidence-informed education. As noted earlier, the department consults with students and employers to refine its curriculum. The department also stays apprised of published literature on graduate education. The university, for its part, supports the department through regular program reviews.

Reimagining the Arts PhD

Our second example program is an arts PhD program. We present it as a disciplinary PhD, but the example would work equally well, if not better, as an interdisciplinary arts PhD.

Efficient

This PhD program is designed to be completed within four to five years of full-time study. The program has a clear thematic niche, "human migration," and students use disciplinary theory and methods to examine issues related to human migration. The PhD program is lean and focused: students complete two required courses in the fall term, and one required and one restricted elective course in the winter term. In the spring term of the first year, students complete a required pass/fail short course that prepares them for qualifying exam completion. Students write their qualifying exam in the fall of the second year, and then complete two required pass/fail short courses that prepare them for proposal defence and dissertation writing. Students then move into the dissertation phase. Students are also required to complete professional training modules offered by the faculty of graduate studies.

All of the required courses are exclusive to doctoral students and are taught by tenure-stream faculty. Further, the department has engaged in partnerships with a number of disciplinary peer departments at other universities to offer online doctoral seminars co-taught by leaders in the field. This has the added advantage of creating linkages within the discipline across institutions. Within the home university, doctoral students from other units' programs are allowed to register with approval from the graduate chair.

As the PhD program seeks to train advanced researchers, two of each student's four courses focus on research methods. Because the PhD program is modest in size, the department has worked with other units to establish faculty-wide doctoral methods courses. The result of this collaborative effort is a robust selection of introductory and advanced methods courses that meet the needs of doctoral students across programs and have the added advantage of creating an interdisciplinary community among both instructors and students.

For elective courses, the program does not offer program-specific courses. Instead, doctoral students choose a cross-listed MA course or an approved graduate course from another unit. All required and elective courses are clearly and explicitly tied to the program-level learning outcomes.

The PhD program size is limited by the department's permanent faculty size. The admissions committee is careful to ensure that all students admitted to the program have interests that correlate well with at least two faculty members; this prevents students from being "orphaned" in the case of unanticipated supervisory changes or departures. Individual faculty are limited to supervising a maximum of four PhD students at a time, with a maximum of one new PhD student per year to ensure a supervisor's assigned PhD students are at different program stages. Faculty are discouraged from taking on new PhD students in advance of anticipated leaves or retirement.

Deliberate

Unlike typically broad and generic PhD programs, this PhD program has focus and purpose:

> Through inquiry and application of [disciplinary] knowledge, the PhD program equips students to advance understanding of the social dimensions of human migration. Students create new knowledge of how refugee movements, immigration, settler colonialism, and Indigenous displacement have shaped and continue to shape our world. Graduates are prepared to work locally and globally in the academic, public, not-for-profit, and corporate sectors to identify innovative strategies to address future migration challenges.

While the topic does not connect directly with most faculty research projects, almost all faculty teaching and supervising in the program are able to find a theoretical and/or methodological connection to the theme. Critically, the faculty understand that the purpose of the PhD is developing the students, rather than advancing faculty members' personal research agendas.

The clear statement of the purpose of the PhD facilitates deliberate design of the program. It has four learning outcomes, according to the department website:

By the end of the program, graduates are able to:

1. Critically evaluate the discipline and its subfields, considering how the discipline's evolution reflects shifts in understandings of power, equity, and social inclusion;
2. Relate advanced understanding of disciplinary theoretical and methodological approaches to the complex challenges of human migration, with particular attention to issues of gender, race, Indigeneity, and sexuality;
3. Design and complete original independent research that connects disciplinary theories to contemporary

problems to advance understanding of human migration; and
4. Use evidence, cultural understanding, and empathy to communicate complex issues to diverse audiences.

The program structure reflects these learning outcomes through coursework, a qualifying exam, a research proposal, and the dissertation.

Coursework

The only courses required for this PhD program are ones that provide analyses of the discipline or that offer advanced training in research methodologies and professional development. The rigorous coursework allows PhD students the opportunity to engage with core elements of the discipline. Faculty members connect readings and assignments focused on human migration with core disciplinary theories and methodologies. Faculty members are mindful of pedagogy and use the courses as opportunities to challenge students to critically engage with the discipline. As the PhD requires students to make an original research contribution, the coursework also ensures that the student is prepared to conduct advanced research through advanced research skills training and project management training.

Qualifying Exam

This exam requires students to bring core ideas together, to demonstrate both knowledge of the history of the discipline and an understanding of different theoretical and methodological approaches employed within the discipline. Students are assessed on their demonstration of the intellectual tools that allow a scholar to read and engage critically with literature in the discipline in order to contextualize their work.

The program has specifically titled the exam as "qualifying" rather than "comprehensive." The department has no illusions that students will leave the program with a "comprehensive" understanding of the discipline. (None of the faculty members possess such an understanding, after all!) The sheer volume of scholarship makes the idea of understanding the breadth of the discipline an impossible undertaking, and there is no disciplinary consensus on what constitutes the "great works." Rather than pushing students to have broad, superficial knowledge of the full landscape of the discipline, the program's qualifying exam requires students to understand the discipline's intellectual history and range of approaches.

The program has also abandoned the frequently used "hazing ritual" paraphernalia of comprehensive exams such as unreasonable and unfocused reading lists and high-pressure exam practices like requiring students to write with no access to notes or the internet—as though professional practice in the future might require the ability to list important texts spontaneously under pressure. Instead, students are provided with focused reading lists, the rubric faculty will use in evaluating their written answers, and exam preparation training. They write the exam in a take-home format, followed by an oral defence.

Research Proposal

Here, students are required to reflect on choice of method, theoretical grounding, and situating their research in the relevant literature. The PhD candidate is expected to be able to locate themselves within some thread of the discipline's conversations. The candidate is also required to demonstrate realistic project management strategies.

Dissertation

As the program seeks to prepare students to translate their knowledge to a variety of audiences, including but not limited to academia, the department has embraced the suggestion from the Canadian Association for Graduate Studies' 2018 *Report of the Task Force on the Dissertation* to expand conceptions of the dissertation to encourage elements designed to communicate findings to a broader audience. To this end, students complete a portfolio ("three paper") style dissertation (which speaks to scholarly audiences), a policy paper (which speaks to professional audiences), and a three-minute thesis-style presentation (which speaks to a more general audience). Upon request, students may opt to replace the portfolio dissertation with a more traditional "manuscript thesis" style dissertation, while retaining the other two requirements (the policy paper and presentation).

The program is designed to be completed in four to five years of full-time study. Students and supervisors work together to achieve the following milestones:

- Year 1: completion of all coursework, monthly progress check-in with supervisor, monthly meeting with PhD cohort.
- Year 2: completion of qualifying exam, completion of proposal defence and dissertation writing course, completion of proposal defence, monthly meeting with PhD cohort.
- Year 3: dissertation writing and professional development training, monthly meeting with PhD cohort.
- Year 4 (and, if needed, year 5): dissertation writing and professional development training, monthly meeting with PhD cohort, dissertation defence, application for graduation.

Supervisors are provided with ongoing support and professional development. Students are established in peer support groups to build bonds within and across cohorts.

Average time to completion rates are updated annually on the program website, and the department tracks student outcomes carefully. Students graduating or discontinuing the program are invited to participate in an exit study, and this information is used to inform future program-related decisions. The graduate chair's annual report, posted on the department's webpage, includes information about program alumni and celebrates academic and non-academic career achievements equally.

Inclusive

Given the program's focus on issues of migration, it is not surprising that faculty teaching in the program and staff supporting the program are highly attuned to issues of inclusion and diversity. Two of the program's four learning outcomes explicitly mention EDID. The required courses all critically address questions of colonization and racism, and all required courses centre diverse voices in course materials. The department is mindful of issues of representation in its speaker series, and individual faculty members also pay attention to diversity when inviting class speakers. The program design is considerate of how workloads and timelines interact with important cultural dates, including the National Day for Truth and Reconciliation (September 30).

Aware of both the limited diversity in the discipline and the role of PhD programs in training stewards of the discipline, including potential future faculty members, the department has set explicit diversity admission goals. The full department has completed anti-bias and anti-racism training, and the university's zero tolerance for harassment policy is clearly posted in department seminar rooms and public spaces. One faculty member with a particular interest in artwork worked with the university's collections officer to increase the number of Indigenous artistic works in the department's public spaces.

The program sees departmental events as important socialization opportunities for PhD students. To ensure that students of different religious and cultural backgrounds can participate and to avoid creating undue pressure on students with caregiving responsibilities, each term the department asks PhD students to complete an anonymous survey identifying key dates and times that may present barriers to participation.

Talent Developing

The PhD program trains students to develop advanced human literacy and data literacy skills, along with some technological literacy skills. In reimagining its PhD program, the department identified a number of skills that combined the stewards of the discipline approach with talent development. Its selection of skills reflects the needs of future faculty members as well as an assessment of the talent needs of PhDs in the discipline working outside academia. Students create an independent development plan in their first term in the program, in which they identify specific skills they plan to develop in the short and medium term, and then set out a plan for developing them. In annual revisions to the plan, students update and document their skill acquisition and set new objectives for the coming year.

For human literacy, communication skills and the ability to make connections between ideas are obviously critical for PhD students. Given the thematic focus on migration, the department also identified the human literacy skills of cultural understanding and acting ethically and with empathy as key learning outcomes. For data literacy, the department identified robust methodological training as key for stewards of their discipline. This includes explicit training in the use of data analysis software, data interpretation, and critical assessment of data sources. For technological literacy, given the complexity and "wicked problems" nature of migration issues, the department identified design thinking and creative problem solving as a key talent development area for PhD students.

The program learning outcomes reflect these talent development goals. These talent goals are included, in greater detail, in course-level learning outcomes, and faculty members explicitly teach these skills in class, with students' grades reflecting their achievement of these outcomes. Through professional development workshops in collaboration with the university career centre and other arts doctoral programs, PhD students are trained to effectively articulate their human, data, and technological literacy skills.

A big change for the department occurred in its approach to TA and RA positions. All PhD students are required to complete TA training workshops with the teaching and learning centre prior to commencing TA work, and the TA activities stress the human literacy skills of leadership and effective communication. For RA work, PhD students are given support and guidance in setting up effective time and project management skills, and faculty are strongly encouraged to use RAships as an opportunity to advance students' methodological training. Faculty in turn also receive support and training to be effective guides in developing students' talents.

Student Focused

When the department adopted the stewards of the discipline mindset, it engaged in a thoughtful discussion about how the discipline can benefit society both within and beyond academia. In this discussion, the faculty members identified a common purpose: to train students to use [disciplinary] understanding to ethically and empathetically address global migration issues. Appreciating the limited opportunities for PhD graduates in academia, faculty members agreed to continue to train PhD students for academic success while also providing them with the tools for success outside academia.

As most of the faculty members have limited experience outside academia, the department has chosen to work with the faculty of graduate studies and the university career centre to ensure students have tools to match their skills with non-academic career opportunities. The faculty also works with numerous arts departments to provide an annual alumni-student networking event at which the arts PhD students learn about alumni career paths.

The student-focused model led the faculty to limit the program size to match supervisory capacity and to identify reasonable program timeframes. Through the faculty of graduate studies, supervisors are provided with supports to achieve key milestones and are trained in effective supervisory practices.

The department has opted to appoint its graduate chair on a three-year rotation. The graduate chair's responsibilities include monitoring student outcomes data and reporting this to the department. Each year, the graduate chair holds a lunch event with current students to discuss areas of challenge. The department uses the cyclical program review timelines as a motivation to keep its program current and evidence based.

Reimagining Professional Arts Graduate Education

Finally, to encourage consideration of professional doctorates, we consider a hypothetical interdisciplinary professional doctorate program: a DPS (Doctor of Public Service).

Efficient

The DPS program is designed to be completed within three years of study, with most students continuing to work in their related professional job while completing their degree requirements. As Canada's first and only DPS program, this interdisciplinary program is unique not only within the university but also among the university's main competitors. The DPS program is structured for efficiency: students complete coursework over four semesters (fall, winter, spring, fall). Over that sixteen-month period, students complete a total of six courses, all of which are core to the DPS program. The fall and winter courses are offered online, while the spring courses are delivered as an in-person two-week intensive residency.

After their coursework is completed, students write a review paper that synthesizes knowledge in a specific area of public service study. After this, students move to the dissertation phase. Because most students are working professionals, the program has partnered with the doctor of business administration program offered at their university to provide customized professional training workshops that address the needs of mid-career professionals.

All of the required courses are exclusive to the DPS program, acknowledging the particular learning needs of this cohort (and avoiding considerations related to the differential tuition structure for this program). All courses are clearly and explicitly tied to the program-level learning outcomes. Required courses are taught by tenure-stream faculty or professional affiliates.

The DPS program is offered collaboratively by three arts departments. Supervision assignments are established after the first year of the program, with faculty being assigned a maximum of one new student per year. Faculty are discouraged from taking on new students in advance of anticipated leaves and in the three years immediately preceding retirement.

Deliberate

The DPS aims to develop the leadership and applied research competencies of mid-career professionals working in the public, not-for-profit, and co-operative sectors. Understanding that public service professionals deal regularly with the challenges of wicked problems, the department has ensured the program's learning outcomes emphasize the importance of combining human and data literacy to address complexity. The DPS has six program-level learning outcomes, which are posted on the department website:

By the end of the program, students will be able to:

1. Lead diverse teams to address complex real-world public service challenges;
2. Connect multidisciplinary theoretical approaches to a range of public service contexts and issues;
3. Apply critical data analysis skills to use evidence to inform public service decision making;
4. Assess public sector problems through anti-racist, decolonialist, anti-ableist, and gender lenses to identify equitable and inclusive solutions;
5. Use diverse communication tools and strategies to engage effectively and empathetically with stakeholders and the general public; and,
6. Use design thinking and process assessments to identify opportunities for real-world public sector improvements.

The program is highly applied. Faculty have adopted case-based learning approaches, and they encourage students to draw upon examples from their public sector work in their assignments. Rather than completing a qualifying exam, students are required to work in teams to complete a coauthored review paper that synthesizes a vast body of knowledge. To accompany this, each individual student submits a reflection paper explaining how the knowledge relates to their own work.

The dissertation requires students to apply their theoretical and methodological training to a real-world challenge in their sphere of work. To ensure that students have structure surrounding their dissertation preparation, as part of the program, they are required to register in specially designed courses to structure their dissertation research and writing in their final year. Further, they work with a supervisor and a supervisory committee that includes both academics and practitioners. In addition to defending their dissertation, DPS students create a public artifact (such as an online video, podcast, or executive summary) that allows stakeholders to learn about their research findings.

The DPS program is based on a cohort model and is highly structured. Students have clarity about how to complete the program in the allocated time. Recognizing that "life happens," the program also has opportunities for students to catch up if they need to take a semester off.

The collaborating departments have established a clear evaluation plan and collect student data annually. Students in the program have access to this information on an internal website. The collaborating departments post average degree completion times on the program website.

The program's milestones can be summarized as follows:

- Year 1, fall and winter: online courses
- Year 1, spring: two-week intensive residency courses
- Year 2, fall: online courses
- Year 2, winter: review paper
- Year 2, spring: dissertation work
- Year 3: dissertation work and defence

Inclusive

Given the necessity for public sector leaders to advance Canada's EDID imperative, the DPS program prioritizes training in diversity and inclusion. One of the program's six learning outcomes is focused on diversity and inclusion. Within courses, instructors include learning outcomes and assignments that focus on the Truth and Reconciliation Commission's Calls to Action (2015). Course materials include representation from diverse communities and train students to apply anti-racist, anti-ableist, and gender lenses. Instructors teaching in the program, including faculty and professional affiliates, complete anti-racism training before teaching in the program.

Diversity within the student cohort is a priority for the admissions committee. To facilitate a diverse student cohort, the program has flexible admissions requirements that acknowledge relevant work and life experience. The admissions committee has completed anti-bias training.

The program consists of online courses, in-person "residencies," and considerable group work. Students are provided with clear expectations for respectful engagement in all of these venues at the program orientation, and are reminded of these expectations in all courses. The program design is both rigorous and respectful of the students' mid-career realities. Students are also invited to take part in the faculty of graduate studies' webinars on work-life balance, effective work habits, and mental health.

The residency components of the program feature considerable social engagement to allow for networking and connection. The program incorporates fun activities, such as trivia events and team-building puzzle activities like escape rooms, that allow for the inclusion of all students.

Talent Developing

Given the program's professional focus and student audience, the collaborating departments conducted an assessment of talent needs prior to establishing the program learning outcomes and design. They also established an advisory committee with representatives from the public, not-for-profit, and co-operative sectors to keep them informed about changing and emerging talent needs.

DPS students strengthen a number of human literacy skills, including teamwork, leadership, connections, and communication. Students also develop data literacy skills, including qualitative and quantitative analysis, data presentation and interpretation, and critical assessment of data sources. The program teaches technological literacy skills through training in design thinking and process improvements. These talent development learning outcomes are explicitly taught across the program courses and feature strongly in students' grades.

As a professional doctorate program aimed at mid-career working professionals, the program does not employ students as TAs or RAs.

Student Focused

The DPS program design is centred on students' needs and realities. The program is intended for mid-career students seeking to advance their career and advance their ability to contribute positively to Canada's wicked problems imperative. The program's learning outcomes allow students to develop skills that transfer across a number of sectors, and the program's efficient format allows them to complete the program in a reasonable timeframe. Importantly, the program encourages students to draw their real-world work challenges into their coursework, creating a form of work-integrated learning. The collaborating departments have deliberately kept the program size relatively small to foster cohorts while ensuring sufficient capacity to meet student needs.

As the program instruction includes both faculty members and professional affiliates, the collaborating units have an annual "teaching day" with the university teaching and learning centre in advance of each cohort's entry. At this event, instructors are taught best practices in competency-based learning, effective assessment strategies, and other tools. Instructors are also taught strategies for teaching mid-career learners with unique concerns and interests.

As noted, the collaborating departments have an established evaluation plan for the program. This information is used to refine the program and to inform the university's cyclical review process.

Reimagining Arts Graduate Education

As you read through these hypothetical examples of "excellent" programs above, you may have had a number of reactions. For example, you may have thought, "My university does not provide those graduate studies, teaching and learning, and career centre supports." Or, "My department does not have the capacity to do student surveys and employer consultations." This may be true—and it is also possible that it used to be true and that your university resources are evolving. We encourage you to challenge the inherent assumption that there are no or limited supports available. And, if your assumption is correct, we encourage you to voice your desire for these student supports to your department chair and dean.

Alternatively, you may have thought, "This hypothetical program isn't very innovative. Where is the co-op program? Where is the community-engaged learning? Where is the transdisciplinarity?" We agree. Our point here is that we don't need radical change to move Canada's arts graduate programs from "meh" to excellent. In its own call for reimagining arts (specifically humanities) PhD programs, the Institute for the Public Life of Arts and Ideas writes that "the 'tool kits' of PhDs, whether working within or outside the academy," remain "largely the same: original, critical thinking, effective communication, creativity, empathy, innovation, problem-solving, project management, and leadership." It continues on to propose "not a wholesale revision of the PhD" or a "reorientation" of core principles. Rather, it advocates *"sharpening existing skills by making them more central to PhD training and adding additional competencies to reflect new ways of working.* To the variety of shared and discipline-specific talents and proficiencies, we add enriched collaboration skills, greater interdisciplinary proficiency, a wider range of technology and media competencies, and a more robust, applied understanding of the public character and value of humanities scholarship" (2013, 10; emphasis added). Like the Institute for the Public Life of Arts and Ideas, we propose improving arts graduate education by keeping what works, sharpening our focus, and reimagining the elements that no longer meet societal or student needs. That being said, we do encourage units that have the imagination and will to consider more innovative ideas.

You might also have objected to the themes that we identified to give coherence to the programs. What about the long-standing all-purpose master of arts in sociology, or PhD in geography? After all, arts departments need to employ a faculty complement that offers breadth in a discipline for their undergraduate offerings. If the PhD program is only focused on migration, what are the faculty members not working in that field to do? And how is it fair that some faculty members working in the area are able to supervise these particular PhD students, and those who aren't cannot? Returning to the idea that programs should be student focused, we would reply that students' needs are best met through the development of programs with some thematic coherence and focus, rather than just through spreading activities around evenly.

It is possible to imagine some exciting and powerful programs with the EDITS framework. And we want to stress that this model does not require programs to move to a professional focus, nor does it require programs to abandon research and theory. But it does require us to be mindful of the purpose of arts graduate degrees. For example, seeing the MA program as centring on diverse career preparation changes our approach to the degree. It is not a miniature PhD, and it is not primarily for preparing students for doctoral study. It is also not simply a fifth year of coursework, little different from an undergraduate degree. The master's must be clearly oriented and focused around career preparation and skill building at an advanced level.

Ideally, we would like to see faculty members and departments leading the charge to reimagine arts graduate education. A reimagined arts graduate curriculum that is imposed top-down by deans is likely to result in, at best, boring programs and, at worst, unsustainable programs that fail to embrace a department's interests and realities. The university can provide support in the form of tools and information, staff support, and even incentives to engage in the change process. But the creative reimagining ideally will happen at the unit level.

Change also does not have to all come at once. The EDITS rubric is amenable to incremental steps—using it to assess existing programs, and then identifying areas one by one for change. By seeing the EDITS model as a continuum, units can take steps to "level up" in specific areas or categories, rather than feeling a need to undertake radical change. (Although we are not opposed to radical change for units that are willing to do the work!)

So, what steps can various actors take to move from the present state to these reimagined options? This is where some books end—presenting the vision, but skimping on the implementation. As experienced administrators ourselves, we know that universities and their surrounding contexts are incredibly complicated. Great ideas often go nowhere because of this complexity.

But that is not good enough for us. Nor is it good enough for Canada or for the thousands of students who enroll in Canada's arts graduate programs. So, the next chapter tackles the challenge of implementation, and the actions required to establish arts graduate education for the public good.

Implementing the Vision

In previous chapters, we've laid out the need to reimagine arts graduate education in Canada, the factors that explain the current state of the system, and our vision for renewed arts graduate education. But how do we move from the status quo to this new state?

Implementation of any new idea is always challenging. A strong bias toward the status quo is normal, especially when there are multiple levels of actors and stakeholders, each with their own capacities and interests. This complexity is why many calls for change in universities (or elsewhere) end with a vision or set of recommendations, but not a lot of specifics on how to implement them—how to break out of the status quo. And thus, we remain stranded, as outlined in chapter 4, without first movers, leadership, or actual action.

This book is, at its heart, a call to action for many actors—for Canada's arts faculty members, arts deans and graduate deans, university leaders, provincial and federal policymakers, granting agencies, and academic associations and organizations. Our aspiration is that reading this book (and thank you for doing so) will be the starting point for individuals like, and including, you to make real changes to improve arts graduate education in Canada in ways that align with Canada's public good.

Calls to Action for Programs, Institutions, and Government: Vision, Culture, and Resources

Since we want you (yes, you) to take up our call to action, in this chapter we provide clarity on the exact actions needed and by whom. We get down to the nitty-gritty details, presenting a roadmap for how Canada can move from our current suboptimal spot to our envisioned stronger position. Specifically, we outline the engagement required from three levels of actors:

- Program level: individual arts faculty members and units offering arts graduate programs
- Institution level: university administrators and leaders
- System level: governments, grant agencies, and employers

Each level differs in its role and capacities. Change and initiative need to come from all levels, and so we start by discussing how each of the three levels can act independently. The point of doing so is to demonstrate that no level needs to wait for the other. All have the agency to initiate and make change.

We lay out actions for each level in three areas: vision, culture, and resources. Vision is needed to move forward. Culture needs to be incorporated, and possibly changed, to do so. And, while good intentions and effort are important, resources are inevitably key to incentivizing and shaping behaviour.

Finally, because each level is responsive to incentives, pressures, and information from other levels, we identify how the three levels can coordinate efforts effectively. True success will involve coordination among these different actors, and we outline how the three levels can move forward in a concerted fashion.

We believe that change at all levels and coordination among the levels are both challenging and achievable. We also strongly believe that they need to be achieved.

So, let's get to work, shall we?

Program-Level Calls to Action

The program level primarily means individual faculty and units. We start at this level for two reasons. First, we believe strongly in collegial governance, which we define as faculty working on and overseeing things collaboratively, rather than relying entirely on hierarchies and being told what to do. Top-down impositions on academic programming are unlikely to be effective, much less innovative. Effective arts graduate programs for the public good must be firmly grounded at the program level to be effective and sustainable. Faculty and units have the subject-matter expertise, the connections to students, and the day-to-day involvement needed to produce real change.

Second, we believe it is in the interest of arts faculty members and units to be early movers in reimagining arts graduate education. If faculty and units are slow to advance change, there is a risk that other less appropriate actors will fill the void, likely creating new problems and pathologies.

If you are an arts faculty member, the following calls to action are directly for you.

Vision

The first step: all arts units offering graduate programming need to bring their faculty together for a frank discussion—or series of discussions—to explicitly decide why they are in the graduate education business at all.

In these discussions, it will be tempting to point the finger at the university and system levels. And fair enough. As we outlined in chapter 4, there is good reason to do so. But in addition to blaming the university for pushing units to create and expand programs, squeeze in more students, and stretch resources, and upbraiding SSHRC for rewarding research applications that provide funding for graduate students, arts units must take responsibility as well. Many arts units have allowed their graduate programs to drift with the winds, rather than taking a serious look at why they exist, and in particular whether or not their programs serve the best interests of students.

It is time for the drift to stop.

Individually and collectively, arts faculty need to ask, "why do we have a graduate program?" If the answers are "because we've always had one," "because every other unit in the faculty has one," "because students keep applying," "because we need TA support for our undergrad programs," or "so that faculty will have students to supervise and research assistants to support their research agendas," the unit needs to dig a bit deeper to find a more noble purpose that goes beyond individual and/or unit self-interest. Faculty members need to find a more meaningful "why" for continuing to offer arts graduate programming.

The vision we present is to capitalize on the possibilities for arts graduate education to serve Canada's public good. We see this as a compelling vision—one that benefits Canada, students, and the arts disciplines. We have presented the EDITS framework and examples of reimagined programs to provide tools and inspiration for faculty and units to turn the "arts graduate education for the public good" vision into reality. To be sure, units may need to do some work to translate them to specific disciplinary contexts. But we challenge all arts faculty and units in Canada to think broadly about how they can reimagine their graduate programs around a vision of the public good.

How can arts units move forward to discuss their collective vision for their graduate programs? Here are some possible actions that could be initiated by a department chair, a graduate chair, or even an individual faculty member:

- Hold a brown bag lunch discussion about the graduate program's role in students' lives and careers;
- Conduct an internal anonymous survey of faculty members using open-ended questions to obtain top-of-mind thoughts on the purpose of graduate programs in the unit;
- Host a half-day, facilitated workshop to establish a clear vision for the unit's graduate programs;

- Engage in individual discussions with other faculty members about the graduate programs' purpose;
- Establish a small working group to draft a one-page vision for the unit's graduate programs and then invite all faculty to respond to this vision;
- Hire an RA to identify five to ten examples of innovative graduate programs in the discipline or across disciplines at other universities, and use the summary report as a starting point for discussion at a department meeting;
- Ask the faculty of graduate studies to provide program-specific student data for time to completion, completion rates, and student funding over the past five years. Combine this information with the national data we presented in chapter 3, and use this information as a starting base for hallway discussions about how the unit's graduate programs are or are not benefiting students;
- Conduct a survey of current students and recent graduates, as well as recent discontinued students, and ask them how the program might better serve future students. Invite faculty members to a brainstorming session to reflect on the feedback; and/or
- Use any opportunity offered by a mandated unit review or curriculum review to spark conversations about the graduate program.

The starting point for meaningful change is for units to work together to set a clear vision for why a specific graduate program exists, how it serves students, and how it serves the public good. This requires someone to get these conversations started, either personally or by requesting that the department/unit leadership do so. That someone could be you.

Culture

Vision is good, but we adhere to the aphorism that "culture eats strategy for breakfast." In the very decentralized environment of academic departments, there are three particular challenges with respect to culture and attitudes: simple resistance to the idea that change is needed; the belief that change is somebody else's job; and a belief that colleagues won't be able to agree on a path forward, so why bother?

One way to address resistance to change is to compare the program vision with the program reality. Here are some possible actions that a department chair or a graduate chair could initiate to assist with this comparison:

- Establish a working group to assess the current graduate program against the EDITS rubric. (If the unit has more than one graduate program, it might be useful to focus on a single program to start.) Ask the group to report back with its assessment along with recommendations with small (or not small) steps to improve the program's score on the rubric metrics;
- As part of a departmental retreat, have small groups of faculty members work together to assess the current graduate program against the EDITS rubric. In a large group discussion, identify areas where there is consensus about room for improvement;
- Conduct an anonymous internal survey of faculty members that has them assess their current graduate program against the EDITS rubric. Share the results with the department to launch a discussion about areas in need of change; and/or
- Invite the graduate students in the program to evaluate the program using the EDITS rubric and share their findings.

These assessments should provoke discussion and information to help counter naysayers who feel change is unnecessary. Unless, of course, your program is performing well. In that case, keep doing what you're doing!

Once there is consensus, or at least sufficient agreement, that the graduate program needs changes, the next step is to do the work to turn visions and aspirations into reality. Here it is important for faculty members and units to take responsibility for making the changes necessary to make their graduate programs student focused. Units and faculty must take ownership of their programs and the changes that need to be made. And for units that house diverse perspectives, the process will involve a concerted effort to find the points of consensus.

In some academic units (those with clearer governance and administrative models and/or with strong staff support), the way to move change forward is clear. The graduate chair leads their graduate committee colleagues and works with the support of the graduate administrator to create and implement plans. The role of other faculty members is simply to be supportive and to resist the urge to hover in the background with a veto.

In other academic units, clarity of responsibilities is less defined and staff support is non-existent. In such units, change management tends to fall to the already overburdened department chair or graduate chair. Other faculty voice vague moral support and no actual assistance. "Yes," many will say, "these are important changes that must happen. I am in complete support of them (or at least those changes that don't affect what I personally want to do). However, I myself need to focus on my own research and teaching." The result is predictable, with the status quo prevailing as change gets kicked down the road until "later," "when the next chair takes over," "when money isn't so tight," or "when [difficult colleague] retires."

Adopting a culture of shared departmental ownership means that improving the graduate programs is not somebody else's job—it is everybody's job. This means that if there isn't an existing committee responsible for managing the necessary changes, the department members need to agree to form a working group that is empowered to do the work and actually given the space and authority to do it.

Concrete actions to create a culture of shared departmental ownership of the graduate programs may include:

- Regularly reminding colleagues that the graduate program is the responsibility of all faculty members;
- Regularly reminding colleagues that, whatever their differences with one another, they share a commitment to graduate students;
- Including graduate program renewal as an action update item at all department meetings;
- Creating a working group responsible for graduate program renewal, with clear timelines and accountabilities defined in a terms of reference;
- Recognizing educational leadership in graduate program renewal in faculty merit pay and promotion processes; and/or

- Assessing potential new faculty hires based on their ability to contribute to deliberate and focused graduate education, in addition to their research prowess and classroom teaching.

Resources

We know what many arts faculty members (and particularly department chairs) want to read here: arts units need more resources from their dean or university to do this work. And while our next section will in fact argue that arts units should be supported in doing this work, we are not going to make that argument here.

Instead, we boldly suggest that in most cases, sufficient resources are already present for arts units to make many if not all of the changes needed. Arts units don't necessarily need new faculty hires to expand course offerings or new staff hires to provide student career counselling and writing support. There is a tremendous amount of improvement that units can achieve with their existing resources—provided they are willing to consider a different approach to allocating those resources.

As we discussed in chapter 6, there is an opportunity for arts graduate programs to become more efficient (the "E" in EDITS). Far too many disciplinary graduate programs are plagued by low numbers or low quality or both, but faculty in their host unit are not able or willing to consider alternatives. Arts units can do far more to share resources and coordinate beyond their own unit walls. This may mean more cross-listed courses, cross-unit courses and supervisions, joint programs, and other collaborations. These are not unusual ideas, but they are often underutilized ones.

Joint arts graduate programs are often limited to interdisciplinary areas where there is no pre-existing department structure to build on. When disciplinary programs send students to another unit for some of their coursework, it's usually seen as an aberration due to a particular student's interest area or to cover a short-term teaching gap.

We need to go beyond this. Disciplinary arts graduate program leaders could build collaboration and shared resources into the foundations of their programs. The best illustration of potentially shared resources, and one of the most long-standing conversations in graduate education, is consolidated research methods courses. Nearly all disciplines and programs strongly argue that they need to run their own research methods courses, tailored to the discipline. But the vast majority of students, especially at the master's level, are not planning careers in the discipline. Letting go of this, and creating a smaller number of well-designed methods courses, taught by instructors who really want to be there, will be more effective while freeing up resources for the rest of the program.

Cooperation across programs to offer elements of professional development or skills acquisition also conserves resources, and can help build trust and mutual knowledge that could be the foundation for greater cooperation in the future.

Beyond these first steps, units need to be active agents in reinventing their own programs and coordinating and linking everything together. Concrete actions here may include:

- Creating strong joint graduate courses shared across multiple arts departments;
- Collaborating with other cognate arts disciplines in the institution to replace a number of weak disciplinary or interdisciplinary graduate programs with a single strong and sustainable program; and/or
- Continuing conversations with others so that even if consolidation/shared resources are not immediately appropriate, these can be continually considered as an option.

The unit that waits for resources to fall from above risks waiting forever. In the event that resources do come, it is possible that they will be tied to conditions that are inappropriate for the discipline and its students. To make changes, arts faculty members and units need to maximize their agency and work with the resources they do have. To be clear, we still advise asking the dean, the teaching and learning centre, and the careers centre for support in the form of knowledge, staff time, and money. We just don't think you should wait for it before moving forward.

University-Level Calls to Action

The university level refers to senior leaders and institutional units beyond the academic units offering arts graduate programs. Here we include arts and graduate studies deans and associate deans and their staff; research vice presidents and their staff; teaching and learning vice provosts and their staff; vice provosts and other leaders responsible for equity, diversity, inclusion, and Indigenous engagement; provosts; presidents; university libraries; career centres; and the myriad other parts of the university that directly or indirectly touch upon arts graduate education.

The university level creates and sustains the incentives, structures, and supports available to units. It can facilitate change—or stymie and discourage it. The university level can create perverse incentives (as it has done; see chapter 4) or positive incentives. It can lobby governments and granting agencies for additional changes. Effective arts graduate programs for the public good must be championed and supported at the university level to create systemic change.

If you are a university senior leader or a member of a university unit, the following calls to action are directly for you.

Vision

We've explored throughout this book how arts graduate education has been largely shaped by incidental forces, especially financial incentives and the prioritization of research intensity. To bring change, nearly all institutions need a stronger central vision for graduate education, and specifically arts graduate education. University leaders need to think more clearly about how to envision graduate programs in their own right, especially the distinctive paths of arts versus STEM models.

While undergraduate programs are clearly associated with the teaching mission of universities, graduate programs typically sit uneasily between the teaching and research missions of the institution. In fact, historically, many institutions once even had combined facilities of "research and graduate studies," or positioned the faculty of graduate studies under the portfolio of the "vice president, research" rather than the portfolio of the "vice president, academic." At present, most Canadian universities have standalone faculties of graduate studies or a vice provost responsible for graduate education, but the affinity of graduate programs to the research mission of the university remains.

The connection between graduate studies and research is unsurprising since graduate students often perform independent research and work as assistants on faculty research projects. Many then go on to postdoctoral fellowships, which are typically entirely research based. However, there are two problems with framing arts graduate programs exclusively or even primarily as serving universities' research missions.

The first is that not all arts graduate students are research students. As we discussed in chapter 5, there are many professional arts graduate degree programs (and considerable potential for universities to expand in this space). The graduate-research connection leaves these programs as an anomaly to the "main" graduate programs, creating a hierarchy of sorts.

The second problem is that framing arts graduate programs primarily as part of the research mission of the faculty undermines the reality of arts graduate students as students and learners—many of whom are not destined for research careers. While in many STEM disciplines, there is a strong connection between academic research and industry research, with easier connections between graduate research and future careers, this is often not the case for the arts. As we've noted throughout the book, most arts graduate students work on theses and dissertations entirely separate from their supervisor's own research projects, even if the students are also hired to work as RAs on those projects. A STEM model for graduate education is inappropriate for most arts disciplines. The research framing for arts graduate programs centres the university's needs over arts graduate students' needs. At best, it is short-sighted and neglectful. At worst, it is exploitative. Arts graduate students become fodder in the pursuit of rankings and quantitative reputation indicators.

The solution is for universities to appreciate the arts as distinctive from STEM, and to adopt a vision for arts graduate education that celebrates this distinctiveness. This vision needs to see the potential for arts graduate education to add value to society rather than (solely, or even primarily) to universities.

Our recommendation, unsurprisingly, is that this vision should focus on the potential for arts graduate education to advance Canada's public good through attention to the wicked problems, EDID, and talent imperatives. This does not mean that research needs to be diminished in graduate education. As we discussed in chapter 5, thoughtful approaches to arts graduate degrees can connect research training to Canada's public good and to students' career futures.

We call upon university leaders to use their power to convene and set a direction to foster and champion a public good vision for arts graduate education at their institutions. And we believe that deans of arts and deans of graduate studies are the most critical actors here. They may not have the power and resources to transform things alone, but they are central to the vision of change and doing things differently. Arts deans sit between arts units and the rest of the university, while graduate studies deans have responsibilities that cross the university. If these deans aren't at the forefront of changing graduate education, little will happen. Concrete actions here may include:

- Establishing an arts graduate education working group to identify a clear mission statement for arts graduate programs at the university;
- Holding a university symposium about arts graduate study and Canada's public good (or any of the three public good imperatives);
- Collecting and sharing university-specific data on arts graduate student outcomes;
- Hosting discussions with arts units, research offices, and the faculty of graduate studies about arts graduate studies as studies, rather than just as feeding the research pipeline;
- Offering teaching and learning workshops that support arts faculty in connecting their programs to the three public good imperatives; and/or
- Consulting with arts graduate chairs about how existing university structures can be adjusted to better accommodate the distinctive disciplinary standards and practices of the arts.

Culture

The university culture is critical to achieving the reimagined arts graduate education vision.

Experienced university observers are well aware that wonderful visionary ideas are often stymied, not by outright opposition but rather by complex existing processes and change-resistant cultures. Change is HARD. A great idea quickly gets chewed up in the inter-faculty or inter-departmental buzzsaw of different units, each focused, quite reasonably, on pursuing its own core mandate and responsibilities. Change and innovation are stalled by those who say "it can't be done" because it's too hard right now, and/or because there are special circumstances and reasons why everything needs to stay the way it is. The status quo enjoys the default position because change requires effort and leadership, including tackling genuinely tricky issues and obstacles.

This is where senior leadership is most essential. Senior leaders set the tone and the agenda. By giving a matter consistent attention and regularly circling back to ask for updates and actions, they signal what is (and is not) a priority. If senior leaders delegate responsibility to people or units that share the vision for change and have the capacity to effect it, change is possible. If senior leaders fail to appoint effective leaders or set vague aspirations, change is unlikely—and frustration and conflict are almost inevitable.

If senior leaders are committed to reimagining arts graduate education and achieving a new vision, they need to be willing to foster attitudinal changes within university units, such as faculties of graduate studies and of arts, teaching and learning centres, and offices of vice presidents, research. This attitude change includes recognizing and celebrating that the arts disciplines bring values distinct from those of STEM disciplines, and thus distinct approaches to arts graduate studies are required. It requires a willingness to consider how university processes might impede rather than facilitate arts graduate program excellence, how university systems might promote competition rather than collaboration among arts units, and how existing models might exploit rather than support arts graduate students—and a shared understanding that these problems must be addressed.

Reimagined arts graduate programs can't just be bolted onto what is already there. In fact, many of the current problems exist because the system has grown incoherently and with numerous contradictions. Senior leaders can promote change by making it clear to all parts of the university that the arts matter, that arts graduate education matters, and that there is a shared responsibility to realize the potential of the arts—and then giving the arts the space and support to actually reach that potential.

Senior leaders also need to be alert to collateral damage from other visions and priorities. Again, this is largely how arts graduate education got to the stage it is at today—the result of competing and overlapping priorities. A push to rise in research rankings or to fix financial problems through enrollment growth will derail efforts to align arts graduate education with Canada's public good, unless there is clear anticipation and planning for how to reconcile competing visions. Concrete actions here for senior leaders may include:

- Signalling the importance of a new vision for arts graduate education through formal messaging and informal conversations;
- Sharing progress and concrete actions with academic senates, boards of governors, and other accountability bodies through ongoing placement on meeting agendas for these bodies;
- Encouraging units to undertake the kind of self-evaluation already discussed, whether in the context of regular quality assurance exercises or independent of them;
- Setting timelines and milestones for change, and ensuring they are met;
- Appointing a key champion who shares the vision and has the skills and networks to collaborate and build a common front for change across all key actors. Warning: only do this if there is a high chance of success for the person; and/or
- Anticipating and listening to key concerns and objections, and being prepared to selectively modify the vision if necessary to accommodate these—without losing the overall focus.

Resources

In chapter 4, we noted that while the current system of arts graduate education in Canada has not come into being by overall design, it is actually quite logical. It responds to a number of different and often conflicting incentives that, together, encourage the growth of graduate programs in all directions. Without a clear vision guiding arts graduate education, arts graduate programs simply follow the money. Universities, faculties, units, and individual faculty members are all generally encouraged to create more graduate programs and take in more graduate students, but for reasons not necessarily related to the students' own interests nor related to any larger societal interest. To reverse and reform that trend, university leaders need to assess the incentives in place and adjust them to support change.

We recognize the complexity of what we are asking here. University budget models can differ considerably, but as we showed in chapter 4, enrollments are typically important elements of the model. Systems such as "responsibility-centred" or "activity-based" budgeting put the onus on individual line faculties (and in some cases individual units) to make sure they are bringing in enough revenue to cover their costs, and enrollment growth is by far the most important revenue source. Historically based budgets remove that particular stress from faculties and units, but units are still pressed to demonstrate growth and success. Regardless of the system, if a unit is not growing and taking in more students (particularly undergraduate students), it is probably at risk of losing resources, including replacements for faculty retirements. Graduate students serving as TAs help units grow their undergraduate programs, and by extension help units maintain or grow in size. The other way for units to gain and keep resources? Research intensity: securing grants, Canada Research Chairs, prizes, and so forth. Achieving that intensity typically requires lots of graduate students, and as we've hopefully made clear by now, this can be a problem. Senior leaders cannot reasonably ask arts units to focus on "better" rather than "more" without addressing the risks to them for doing so.

We are sympathetic to the reality that university budgets must be balanced. We cannot guarantee that reimagining arts graduate education to support the public good will be an instant money bonanza for universities. But we do encourage senior leaders to thoughtfully consider whether arts graduate education at their university is currently on a sustainable path. It may bring in short-term revenue, but will it create long-term reputational damage, as more and more alumni question the worth of their degrees and governments and the public question why we need these disciplines at all?

As we have argued, a reformed approach to arts graduate education will contribute to achieving Canada's public good. In turn, this will encourage robust and sustainable arts graduate programs that pay their own way—ideally while fostering alumni connection, donor support, and government appreciation. Achieving this may require universities to make strategic investments in arts graduate programming through targeted incentives for reinvention and reimagination.

This university-level strategic investment should not be seen as an altruistic gesture to the arts disciplines. In crass university budget terms, arts graduate education may deliver some of the best bangs for the buck. Unlike most STEM disciplines, arts graduate education generally requires no special equipment, lab space, or other costly extras. Courses can be cross-listed with undergraduate courses (just not all of them, please!), and often with other cognate programs (as we've suggested at the program level). Students are funded, but often work as TAs for a significant portion of that funding. Faculty are typically not compensated for supervising dissertations and research papers, work that comes on top of their regular teaching assignments, thus keeping teaching costs down, but students still pay tuition and universities get funded for these students. We don't advocate running programs on a shoestring or exploiting people's labour. But the fact is that well-run arts programs provide value for money, and they deserve university support for reimagination and realignment to reach or maintain that state. In many cases, it is far overdue.

In addition to providing strategic resource support, senior leaders need to recognize and address processes that pit units against one another, making it difficult to cooperate and collaborate. Units and programs must be incentivized to cooperate, not punished for it or left to worry they are chumps if they don't fight for their share. These incentives should focus on using collaboration to improve quality, rather than simple cost control. For example, if several arts graduate programs in different disciplines can be convinced to collaboratively offer a single research methods course, it has to be because the course is superior to what any of them can offer on their own. And if the result of combining courses is that each unit takes a budget hit because they don't need as much money anymore, that will mean the end of any further cooperation.

Every institution is different, but some concrete actions here might include:

- Not penalizing arts units that decline to add or expand a graduate program;
- Providing funding for educational design support to arts unit leaders who wish to redesign their graduate programs;
- Providing arts unit faculty and staff with EDID training and supports to assist them in updating their programs to address the EDID imperative;
- Allocating designated faculty positions strategically to increase diversity in arts faculty complements;
- Identifying and addressing pressures and incentives for the creation or expansion of graduate programs solely because of their revenue potential;
- Not penalizing units that experience a strategic drop in graduate enrollments due to program changes and cancellations;
- Assessing and funding programs based on graduate outcomes, not their ability to put bums in seats;
- Identifying and addressing barriers to cross-unit collaborations to make it as easy as possible to collaborate and share;
- Incentivizing the creation of joint courses and other inter-unit collaborations, both through resources and with simplified processes;
- Offering faculty-level and/or central graduate student training programs and graduate supervisor training programs to support arts units' efforts to transform TAships and RAships into career development opportunities;
- Offering faculty-level and/or central professional development, career management, and skills training programs tailored for the needs of arts graduate students;
- Supporting arts units in connecting with organizations (non-profit, government, and industry) where students can find meaningful employment that makes use of their talents;

- Celebrating and rewarding arts departments that reimagine and update their graduate programs to align with a university vision to advance the public good;
- Demanding that national granting agencies (particularly SSHRC) and provincial governments address their own incentives for unsustainable arts graduate programming; and/or
- Calling upon national granting agencies (particularly SSHRC) to create incentives for arts graduate programs that work toward Canada's public good.

System-Level Calls to Action

The system level includes provincial ministries responsible for postsecondary education, the Council of Ministers of Education, Canada (CMEC), the federal government through its funding of national research agencies, and the national research agencies (particularly SSHRC). We also see an important lobbying and education role here for national arts disciplinary associations, the Federation for the Humanities and Social Sciences, the U15 Group of Canadian Research Universities, arts and graduate studies deans' associations (such as the Western Canadian Deans of Graduate Studies), and the Canadian Association for Graduate Studies. We also see an important role for employers and private sector organizations like the Conference Board of Canada.

Keen readers will already see a problem in the above list—it's a wide range of "everybody." While the micro (unit/department) and meso (university) levels are confined to specific institutions that have boundaries and hierarchies, the macro (system) level encompasses a tremendous range of actors that may not see that they have much in common, other than a tangential interest in aspects of arts graduate education. Yet they are fundamental to its success.

This system level creates powerful incentive structures for universities. Change must be designed at the unit level. It has to be enabled at the university level. But it won't get very far without action at the system level. Systemic change, by definition, requires system change.

If you are a policymaker or elected official, or associated with a national granting agency, disciplinary association, or other extra-university interests, the following calls to action are directly for you.

Vision

Canada needs a national vision of the future of arts graduate education. The question is, who will provide the leadership for this?

As political scientists whose research focuses on Canadian politics, we are tempted to call for a national commission or task force that updates the work of the Royal Commission on National Development in the Arts, Letters and Sciences (known as the "Massey Commission" after its chair, Vincent Massey). The Massey Commission was established in 1949, tabled its report in 1951, and led to increased university funding, the Canada Council for the Arts, and the National Library of Canada. But as exciting as this idea is to us, we will refrain from calling for this due to pragmatism (we don't see such a commission as likely) and impatience (commissions can be time-consuming).

In lieu of this, we instead call upon the collective wisdom of the crowds and invite all strategic actors to take action to define multiple national visions of a future state in which arts graduate education is aligned with Canada's public good. If multiple strategic actors—including SSHRC, the Federation for the Humanities and Social Sciences, and the Conference Board of Canada—present positions and visions affirming the opportunities of arts graduate education to contribute to Canada and its public good, there will be a growing narrative of the future of arts graduate education. This collective narrative may not be perfectly coordinated. It may include internal contradictions. It may even—be still our authorial hearts—be critical of the vision we have laid out here in *For the Public Good: Reimagining Arts Graduate Programs in Canadian Universities*.

So be it.

Arts graduate education has struggled for decades in Canada due to a lack of vision. We cannot overstate how much arts graduate education has been a tagalong, accompanying other visions—to a more educated mobile society, to scientific innovation and economic growth, and to other worthy goals that nevertheless do not really speak to the specific qualities and contributions of arts graduate education. While we are partial to our own vision of aligning arts graduate education to Canada's public good, we welcome a world that includes multiple compelling visions for the future of arts graduate education in Canada. Multiple visions are preferable to the current state of arts graduate education—being ignored and left adrift, with students left to suffer the consequences.

Through the work of various actors identifying the opportunities for the future of arts graduate education and the challenges of its current state, the gap between the present status quo and a desired future state can be acknowledged. From this, processes and people can adapt and work for a better future.

Concrete actions here may include:

- Research bodies like the Conference Board of Canada and/or think tanks can connect with employers to identify what they need and prioritize from arts graduate education, particularly in the areas of addressing wicked problems, advancing EDID in workplaces, and bringing human literacy, data literacy, and technological literacy skills to bear in their work;
- SSHRC and the Federation for the Humanities and Social Sciences can partner to define a vision document for the future of arts graduate education in Canada;
- The Federation for the Humanities and Social Sciences can act as a catalyst, convening a discussion about the future of arts graduate education in Canada, culminating in a vision document;
- CMEC can commission a study of the linkages between arts education and human literacy training, with attention to the distinction between undergraduate and graduate programs;
- National disciplinary associations can follow the lead of the Canadian Historical Association and complete their own task force reviews of the state of graduate education and outcomes in their disciplines. Building from this, disciplinary associations can establish clear visions for the future of graduate education in their fields of study; and/or
- National disciplinary journal editorial boards can issue calls for papers for special issues on the future of graduate training in the discipline, culminating in workshops to establish discipline-specific visions.

Culture

Canada has long undervalued the necessity and contributions of the arts. Understanding humans and human systems is critical for identifying approaches and solutions to address wicked problems. Appreciation of equity, diversity, inclusion, and decolonization is essential for successful interactions in our contemporary society. Human literacy is a vital skill set in our increasingly automated world. This undervaluing of the arts in Canadian society has been to the detriment of the public good.

We won't reiterate all of chapters 1 and 2 here. But what we will stress is that achieving the vision for arts graduate education requires individuals working outside universities—public servants, elected officials, and those working in industry—to acknowledge that arts education has a unique value for Canada and the public good.

Some of these attitudinal shifts may occur naturally with increased labour market demand for human literacy skills. This attitude change could be expedited by increased employer understanding of what universities can and cannot do with regard to producing "job-ready graduates" in the arts.

Currently, we see an unproductive dialogue between two extremes here: one that argues for education as career training, and another that recoils at the idea that education is just about jobs. We suggest a middle ground, one that develops students' talents and literacies without preparing them narrowly for particular careers. We see an opportunity for employers to work with universities to identify how they can support the development of talent through experiential learning and similar university-employer connections.

Governments, as major employers themselves, need to also lead the way in hiring and recruiting arts graduate students. There is an irony that while some parts of governments subsidize and incentivize the production of arts PhDs in particular, other parts do not necessarily seek out and value candidates with advanced degrees. Indeed, and anecdotally, we have each individually heard from government officials that they do not see value in hiring MA or arts PhD graduates—a discouraging and troubling reality. This points to the need for greater government-university dialogue, both for governments to learn the value of these graduates and for universities to learn why this value is not self-evident (and how to address this).

Specific to granting agencies, we believe there is work to be done to create a clearer understanding of the differences between arts and STEM when it comes to graduate education. We recognize that much progress has been made in recent years in making the training of "highly qualified personnel," or HQPs, an integral part of grant criteria. But beyond the funding and the training, it is not clear that faculty-tied research funding is necessarily beneficial for the long-term success of graduate students, given the typical disconnect between arts faculty research agendas and arts graduate students' own projects and academic progress. It is possible that reducing the emphasis on graduate research funding in faculty research grants and simply increasing direct student research funding would be more effective.

Finally, public agencies need to better understand universities and their complex processes, and how Canadian public universities are heavily motivated for growth and will almost always take any public money they can find. Governments need to understand how their own dispersed nature and often short-term decisions tied to electoral cycles and shifting leadership discourage universities from long-term focused thinking, given their heavy dependence on public funding and regulation.

Concrete system-level actions in the area of attitudes and culture include:

- Organizations can refrain from using the language of "soft skills" and "hard skills" and instead speak of "human literacy," "data literacy," and "technological literacy" (see chapter 2);
- Employers, including governments, can connect with universities to identify opportunities for experiential learning and for improved dialogue; and/or
- SSHRC could conduct a review of its granting structures and their underlying assumptions to identify opportunities to best align with arts graduate education needs.

Resources
In Canada, governments control the bulk of university funding, either directly through public grants or indirectly through regulating tuition.

This makes them the most important players of all in the distribution of resources and especially the incentive structures that drive and shape graduate education. As mentioned above, philanthropic actors may be able to make the important contributions of seed funding and experimentation, but only public funders can truly underwrite the vision of arts graduate education for the public good here.

Public resources may need to be reallocated in a way that does more than incentivize growth and/or penalize contraction. The details of this will vary by province and their different funding formulas, and in some cases, provinces are already taking steps in this direction. But we also need more thoughtful and nuanced formulas specifically shaped to support arts graduate education, not just undergraduate arts or graduate education in general. Again, so much of the current system is a by-product of fractured incentives and inappropriate visions borrowed from elsewhere.

In fact, while this will horrify some, we embrace the concept of performance funding that would tie government money to incentivizing EDITS goals. This has to be a robust, thoughtful model, as the problem with performance funding is not the principle, but the way in which it is seemingly used to punish universities (rather than incentivizing them positively) and/or curb entire areas of intellectual activity that do not produce "job-ready" graduates. We call instead for funding formulas that prioritize efficient, deliberate, inclusive, talent-developing, and student-focused (EDITS) programs. Funding also needs to support stronger internal coordination within universities, rather than encouraging overlapping programs chasing the same bums into seats. Cohesion and coordination need to be rewarded as much as or more than just growth.

Looking beyond provincial government funding models, we encourage all system actors to consider how they can create resources in the form of information, programs, and funding to incentivize and support reimagined arts graduate programs. Concrete actions here may include:

- SSHRC's expansion of its partnered research training initiatives program to match the scope and scale of NSERC's CREATE program;
- Careful consideration of the SSHRC scholarship programs, with a view to ensuring that this funding has promotion of diversification

and Indigenization of arts enrollments as a central value, and that it supports and incentivizes graduate program leaders to focus on developing students who are prepared to move into positions beyond the academy;
- Development of provincial and federal government internship and training opportunities specifically targeting arts graduate students;
- Development of provincial and federal incentive programs so employers, including non-profits and small businesses, can seek out and recruit graduates of arts graduate programs. The Mitacs program serves as a partial example, as its chief limitation is that it requires investments from "industry" itself, which is challenging for non-profits;
- Evaluation through an arts lens of Statistics Canada higher education data collection practices and research products. (If you were frustrated by the chapter 3 groupings of "social and behavioural science and law" and the datedness of some of the available data, well, so were we!); and/or
- A national organization such as CMEC or Universities Canada can take the lead in developing better information and tracking of graduate education trends, including employment of graduates, in systematic and comparable ways. This would involve considerable effort and expense, but would be the greatest contribution toward improved postsecondary education at all levels, not just arts graduate education.

Coordination Calls to Action

We've laid out actions for three levels: programs, universities, and system actors. Each can act independently, as much can be done without waiting for the others. Still, the lack of either coordination or shared thinking is a big reason for the system we have today, where individual actors are behaving quite logically toward the incentives before them, but in a way that creates a loose and shapeless system. This undermines the capacity for arts graduate education to serve Canada's public good and undermines the interests of the students who enroll in arts graduate programs.

The coordination issues are present both between and within levels. Departments may be trying to create student-focused programs, while the faculty of graduate studies is pressing units to increase overall enrollments (program-level/university-level miscoordination). The faculty of arts may be encouraging units to build EDID into programs, while the vice president, research office is urging faculty members to focus attention on publishing in high-impact journals to advance university rankings (faculty-level/university-level miscoordination). Universities may be encouraged by the provincial ministries of education to grow co-operative education and internships as much as possible, but the provincial ministries of labour have a strong interest in regulating and controlling these placements; the federal ministry of science and innovation wants to promote research growth and graduate student training, but Canada's department of immigration and citizenship determines the eligibility for international applicants on its own criteria. Each of these views arts graduate education through its own prisms and assumptions.

We wish we had a miracle solution here. The reality is that any issue with multiple players and multiple interests is going to be challenged by its complexity. Coordination failures occur when there is a lack of communication, a lack of shared information, and a lack of trust.

Asking faculty to trust senior administration, units to trust each other, universities to trust governments, governments to trust universities, and so forth requires some foundational work. For this reason, we recommend increasing communication, sharing information, and fostering trusting relationships among stakeholders.

Concrete actions here may include:

- Ensuring transparency about consultation processes regarding visions for arts graduate education;
- Creating opportunities for engagement of multiple parties in creating visions for arts graduate education;
- Making documents outlining visions for arts graduate education publicly accessible; and/or
- Consulting with multiple parties about different strategies to reimagine arts graduate education and incentivize change.

Coordination does not have to be on a grand scale. In fact, the most effective coordination comes through regular dialogue and exchanges of information; recognition and understanding of everyone's different responsibilities and missions; and perhaps most of all, frank conversations that uncover different and sometimes unconscious assumptions that are undermining attempts to work together. Considering the current uncoordinated state of arts graduate education in Canada, there's really only one way to go here—up.

Student Agency

We have laid out the vision-, culture-, and resource-related actions for each level involved in arts graduate education, along with the need for coordination among them all. But one actor we haven't yet included is arts graduate students themselves. One might argue that ultimately it is up to students to demand an arts graduate education system that works for them. We disagree. The onus for action is on the rest of us. We have the duty and tools to do so. Pushing this responsibility onto students who lack the capacity and authority to make the necessary changes is simply a way for the rest of us to allow the status quo to persist.

Yet this is all ultimately for the benefit of students, and so students must have their own agency and voice here. All of the above changes should involve arts graduate student input and collaboration when possible. We recognize that sometimes students may struggle to contribute individual input for a very complex system in which they only have limited involvement. But systematic efforts through tools such as surveys, exit interviews, and focus groups can provide data and insights that will help inform the design and application of arts graduate education for the public good vision.

Students need also to be provided with the tools to be informed consumers. The simplest step is to present them with better and more consolidated information. This could include, for example, transparency on known facts like overall completion rates and time to completion for graduate programs. As we've suggested, nationally comparable data on employment outcomes would be far superior to the current modest and individualized efforts. Also of value would be the establishment of national directories of graduate programs in a discipline or area (a task perhaps best performed by disciplinary associations, especially if they receive modest funding to keep it up to date).

It's not up to students to change the system. In fact, we recognize that much of the current system has been shaped by student demand—students keep applying to arts graduate programs and seeking research careers, and so the system has responded accordingly. But we see our vision as a collaborative one that encourages students to empower themselves and seek out arts graduate programs and outcomes that equip them well to serve the public good. This is an iterative process, and students must be given agency to help shape a system that is truly centred on them.

Changes, Big and Small

The implementation ideas in this chapter range from small (a brown bag lunch discussion) to large (a national commission). Some may seem so modest as to be useless, others so large as to be ridiculous. But we believe that there is something in here for each actor that is feasible to consider. We believe in small changes, and in large changes, and in changes of all sizes in between. Our challenge for you is to find one option in here that you can take on to move forward. Forward is forward, and improving arts graduate education in Canada is our collective responsibility. So, let's each do our part.

10

Moving Forward

As we conclude For the Public Good: Reimagining Arts Graduate Programs in Canadian Universities, let's retrace our journey together.

We have made a number of bold claims in this book. We have asserted that:

- The knowledge and skills from the arts disciplines can be beneficial to Canada's public good (chapter 1), and specifically to Canada's need to address issues related to wicked problems, EDID, and talent (chapter 2);
- Arts education at the graduate level is particularly well positioned to connect the knowledge and skills from the arts disciplines to Canada's public good, by deliberately addressing Canada's needs in the areas of wicked problems, EDID, and talent;
- The current arts graduate education system is underperforming and in need of reimagination and a clear vision (chapter 3); and
- The current arts graduate education system is a result of university, policy, and cultural forces (chapter 4).

We have called on everyone involved with arts graduate education, be it directly through work in Canada's universities or less directly through work in government, granting agencies, or industry, to adopt a new vision for arts graduate education, focusing it on Canada's public good through attention to the wicked problems, EDID, and talent imperatives.

We have provided tools for all arts graduate education actors to achieve this new vision. These tools include:

- A typology of arts graduate credentials (professional and research master's and doctoral degrees, as well as non-degree programs) that can be deliberately aligned with public good objectives (chapter 5);
- A framework model for arts graduate education for the public good, defined around the five characteristics of efficient, deliberate, inclusive, talent developing, and student focused (EDITS; chapter 6);
- A rubric to apply the EDITS model to evaluate existing arts graduate programs (chapter 7), and examples of how the "excellent" column of the rubric can be used to inspire innovation in arts graduate programming (chapter 8); and
- An implementation plan, broken down by level of actors, to achieve the arts graduate education for the public good vision (chapter 9).

So now we pass the baton to you. We encourage, urge, and challenge you to take action from your particular position and areas of agency. If you're not sure where to start, we have one more tool for you. Table 10.1 lists first steps for each of the many actors who have a role to play in reforming arts graduate education.

TABLE 10.1 **First Steps**

If you are a(n)...	Start by doing this...
Arts faculty member	Talk to your colleagues and add a discussion of graduate education to a department meeting agenda.
Arts graduate chair	Give a presentation about the ideas in this book and/or the EDITS framework to your graduate committee to spark a conversation.
Arts department chair	Lend your copy of this book to your graduate chair, and then talk about how this relates to your graduate program, where the department might go with it, and what steps are needed from you.
Arts associate dean, graduate studies	Talk about the ideas in this book at the next regular meeting of arts graduate chairs. If there isn't a regular meeting, set one up. Ask them about their interest in having a deeper conversation about some of the ideas in this book. Lend your copy of this book to your dean.
Arts associate dean, academic	Work with the graduate studies associate dean to initiate a discussion with arts graduate chairs and your dean. Identify areas within your portfolio that can contribute to change or that are getting in the way of it.
Arts dean	Clear some time in your schedule to specifically learn about and reflect on the graduate programs across your faculty, rather than viewing them unit by unit in silos, and how department chairs and graduate chairs see them. Have a coffee with the dean of graduate studies and get their impression. Add graduate education to your list of priorities, or move it up on your list, for the coming year.
Graduate studies associate dean	Work with the arts associate deans to invite yourself to the regular meeting of arts graduate chairs to talk about the ideas in this book. Or, set up such a meeting.
Graduate studies dean	Take the dean of arts for coffee or lunch. Lend them your copy of this book and talk about how the ideas fit within the context of your institution. Ask how the faculty of graduate studies can help. Identify together some low-hanging fruit/easy wins.
Career services director	Send an email to arts graduate chairs asking whether current offerings are meeting the needs of their students, and whether they have any interest in working together to develop and/or enhance offerings tailored to arts graduate students' needs.

TABLE 10.1 *continued*

If you are a(n)...	Start by doing this...
Teaching and learning centre director	Send an email to arts department chairs to let them know how your centre can assist them in reimagining arts graduate education.
Vice president, research	Reflect specifically on the role of arts graduate students in university research and whether they are being supported according to the EDITS criteria. Initiate conversations with the vice president, academic, the dean of graduate studies, and the dean of arts about how to advance the ideas in this book.
Vice provost, teaching and learning	Have coffee with your dean of arts and dean of graduate studies to discuss how you can help promote change.
Provost/Vice president, academic	Ask your dean of arts and your dean of graduate studies whether they've read this book, and what they think. Schedule a time to talk with them about arts graduate education.
University president	Tell your dean of arts you've read this book and think it's interesting and worth further discussion. Let the provost and the dean of graduate studies know, too.
Academic senate/ Faculty council member	Ask for arts graduate education to be placed on the next meeting agenda. Prepare a short presentation outlining the EDITS vision and suggest that a senior administrator chair a task force to consider change.
University board member	Ask the university president for their opinion about *For the Public Good: Reimagining Arts Graduate Programs in Canadian Universities*. If they haven't read it yet, ask them to schedule a time for a future discussion with you once they have had a chance to do so. Follow up with them to ensure the conversation occurs.
Provincial public servant in ministry responsible for postsecondary education	Mention this book when you're meeting with university leaders. Ask if they've read it. Add it to a future meeting agenda. Ask how the province can help by introducing, changing, and/or eliminating policies and processes. Write a briefing note for your deputy minister outlining the issues concerning arts graduate education.

TABLE 10.1 *continued*

If you are a(n)...	Start by doing this...
Provincial elected official (MLA, MPP, MNA, or MHA)	Talk to both local university leaders and provincial public servants to inform yourself about the provincial policy framework for graduate education. Build a big picture understanding of how the different parts work (or don't work) together and facilitate further dialogue between actors.
Municipal elected official	Offer to facilitate discussions between your community's universities and employers on how arts graduate education can meet local talent needs. Identify changes needed on both sides.
Federal public servant	Consider how your university-related programs align with federal and provincial policies. Initiate interdepartmental and intergovernmental discussions to identify departments working at cross-purposes and how to mitigate this. Write a briefing note for your deputy minister outlining the issues concerning arts graduate education.
Federal elected official (MP)	Inform yourself on how federal policies impact universities in your province and/or community. Identify opportunities for adjustment or change and generally build non-partisan expertise on the subject.
SSHRC leadership	Add a discussion of the ideas in this book to the next meeting of your leadership group and governing council. Discuss ways some of the ideas could be integrated into the next restructuring of scholarships and other programming.
SSHRC staff	Talk about this book at your next team meeting and ask your manager if they have read it. Offer to lend them your copy.
National academic association board member	Request that a discussion of a national review of arts graduate student outcomes be added to the next board meeting agenda.
Executive director of a disciplinary or pan-disciplinary national association	Put together a short brief about the importance and potential of arts graduate education. Suggest to the president of the association/chair of the board that it be added as an item for discussion at the next board meeting. Suggest graduate education as a priority item for your organization's next strategic plan.

TABLE 10.1 *continued*

If you are a(n)...	Start by doing this...
Think tank, industry association, or Chamber of Commerce member	Reach out to universities, programs, and disciplinary associations to offer pathways and advice on how arts graduate programs can best build career-ready talent. Reach out equally to firms and employers to show how arts graduates can meet their needs. Back up this advice with specific actions to match everyone together.
Prospective arts graduate student	Ask arts programs to provide you with data on time to completion, graduation rates, and career outcomes before accepting admissions offers. If they cannot provide such data, ask the faculty of graduate studies for this information.
Current arts graduate student	Talk to your counterparts about the ideas in this book. Ask student representatives to request a discussion of the ideas at the next department meeting. Offer to organize a student-led assessment of the program using the EDITS framework.
Graduate students' association member	Talk with your fellow association members about this book. Request a discussion with the dean of graduate studies about the future of arts graduate education at your university.
Arts graduate alumni	Send an email to faculty members you remember and/or to the current department head. Tell them about how the ideas in this book resonated with you, given your experience. Offer to come to speak to students and/or faculty.
Member of the general public	Email the provost or president of your local university and ask them their thoughts on the ideas in this book.

Big changes start with small steps, with conversations and the sharing of ideas, with openness to the idea that things can be better. And when it comes to arts graduate education in Canada, things can be better.

Canada's arts graduate students deserve better than the status quo. Canada deserves better than the status quo. And there is so much potential to be achieved.

So, let's all get busy.

Appendix 1

EDITS
Rubric

Efficient

	Unsatisfactory	Satisfactory	Good Meets all satisfactory criteria, plus:	Excellent Meets all good criteria, plus:
Capacity	☐ Offering unit relies on contingent faculty to support program delivery, including supervision	☐ Offering unit has sufficient permanent faculty to support program delivery, including supervision	☐ Offering unit has a multi-year admissions plan that accounts for anticipated changes in faculty complement (sabbaticals, retirements, etc.) ☐ All courses have a minimum number of students ☐ Individualized supervision is required only where necessary to achieve program-level learning outcomes	☐ Program size is below offering unit's maximum capacity to allow for unanticipated changes in faculty complement ☐ Faculty supervisions are limited to areas of faculty expertise
Program Length	☐ Program length is disconnected from program purpose	☐ Program length is as short as possible relative to program purpose		
Course Purpose	☐ Courses are not explicitly tied to program-level learning outcomes	☐ All courses are explicitly tied to program-level learning outcomes		
Course Focus	☐ Most or all courses are cross-listed with undergraduate courses	☐ Most courses are program-specific (i.e., are not cross-listed with undergraduate courses)	☐ Program is comprised primarily of core required courses, and electives are limited	☐ Elective courses outside program are encouraged, provided there is a clear link to program-level learning outcomes
University Connection	☐ Students in other programs are prohibited from enrolling in program courses	☐ Courses are available to students in other programs and may be cross-listed with other programs, and/or arrangements are in place with other institutions for reciprocal course enrollment	☐ Where possible and appropriate, program requires students to participate in faculty- or university-level offerings (e.g., professional development) rather than program-specific offerings	☐ Program is clearly differentiated from other programs at the university and from similar offerings at other universities

Deliberate

	Unsatisfactory	Satisfactory	Good Meets all satisfactory criteria, plus:	Excellent Meets all good criteria, plus:
Purpose	☐ Program's purpose is unspecified ☐ Program's learning outcomes are unspecified or vague	☐ Purpose of program is clearly stated ☐ Program has explicit, clearly stated learning outcomes	☐ Program is explicitly linked to one or more of Canada's public good imperatives ☐ Program learning outcomes are directly tied to program's purpose	☐ Program's structure is thoroughly connected to one or more of Canada's public good imperatives
Requirements	☐ Connection between program requirements and program learning outcomes is unclear	☐ All program requirements are explicitly tied to program learning outcomes	☐ Program requirements are truly necessary for program learning outcomes	☐ Program learning outcomes are thoughtfully coordinated with course-level learning outcomes ☐ Program electives are limited and explicitly tied to program learning outcomes
Timelines	☐ Degree completion guidelines are unstated or unrealistic	☐ Program has explicit and realistic degree completion guidelines	☐ Program has explicit pathways for students to realistically complete the degree in a specified timeframe	☐ Program website provides clear information about degree completion timelines over the past five years
Pedagogy	☐ Pedagogical approaches are disconnected from program learning outcomes	☐ Program explicitly matches pedagogical approaches to program learning outcomes	☐ Program uses research training purposively, with research products matched to program-level learning outcomes	☐ Program integrates experiential and/or work-integrated learning to support program-level learning outcomes
Evidence based	☐ Offering unit has no plans or measures to evaluate program success	☐ Offering unit has a clear evaluation plan to use student outcomes to assess program success and inform curriculum refinement	☐ Offering unit consults with current and former students, including students who discontinued studies, to obtain feedback on how well their graduate education prepared them for work they are doing	☐ Offering unit openly shares student outcomes and feedback data and how it is continuing to refine curricula

Appendix 1 **257**

Inclusive

	Unsatisfactory	Satisfactory	Good Meets all satisfactory criteria, plus:	Excellent Meets all good criteria, plus:
Admissions	☐ Program does not have admissions goals	☐ Program's admissions goals include attention to student diversity	☐ All faculty and staff involved in admissions decisions have completed anti-bias training ☐ Admissions requirements and processes are designed to promote diversity	☐ All faculty, instructors, and staff have completed anti-racism training
Culture	☐ Program does not have harassment policies	☐ Program actively works to create a clear welcoming tone with zero tolerance for harassment in classes, at events, and in other spaces		☐ Offering unit undertakes ongoing efforts to promote inclusion as a shared commitment
Events and Extra-curriculars	☐ Program's social and extracurricular events centre on alcohol	☐ Program proactively avoids social and extra-curricular events that exclude identifiable groups	☐ Offering unit ensures inclusion and diversity in invited speakers and guests	☐ Offering unit offers innovative and inclusive events
Faculty and Staff Complement	☐ No awareness of areas of non-diversity	☐ Program balances areas of non-diversity with appropriately compensated external expertise	☐ Offering unit's faculty and staff complement plans include diversity as a key criterion	☐ Offering unit's faculty and staff complement plans prioritize diversity
Course Materials	☐ Course instructors are unaware of how representative their course materials are	☐ Course instructors have assessed their course materials with an eye to represen-tation and the centring of diverse voices	☐ Course instructors include consideration of decolonization and anti-racism among course learning outcomes	☐ Program-level learning outcomes include consideration of decolonization and anti-racism
Assessment	☐ Program assessment practices exclude or disadvantage some students	☐ Course instructors have assessed their course assessments with an eye to inclusion of students with diverse abilities and from diverse backgrounds	☐ Course instructors communicate assessment expectations and grading criteria clearly and in advance	☐ Course instructors allow students to choose among a number of assessment options
Well-Being	☐ Program design, including workloads and structure, is uncoordinated and haphazard	☐ Program design, including workloads and structure, prioritizes student well-being and mental health	☐ Offering unit's culture prioritizes student well-being and mental health	☐ Faculty, university, and/or offering unit provide students with tools to build their well-being and mental health

Talent Developing

	Unsatisfactory	Satisfactory	Good Meets all satisfactory criteria, plus:	Excellent Meets all good criteria, plus:
Program Learning Outcomes	☐ Program-level learning outcomes are limited to content/ knowledge learning	☐ Program-level learning outcomes explicitly include numerous human literacy skills	☐ Program-level learning outcomes explicitly include numerous human literacy skills and some data literacy and/or technological literacy skills	☐ Program-level learning outomes explicitly include numerous human literacy skills and numerous data literacy and/or technological literacy skills
Course Learning Outcomes	☐ Course-level learning outcomes are limited to content/ knowledge learning	☐ All courses include literacy development among course-level learning outcomes	☐ Faculty members devote class time to literacy development	☐ Faculty, university, and/or offering unit provide students with tools to connect their TA and RA work to their literacy skills
Assistants	☐ Faculty members view TAships and RAships primarily as teaching/ research support	☐ Faculty members view TAships and RAships primarily as talent development rather than teaching/ research support	☐ Faculty, university, and/or offering unit provide students with skills training programs to support their TA and RA work	
Evaluation	☐ Talent development learning outcomes are not formally evaluated	☐ Offering unit uses summative evaluation to assess students' achievement of talent development learning outcomes		
Connection to External World	☐ Program is not proof tested against the real world	☐ Faculty, university, and/or offering unit provide students with tools to explicitly recognize and articulate their literacy skills	☐ Offering unit regularly considers information on Canada's talent needs to inform its curriculum refinements	☐ Offering unit regularly consults with dominant industries that employ its graduates to understand emerging talent needs to inform its curriculum refinements

Student Focused

	Unsatisfactory	Satisfactory	Good Meets all satisfactory criteria, plus:	Excellent Meets all good criteria, plus:
Student Needs	☐ Connection between program's purpose and student needs is unclear	☐ Program's stated purpose clearly prioritizes student needs over other considerations	☐ Program admissions are based on and limited by offering unit's capacity to meet students' needs over the entirety of their degree	☐ Student TA and RA assignments prioritize student training over other considerations
Career Connection	☐ Program is not positioned as tied to career preparation of any sort or is limited to academic career preparation	☐ Program explicitly promises to prepare students for diverse careers	☐ Faculty, university, and/or offering unit provide students with tools for explicitly tying their literacy skills to diverse careers	☐ Faculty, university, and/or offering unit provide students with opportunities for work-integrated learning, network development, and alumni connection
Milestones and Support	☐ Program milestones cannot realistically be achieved in a reasonable timeframe	☐ Program milestones are achievable in a reasonable timeframe	☐ Faculty members are responsive to students' concerns and unique situations	☐ Supervisors are trained and appropriately mentored to provide student support and meaningful feedback
Student Consultation	☐ Offering unit does not consult with current and former students to obtain feedback on the program	☐ Offering unit consults with current and former students, including students who discontinued studies, to obtain feedback on the program, and uses this information to refine its program	☐ Offering unit consults published literature for best practices in graduate programming and uses this information to refine its program	☐ University and/or faculty provide support for regular program reviews

Appendix 2

EDITS Program Rubric, "Excellent" Column Focus

Efficient

Excellent

- ☐ Offering unit has sufficient permanent faculty to support program delivery, including supervision

- ☐ Offering unit has multi-year admissions plan that accounts for anticipated changes in faculty complement (sabbaticals, retirements, etc.)

- ☐ Program size is below offering unit's maximum capacity to allow for unanticipated changes in faculty complement

- ☐ Individualized supervision is required only where necessary to achieve program-level learning outcomes

- ☐ Faculty supervisions are limited to areas of faculty expertise

- ☐ Program length is as short as possible relative to program purpose

- ☐ All courses are explicitly tied to program-level learning outcomes

- ☐ Most courses are program specific (i.e., not cross-listed with undergraduate courses)

- ☐ All courses have a minimum number of students

- ☐ Courses are available to students in other programs and may be cross-listed with other programs, and/or arrangements are in place with other institutions for reciprocal course enrollment

- ☐ Program is comprised primarily of core required courses; electives are limited

- ☐ Elective courses outside program are encouraged, provided there is a clear link to program-level learning outcomes

- ☐ Where possible and appropriate, program requires students to participate in faculty- or university-level offerings (e.g., professional development), rather than program-specific offerings

- ☐ Program is clearly differentiated from all other programs at the university and from similar offerings at other universities

Deliberate | **Excellent**

- ☐ Purpose of the program is clearly stated
- ☐ Program is explicitly linked to one or more of Canada's public good imperatives
- ☐ Program's structure is thoroughly connected to one or more of Canada's public good imperatives
- ☐ Program has explicit, clearly stated learning outcomes
- ☐ Program learning outcomes are directly tied to program's purpose
- ☐ All program requirements are explicitly tied to learning outcomes
- ☐ Program requirements are truly necessary for learning outcomes
- ☐ Program explicitly matches pedagogical approaches to program learning outcomes
- ☐ Program uses research training purposefully, with research products matched to program-level learning outcomes
- ☐ Program integrates experiential and/or work-integrated learning to support program-level learning outcomes
- ☐ Program learning outcomes are thoughtfully coordinated with course-level learning outcomes
- ☐ Program electives are limited and explicitly tied to learning outcomes
- ☐ Program has explicit and realistic degree completion guidelines
- ☐ Program has explicit pathways for students to realistically complete the degree in a specified timeframe
- ☐ Program website provides clear information about degree completion timelines over the past five years
- ☐ Offering unit has clear evaluation plan to use student outcomes to assess program success and inform curriculum refinement
- ☐ Offering unit consults with current and former students, including students who discontinued studies, to obtain feedback on how well their graduate education prepared them for the work they are doing
- ☐ Offering unit openly shares student outcomes and feedback data and how it is continuing to refine curricula

Inclusive	**Excellent**
	☐ Program admissions goals include attention to student diversity
	☐ Admissions requirements and processes are designed to promote diversity
	☐ All faculty and staff involved in admissions decisions have completed anti-bias training
	☐ Program actively works to create a clear welcoming tone with zero tolerance for harassment in classes, events, and other spaces
	☐ All faculty, instructors, and staff have completed anti-racism training
	☐ Program proactively avoids social and extracurricular events that exclude identifiable groups
	☐ Offering unit ensures inclusion and diversity in invited speakers and guests
	☐ Offering unit undertakes ongoing efforts to promote inclusion as a shared commitment
	☐ Offering unit offers innovative and inclusive events
	☐ Program balances areas of non-diversity with appropriately compensated external expertise
	☐ Offering unit's faculty and staff complement plans include diversity as a key criterion
	☐ Offering unit's faculty and staff complement plans prioritize diversity
	☐ Course instructors have assessed their course materials with an eye to representation and the centring of diverse voices
	☐ Course instructors include consideration of decolonization and anti-racism among course learning outcomes
	☐ Program-level learning outcomes include consideration of decolonization and anti-racism
	☐ Course instructors have assessed their course assessments with an eye to inclusion of students with diverse abilities and from diverse backgrounds
	☐ Course instructors communicate assessment expectations and grading criteria clearly and in advance

	Excellent
Inclusive *continued*	☐ Course instructors allow students to choose among a number of assessment options ☐ Program design, including workloads and structure, prioritizes student well-being and mental health ☐ Offering unit's culture prioritizes student well-being and mental health ☐ The faculty, university, and/or offering unit provides students with tools to build their well-being and mental health ☐ Program-level learning outcomes explicitly include numerous human literacy skills
Talent Developing	☐ Program-level learning outcomes explicitly include numerous human literacy skills and some data literacy and/or technological literacy skills ☐ Program-level learning outcomes explicitly include numerous human literacy skills and numerous data literacy and/or technological literacy skills ☐ All courses include literacy development among course-level learning outcomes ☐ Faculty members devote class time to literacy development ☐ Faculty members view TAships and RAships primarily as talent development rather than teaching/research support ☐ The faculty, university, and/or offering unit provides students with tools to connect their TA and RA work to their literacy skills ☐ The faculty, university, and/or offering unit provides students with skills training programs to support their TA and RA work ☐ Offering unit uses summative evaluation to assess students' achievement of talent development learning outcomes ☐ The faculty, university, and/or offering unit provides students with tools to explicitly recognize and articulate their literacy skills ☐ Offering unit regularly considers information on Canada's talent needs to inform its curriculum refinements ☐ Offering unit regularly consults with dominant industries that employ its graduates to understand emerging talent needs to inform its curriculum refinements

	Excellent
Student Focused	☐ Program's stated purpose clearly prioritizes student needs over other considerations
	☐ Program explicitly promises to prepare students for diverse careers
	☐ Program milestones are achievable in a reasonable timeframe
	☐ Offering unit consults with current and former students, including students who discontinued studies, to obtain feedback on the program, and uses this information to refine its program
	☐ Program admissions are based on and limited by offering unit's capacity to meet student needs over the entirety of their degree
	☐ The faculty, university, and/or offering unit provides students with tools for explicitly tying their literacy skills to diverse careers
	☐ Faculty members are responsive to students' concerns and unique situations
	☐ Offering unit consults published literature for best practices in graduate programming and uses this information to refine its program
	☐ Student TA and RA assignments prioritize student training over other considerations
	☐ The faculty, university, and/or offering unit provides students with opportunities for work-integrated learning, network development, and alumni connection
	☐ Supervisors are trained and appropriately mentored to provide student support and meaningful feedback
	☐ The university or faculty provides support for regular program reviews

Appendix 3

EDITS for Supervisors

Our hope is that this book will inspire arts faculty members to work toward reforming the graduate programs in which they teach and supervise. But we recognize that there are units that aren't ready for change. If you find yourself in such a unit, or even if you do not, we offer some suggestions about how you can revise your own supervisory practice to embody the EDITS principles.

Efficient

When we talk about efficiency in the context of graduate program design, we place emphasis on the idea that time is a scarce and precious resource—for both faculty members and students. The embedded practices of graduate supervision in many of the arts disciplines tend to be time-consuming for supervisors. And the times to completion for arts students—almost always longer than for STEM students—suggest that these practices are not set up to treat students' time as valuable either.

To develop a supervisory practice that values your time, you should:

- Borrow the concept of the research group (or lab) from the STEM disciplines. Meet with your graduate students as a group, and encourage more senior students to mentor more junior ones. Regular group meetings will help you keep track of progress, create a sense of camaraderie and accountability among students, and encourage conversations focused on various aspects of professional development. And these group meetings should save you time.
- Spend time with students early in their program to ensure that they have defined a manageable and well-designed research project, rather than leaving them to explore and require significant course correction later in their program.
- Be a mentor, not a line editor. It's important to provide detailed feedback on students' writing, but they will learn more if they undertake the editing. So only edit a page or two, and then give explicit instructions for changes that need to be made throughout (e.g., "Go through and check each paragraph to ensure it has a topic sentence. See example on page x.").

To develop a supervisory practice that values your students' time, you should:

- Start with a conversation about the idea of opportunity costs of graduate school. Return to this conversation periodically over the student's program.
- Ensure that the student has defined a manageable and well-designed research project.
- Scaffold a student to help them move through the degree in a timely fashion, through the provision of deadlines, scheduled check-ins, and advice to avoid the consequences of "drift." (E.g., "If you are routinely unable to meet deadlines that we have agreed on, then we will have a conversation about whether this signals your time would be better spent otherwise.")

- Provide constructive and timely feedback on all student writing. Agree on deadlines for submission and feedback to keep you both on track and accountable.

Deliberate

When we talk about the deliberate design of graduate programs, we say that "A deliberate curriculum starts with a clear sense of the purpose of the credential. Faculty members should be able to make a compelling pitch for why their graduate program exists." This is also true of an individual student's program.

As a supervisor, you can encourage your students to articulate their own sense of purpose and help them design their program accordingly. This starts with an early conversation about why the student is pursuing the degree and where they hope it will take them. For PhD students whose answer is an academic career, it's essential to offer a clear message that this may not be an achievable goal because of the mismatch between the number of new PhD graduates and the number of tenure-track positions. Insist that the student research alternatives and develop a backup plan beyond the academy. Talk to them about the public good imperatives and encourage them to link their personal objective to at least one of them.

Once your student has their objective(s) set, work with them to think about the kinds of skills they need and the experiences that will help them to build those skills. Ask them to develop a plan for acquiring the skills, and then insist that they document their skill acquisition. Think of this as an iterative process: as students progress in a degree, their objective(s) changes and their understanding of the skills they need to hone changes with it. Revisit their objective(s) and plan periodically. (If this sounds like a lot of work, remember that a group approach to supervision can help efficiency. Make objectives and skill/talent development a standing item on the agenda for your group meetings, and encourage students to support one another in developing and executing their plans.)

Inclusive

Graduate supervision is very much about building and maintaining functional interpersonal relationships. This is complicated by the multi-faceted role of the graduate supervisor: mentor, advocate, and gatekeeper/authority figure. Under even the simplest circumstances, shifting between these roles while building and maintaining a positive relationship is challenging.

Fifty years ago, the graduate student-supervisor relationship was often grounded in a set of common experiences and social locations: older white men supervising younger white men—i.e., junior versions of themselves—who sought to transition from student to colleague. Today, the growing diversity of both the graduate student population and the arts professoriate adds differences of gender, race, culture, and more into the mix. Inclusive supervision is necessarily a highly individualized undertaking that takes into account the social identities of both you—the supervisor—and the supervisee.

A supervisory practice committed to equity, diversity, inclusion, and decolonization will start with careful reflection on both your and the student's identities, and the ways they interact. Do these social locations exacerbate power differentials? Are they likely to foster miscommunication? To the extent that they do, think about how to have a conversation that sets the stage for better communication.

If your students are from equity-deserving groups and you are not, you have a unique opportunity to improve your understanding of the challenges they face and ways in which the academy looks to them to be inhospitable. Undertake a practice of "reverse mentorship" in which your students have the opportunity, if they choose, to mentor you to improve your understanding of the barriers to diversity in the academy (Jordan and Sorell 2019).

An inclusive supervisory practice also involves attention to diversity: try to ensure your approach to accepting students to supervise includes being conscious of potential bias, and seek out opportunities to increase the diversity of the students that you do supervise.

And finally, ensure that your research group is an inclusive environment. Set an appropriate tone, talk about issues of diversity and inclusion at group meetings, encourage positive cross-cultural communication, and respond immediately to any concerns brought to you. And, of course, avoid social events that might exclude some group members, such as a lunch held during Ramadan, group meetings held in pubs, or social outings that exclude students with disabilities.

Talent Focused

Many supervisors of graduate students see their primary role as guiding students to complete a passable thesis. That is, of course, the visible measure of success. Beyond this, many supervisors try to equip PhD students to succeed in the highly competitive academic job market by encouraging them to publish journal articles and gain experience with teaching.

A talent-focused approach to graduate supervision places as much priority on explicit talent development beyond the academic track as it does on supporting research and writing and mentoring on the way to an academic job. The "deliberate" approach to graduate supervision we suggest lends itself to supporting students in the development of talent, and particularly tied to the literacies we set out in chapter 2. Help your students to locate their ambitions relative to these literacies, and then talk about what talents they will develop while engaging in research and writing their thesis and which they will develop through other means.

To develop human literacy as they research and write their thesis, students could:

- Engage in a research project that is part of a broader multidisciplinary research project, and gain skills in working in multidisciplinary teams;
- Engage in a research project in partnership with an organization outside the university, such as through a Mitacs-funded research internship;
- Acquire specific training in cross-cultural communication in preparation for fieldwork; and/or
- Reflect on ethical approaches to research in preparation for, and in writing, their thesis.

Data literacy is an integral part of research in many of the arts disciplines, whether or not the research involves the collection or analysis of data, quantitative or qualitative. Supervisors can encourage students to reflect on the skills they are acquiring as they undertake this research, with attention not only to the more technical aspects (e.g., "can analyze text using NVivo") but also to the more fundamental (e.g., "can assess data sources and analyses critically" and "can draw appropriate conclusions from data analysis").

The process of conducting thesis research may require some acquisition of skills associated with technological literacy, such as coding or numeracy. Again, you should encourage students to identify these literacies as they acquire them and to document them appropriately for when they embark on their subsequent career.

A supervisory practice that emphasizes talent development also ensures that students have ample opportunity to develop the three literacies outside of their research and thesis writing. Experiential learning opportunities such as internships give students significant opportunity to develop these literacies, and having their supervisor's blessing and encouragement to undertake these opportunities is essential.

Supervisors often employ the students they are supervising as research assistants or have them assigned as teaching assistants. When this is the case, a talent-focused approach to supervision will connect the work to be done to the acquisition of skills. Help teaching assistants assigned to run tutorial sessions to acquire skills associated with group facilitation, and coach teaching assistants assigned to grade papers on the skill of providing constructive feedback. Design research tasks to ensure that students gain knowledge of the associated technical or data analysis skills. You can also ask your students to share their own insights and thoughts on the research, encouraging them to see themselves as a peer providing feedback rather than simply as an assistant completing tasks.

Student Focused

In chapter 6, we described a student-focused graduate program as one that "prioritizes student learning and experience and places emphasis on preparing students for post-graduation employment." The same description can apply to a student-focused approach to graduate supervision.

A student-focused supervisory practice is selective; students are taken on when you believe you can offer those students mentorship that will help them develop their talents. You don't take on students solely in the hopes of improving your own prospects for success in granting competitions or moving your research forward. And you carefully monitor the number of supervisions to which you commit, to ensure that you can truly provide appropriate supervision. Sometimes this means saying no to students asking for supervision, because you're not confident you can serve the student well.

A student-focused supervisory practice is generous. Its central focus is the student's best interest, and if you are no longer the best equipped to provide mentorship and guidance, you open the door to alternative or shared supervision.

And, finally, a student-focused supervisory practice is one that develops students' talents and prepares them for their future career, employing many of the suggestions set out above.

References

Alberta. 2018. *Alberta Credential Framework* (ACF). May 7, 2018. https://open.alberta.ca/dataset/c8ff10eb-eccc-448b-92f6-c91ac8e3b482/resource/ea7b90da-52bb-4265-84d4-5d0eb34a5181/download/alberta-credential-framework.pdf.

Anders, George. 2017. *You Can Do Anything: The Surprising Power of a "Useless" Liberal Arts Education*. New York: Little Brown.

Anonymous. 2022. "The Precarious Worklife of Sessional Instructors" *University Affairs*, August 12, 2022. https://www.universityaffairs.ca/opinion/in-my-opinion/the-precarious-worklife-of-sessional-instructors-2/.

Aoun, Joseph E. 2017. *Robot-Proof: Higher Education in the Age of Artificial Intelligence*. Cambridge: MIT Press.

Australian Public Service Commission. 2007. *Tackling Wicked Problems: A Public Policy Perspective*. http://www.enablingchange.com.au/wickedproblems.pdf.

Ayres, Zoë J. 2022. "Dismantling the Ivory Tower: Systemic Issues That Might Impact Your Mental Health." In *Managing Your Mental*

Health During your PhD: A Survival Guide, 103–34. Springer. https://doi.org/10.1007/978-3-031-14194-2_8.

Bamber, Veronica. 2015. "Mixing Decks: Frameworks for Master's Scholarship." *Higher Education Quarterly* 69 (July): 221–36. https://doi.org/10.1111/hequ.12070.

Barreira, Paul, Matthew Basilico, and Valentin Bolotnyy. 2018. "Graduate Student Mental Health: Lessons from American Economics Departments." Working Paper. https://scholar.harvard.edu/files/bolotnyy/files/bbb_mentalhealth_paper.pdf.

Benham, Jamie L., Omid Atabati, Robert J. Oxoby, Mehdi Mourali, Blake Shaffer, Hasan Sheikh, Jean-Christophe Boucher, et al. 2021. "COVID-19 Vaccine-Related Attitudes and Beliefs in Canada: National Cross-Sectional Survey and Cluster Analysis." *JMIR Public Health and Surveillance* 7 (12): e30424. https://doi.org/10.2196/30424.

Bennett, Zoe. 2014. *Your MA in Theology: A Study Skills Handbook*. London: SCM Press.

Berdahl, Loleen, and Jonathan Malloy. 2018. *Work Your Career: Get What You Want from Your Social Sciences or Humanities PhD*. North York: University of Toronto Press.

Berdahl, Loleen, and Jonathan Malloy. 2019. "Departmental Engagement in Doctoral Professional Development: Lessons from Political Science." *Canadian Journal of Higher Education* 49 (2): 37–53. https://doi.org/10.47678/cjhe.v49i2.188226.

Berdahl, Loleen, Jonathan Malloy, and Lisa Young. 2020. "Faculty Perceptions of Political Science PhD Career Training." *PS: Political Science & Politics* 53 (4): 751–56. https://doi.org/10.1017/S1049096520000839.

Berdahl, Loleen, Jonathan Malloy, and Lisa Young. 2022. "Doctoral Mentorship Practices in Canadian Political Science." *Canadian Journal of Political Science* 55 (3): 709–20. doi:10.1017/S0008423922000440.

Blu Waters, Laureen, Randy Pitawanakwat, Darcey Dachyshyn, Alex Venis, Gina Catenazzo, Naomi Go, Born in the North, et al. 2022. *Skoden*, Seneca College. https://ecampusontario.pressbooks.pub/skoden/part/introduction/.

Bouchard St-Amant, Pier-André, Alexis-Nicolas Brabant, and Éric Germain. 2020. "University Funding Formulas: An Analysis of the Québec Reforms and Incentives." *Canadian Journal of Higher Education* 50 (1): 1–27. https://www.erudit.org/en/journals/cjhe/1900-v1-n1-cjhe05311/1069648ar.pdf.

Braith, Melanie, Mavis Reimer, and Jo-ann Archibald Q'um Q'um Xiiem. 2020. *Reconciliation in Canadian Indigenous Graduate Education: Report for the Canadian Association for Graduate Studies.* https://www.ufv.ca/media/assets/school-of-grad-studies/CAGS-Report---Reconciliation-in-Canadian-Indigenous-Graduate-Education-(September-2020)-(1).pdf.

Cameron, David M. 2004. "Collaborative Federalism and Post-Secondary Education: Be Careful What You Wish For." John Deutsch Institute for the Study of Economic Policy. Kingston: Queen's University. http://jdi-legacy.econ.queensu.ca/Files/Conferences/PSEconferencepapers/Cameronconferencepaper.pdf.

Cameron, David M. 2005. "Ontario's Rae Report: Investing in Growth." *Canadian Public Administration* 48 (2): 280–87. https://doi.org/10.1111/j.1754-7121.2005.tb02193.x.

Canada's Fundamental Science Review (CFSR). 2017. *Investing in Canada's Future: Strengthening the Foundations of Canadian Research.* Advisory Panel on Federal Support for Fundamental Science. https://sciencereview-examenscience.ised-isde.canada.ca/site/canada-fundamental-science-review/sites/default/files/attachments/2022/ScienceReview_April2017-rv.pdf.

Canada, Government of. 2018. *Opportunity for All—Canada's First Poverty Reduction Strategy.* https://www.canada.ca/en/employment-social-development/programs/poverty-reduction/reports/strategy.html.

Canadian Association for Graduate Studies (CAGS). 2003. *The Completion of Graduate Studies in Canadian Universities: Report and Recommendations, October 2003.* Revised in November 2004. https://cags.ca/documents/publications/working/completion_grad_studies_2004.pdf.

Canadian Association for Graduate Studies (CAGS). 2018. *Canadian Association for Graduate Studies: Report of the Task Force on* the Dissertation. Ottawa: Canadian Association for Graduate Studies. https://gradstudents.carleton.ca/wp-content/uploads/CAGS-Dissertation-Task-Force-Report-1.pdf.

Canadian Association for Graduate Studies (CAGS). 2023. "Canadian Graduate and Professional Student Survey (CGPSS)." https://cags.ca/cgpss/.

Canadian Historical Association (CHA). 2022. *CHA Committee on the Future of the History PhD in Canada Report*. https://cha-shc.ca/wp-content/uploads/2023/01/CHA-Task-Force-Report-Final.pdf.

Canadian Information Centre for International Credentials (CICIC). 2022. "Qualification Frameworks in Canada." https://www.cicic.ca/1287/provincial_and_territorial_qualifications_frameworks.canada.

Carlucci, Daniela, Giovanni Schiuma, and Francesco Santarsiero. 2018. "Toward a Data-Driven World: Challenges and Opportunities in Arts and Humanities." In *Big Data in the Arts and Humanities: Theory and Practice*, edited by Giovanni Schiuma and Daniela Carlucci, 15–26. Boca Raton: CRC Press.

Casey, Daniel, Serrin Rutledge-Prior, Lisa Young, Jonathan Malloy, and Loleen Berdahl. 2023. "Hard Work and You Can't Get It: An International Comparative Analysis of Gender, Career Aspirations, and Preparedness Among Politics and International Relations PhD Students." PS: Political Science & Politics 56, no. 3 (July): 402–10. doi:10.1017/S1049096523000057.

Cassuto, Leonard, and Robert Weisbuch. 2021. *The New PhD: How to Build a Better Graduate Education*. Baltimore: Johns Hopkins University Press.

Centre de recherche et d'intervention sur l'éducation et la vie au travail [Centre for Research and Intervention on Education and Life at Work] (CRIEVAT). 2019. *Canadian Graduate and Professional Student Survey: 2019 Summary Report, All Students: National Report*. CRIEVAT, University of Laval. https://secureservercdn.net/45.40.150.54/0zz.a2b.myftpupload.com/wp-content/uploads/2020/08/NATIONAL_CGPSS_2019_ALL.pdf.

Choi, Youjin, Eden Crossman, and Feng Hou. 2021. "International Students as a Source of Labour Supply: Transition to

Permanent Residency." Statistics Canada. https://doi.
org/10.25318/36280001202100600002-eng.

Council of Canadian Academies (CCA). 2021. *Degrees of Success: The Expert Panel on the Labour Market Transition of PhD Graduates.* https://www.cca-reports.ca/wp-content/uploads/2021/01/Degrees-of-Success_FullReport_EN.pdf.

Council of Graduate Schools. 2008. *Graduate Education and the Public Good.* https://www2.ed.gov/policy/highered/reg/hearulemaking/2018/gradedpublicgood.pdf.

Council of Ministers of Education, Canada (CMEC). 2007. *Ministerial Statement on Quality Assurance of Degree Education in Canada.* https://www.cmec.ca/Publications/Lists/Publications/Attachments/95/QA-Statement-2007.en.pdf.

Council of Ontario Universities. 2023. *A Plan for Prosperity: Ensuring the Financial Sustainability of Ontario's Universities.* https://ontariosuniversities.ca/wp-content/uploads/2023/07/Plan-for-Prosperity-July-2023.pdf.

Czuy, Kori, and Melitta Hogarth. 2019. "Circling the Square: Indigenizing the Dissertation." *Emerging Perspectives* 3 (1): 1–16. https://cjc-rcc.ucalgary.ca/index.php/ep/article/view/52758.

Deller, Fiona, Amy Kaufman, and Rosanna Tamburri. 2019. *Redefining Access to Postsecondary Education.* Toronto: Higher Education Quality Council of Ontario. https://heqco.ca/wp-content/uploads/2020/02/Formatted-Access-Paper.pdf.

Desjardins, Louise. 2012. *Profile and Labour Market Outcomes of Doctoral Graduates from Ontario Universities.* Ottawa: Statistics Canada. https://heqco.ca/pub/profile-and-labour-market-outcomes-of-doctoral-graduates-from-ontario-universities/.

Diversity Gap Canada. 2019. "U15 Leadership Remains Largely White and Male Despite 33 Years of Equity Initiatives." https://www.thediversitygapcanada.com/uploads/1/3/0/4/130476297/1._u15_leadership_remains_largely_white_and_male_despite_33_years_of_equity_initiativesnal-1.pdf.

Dorn, Charles. 2017. *For the Common Good: A New History of Higher Education in America.* Ithaca: Cornell University Press.

Duklas, Joanne. 2015. *New Program Approval Practices: A Summary of Current Program Development Typologies at Ontario Colleges and Universities*. Ontario Council on Articulation and Transfer. https://www.oncat.ca/sites/default/files/research/2014-39-Final-Report-New-Program-Governance-Protocols.pdf.

Fauci, Anthony S. 2021. "The Story Behind COVID-19 Vaccines." *Science* 372 (6538): 109. https://doi.org/10.1126/science.abi8397.

Fecher, Benedikt, Freia Kuper, Nataliia Sokolovska, Alex Fenton, Stefan Hornbostel, and Gert G. Wagner. 2021. "Understanding the Societal Impact of the Social Sciences and Humanities: Remarks on Roles, Challenges, and Expectations." *Frontiers in Research Metrics and Analytics* 6 (July): 696804. https://doi.org/10.3389/frma.2021.696804.

Frenette, Marc. 2014. *An Investment of a Lifetime? The Long-Term Labour Market Premiums Associated with a Postsecondary Education*. Ottawa: Statistics Canada. https://www150.statcan.gc.ca/n1/pub/11f0019m/11f0019m2014359-eng.htm.

Future Skills Centre—Centre des Compétences futures (FSC-CCF). 2022. *Lost Opportunities: Measuring the Unrealized Value of Skill Vacancies in Canada*. https://fsc-ccf.ca/wp-content/uploads/2022/03/FSC-issue-briefing-skills-vacancies.pdf.

Galarneau, Diane, and Laura Gibson. 2020. *Trends in Student Debt of Postsecondary Graduates in Canada: Results from the National Graduates Survey, 2018*. Statistics Canada. https://www150.statcan.gc.ca/n1/en/pub/75-006-x/2020001/article/00005-eng.pdf?st=zbuwt_cy.

Gaudry, Adam, and Danielle Lorenz. 2018. "Indigenization as Inclusion, Reconciliation, and Decolonization: Navigating the Different Visions for Indigenizing the Canadian Academy." *AlterNative: An International Journal of Indigenous Peoples* 14 (3): 218–27.

Golde, Chris M., and George E. Walker, eds. 2006. *Envisioning the Future of Doctoral Education: Preparing Stewards of the Discipline*. San Francisco: Jossey-Bass.

Hanlon, Aaron. 2022. "The Humanities Are Facing a Credibility Crisis." *The Washington Post*, April 15, 2022. https://

www.washingtonpost.com/outlook/2022/04/15/humanities-sciences-credibility-crisis-public-trust/.

Hazelkorn, Ellen, and Georgiana Mihut. 2021. "Introduction: Putting Rankings in Context—Looking Back, Looking Forward." In *Research Handbook on University Rankings: Theory, Methodology, Influence and Impact*, edited by Ellen Hazelkorn and Georgiana Mihut, 1–17. Cheltenham: Edward Elgar Publishing. https://doi.org/10.4337/9781788974981.

Head, Brian W. 2022. "The Rise of 'Wicked Problems'—Uncertainty, Complexity and Divergence." In *Wicked Problems in Public Policy*, edited by Brian W. Head, 21–36. Palgrave Macmillan. https://doi.org/10.1007/978-3-030-94580-0_2.

Henry, Frances, Enakshi Dua, Carl E. James, Audrey Kobayashi, Peter Li, Howard Ramos, and Malinda S. Smith, eds. 2017. *The Equity Myth: Racialization and Indigeneity at Canadian Universities*. Vancouver: UBC Press.

Hewitt, Ted. 2018. "Underemployment of PhDs Hurts Research." *SSHRC, President's Desk*. January 3, 2018. https://www.sshrc-crsh.gc.ca/about-au_sujet/president/2018/underemployment-of-phds-hurts-research-2018-eng.aspx?pedisable=true.

Higher Education Quality Council of Ontario (HEQCO). 2015. "The Ontario University Funding Model in Context." https://heqco.ca/wp-content/uploads/2020/03/Contextual-Background-to-the-Ontario-University-Funding-Formula-English.pdf.

Higher Education Strategy Associates (HESA). 2022. *The State of Postsecondary Education in Canada 2022*. https://higheredstrategy.com/the-state-of-postsecondary-education-in-canada-2/.

Ibrahim, Awad, Tamari Kitossa, Malinda S. Smith, and Handel K. Wright, eds. 2022. *Nuances of Blackness in the Canadian Academy: Teaching, Learning, and Researching While Black*. Toronto: University of Toronto Press.

Institute for the Public Life of Arts and Ideas (IPLAI). 2013. *White Paper on the Future of the PhD in the Humanities*. Montreal: Institute for the Public Life of Arts and Ideas, McGill University. https://www.acfas.ca/sites/default/files/fichiers/1536/

white_paper_on_the_future_of_the_phd_in_the_humanities_dec_2013_1.pdf.

Jay, Paul. 2014. *The Humanities "Crisis" and the Future of Literary Studies*. New York: Palgrave Macmillan. https://doi.org/10.1057/9781137398031_2.

Jordan, Jennifer, and Michael Sorell. 2019. "Why Reverse Mentoring Works and How to Do It Right." *Harvard Business Review*, October 3, 2019. https://hbr.org/2019/10/why-reverse-mentoring-works-and-how-to-do-it-right.

Karp, Paul. 2020. "Australian University Fees to Double for Some Arts Courses, But Fall for Stem Subjects." *The Guardian*, June 18, 2020. https://www.theguardian.com/australia-news/2020/jun/19/australian-university-fees-arts-stem-science-maths-nursing-teaching-humanities.

Katz, Philip M. 2005. *Retrieving the Master's Degree from the Dustbin of History: A Report to the Members of the American Historical Association*. Washington, DC: American Historical Association.

Keen, Paul. 2014. "'Imagining What We Know': The Humanities in a Utilitarian Age." *Humanities* 3: 73–87. https://doi.org/10.3390/h3010073.

Ketchen Lipson, Sarah, S. Michael Gaddis, Justin Heinze, Kathryn Beck, and Daniel Eisenberg. 2015. "Variations in Student Mental Health and Treatment Utilization Across US Colleges and Universities." *Journal of American College Health* 63 (6): 388–96.

Krackov, Sharon K., and Henry Pohl. 2011. "Building Expertise Using the Deliberate Practice Curriculum-Planning Model." *Medical Teacher* 33 (7): 570–75. https://doi.org/10.3109/0142159X.2011.578172.

Lang, Daniel W. 2022. "Financing Higher Education in Canada: A Study in Fiscal Federalism." *Higher Education* 84: 177–94. https://doi.org/10.1007/s10734-021-00761-0.

Leblanc, Deanne Aline Marie. 2021. "The Roles of Settler Canadians Within Decolonization: Re-Evaluating Invitation, Belonging and Rights." *Canadian Journal of Political Science* 54 (2): 356–73. https//doi.org/10.1017/S0008423920001274.

Lei, Ling, and Shibao Guo. 2022. "Beyond Multiculturalism: Revisioning a Model of Pandemic Anti-Racism Education in Post-Covid-19 Canada." *International Journal of Anthropology and Ethnology* 6 (1). https://doi.org/10.1186/s41257-021-00060-7.

Liu, Alan, Abigail Droge, Scott Kleinman, Lindsay Thomas, Dan C. Baciu, and Jeremy Douglass. 2022. "What Everyone Says: Public Perceptions of the Humanities in the Media." *Daedalus* 151 (3): 19–39. https://doi.org/10.1162/daed_a_01926.

Llamas, Jasmín D., Khoa Nguyen, and Alisia G.T.T. Tran. 2021. "The Case for Greater Faculty Diversity: Examining the Educational Impacts of Student-Faculty Racial/Ethnic Match." *Race Ethnicity and Education* 24 (3): 375–91. https://doi.org/10.1080/13613324.2019.1679759.

Looker, E. Dianne. 2018. *44th Statistical Report, 2018: Part I*. Canadian Association for Graduate Studies. https://secureservercdn.net/45.40.150.54/0zz.a2b.myftpupload.com/wp-content/uploads/2019/11/2019-44th-Statistical-Report-Part-1-Englishoct2.pdf.

Mahoney, Kathleen. 2016. "The Roadblock to Reconciliation: Canada's Origin Story." *Canadian Issues* (Summer): 29–36A.

McMaster University. n.d. "Inspiring & Supporting the Next Generation of Indigenous Scholars." Accessed October 13, 2022. https://miri.mcmaster.ca/iusrs/.

Milligan, Ian, and Robert Warren. 2018. "Big Data and the Coming Historical Revolution: From Black Boxes to Models." In *Big Data in the Arts and Humanities: Theory and Practice*, edited by Giovanni Schiuma and Daniela Carlucci, 65–76. Boca Raton: CRC Press.

Moreno, Josephine M. 2021. "Making Graduate Admissions Inclusive." *Inside Higher Education*, May 25, 2021. https://www.insidehighered.com/admissions/views/2021/05/24/its-time-make-graduate-admissions-inclusive-opinion.

Natural Sciences and Engineering Research Council of Canada (NSERC). 2023. "Canada Graduate Scholarships—Master's Program." https://www.nserc-crsng.gc.ca/students-etudiants/pg-cs/cgsm-bescm_eng.asp.

Ontario. 2022. "Ontario Qualifications Framework." https://www.ontario.ca/page/ontario-qualifications-framework.

Pierson, Paul. 2000. "Increasing Returns, Path Dependence, and the Study of Politics." *American Political Science Review* 94 (2): 251–67. https://doi.org/10.2307/2586011.

Policy Horizons Canada. 2018. "The Next Generation of Emerging Global Challenges: A Horizons 2030 Perspective on Research Opportunities. October 19, 2018. https://horizons.gc.ca/wp-content/uploads/2018/10/SSHRC-Emerging-Global-Challenges-ENG-Web-New-1.pdf.

Porter, Susan. 2021. "Doctoral Reform for the 21st Century." In *The Future of Doctoral Research: Challenges and Opportunities*, edited by Ann Lee and Rob Bongaardt, 28–39. London: Routledge.

Posselt, Julie R. 2016. *Inside Graduate Admissions: Merit, Diversity, and Faculty Gatekeeping*. Cambridge: Harvard University Press.

Rajagopal, Indhu. 2002. *Hidden Academics: Contract Faculty in Canadian Universities*. Toronto: University of Toronto Press.

Reid, Alana, Hui (Amy) Chen, and Rebecca Guertin. 2020. *Labour Market Outcomes of Postsecondary Graduates, Class of 2015*. November 17, 2020. Statistics Canada. https://www150.statcan.gc.ca/n1/en/pub/81-595-m/81-595-m2020002-eng.pdf?st=9GTVy4rp.

Reithmeier, Reinhart, Liam O'Leary, Xiaoyue Zhu, Corey Dales, Abokor Abdulkarim, Anum Aquil, Lochin Brouillard, et al. 2019. "The 10,000 PhDs Project at the University of Toronto: Using Employment Outcome Data to Inform Graduate Education." https://doi.org/10.1371/journal.pone.0209898.

Reitter, Paul, and Chad Wellmon. 2021. *Permanent Crisis: The Humanities in a Disenchanted Age*. Chicago: University of Chicago Press.

Riddell, Jessica. 2021. "Tackling Wicked Problems in Higher Education." *Maple Business Council*, August 20, 2021. https://www.maplecouncil.org/momentum-content/2021/8/20/maple-league-article.

Rittel, Horst W.J., and Melvin M. Webber. 1973. "Dilemmas in a General Theory of Planning." *Policy Sciences* 4 (2): 155–69. https://www.jstor.org/stable/4531523.

Robinson, Carol. 2018. "The Landscape of Professional Doctorate Provision in English Higher Education Institutions: Inconsistencies, Tensions and Unsustainability." *London Review of Education* 16 (1): 90–103. https://doi.org/10.18546/LRE.16.1.09.

Royal Bank of Canada (RBC). 2018. *Humans Wanted: How Canadian Youth Can Thrive in the Age of Disruption.* https://www.rbc.com/dms/enterprise/futurelaunch/_assets-custom/pdf/RBC-Future-Skills-Report-FINAL-Singles.pdf.

Schiuma, Giovanni, and Daniela Carlucci. 2018. *Big Data in the Arts and Humanities: Theory and Practice.* Boca Raton: CRC Press.

Schmidt, Benjamin. 2018. "The Humanities Are in Crisis." *The Atlantic*, August 23, 2018. https://www.theatlantic.com/ideas/archive/2018/08/the-humanities-face-a-crisisof-confidence/567565/.

Shah, Hetan. 2020. "Global Problems Need Social Science." *Nature* 577 (7790): 295. https://doi.org/10.1038/d41586-020-00064-x.

Singh, Jakeet. 2014. "The Ideological Roots of Stephen Harper's Vendetta Against Sociology." *The Toronto Star*, August 26, 2014. https://www.thestar.com/opinion/commentary/2014/08/26/the_ideological_roots_of_stephen_harpers_vendetta_against_sociology.html.

Skolnik, Michael L. 2010. "Quality Assurance in Higher Education as a Political Process." *Higher Education Management and Policy* 22 (1). https://doi.org/10.1787/hemp-22-5kmlh5gs3zr0.

Smith, Malinda. 2017. "Disciplinary Silences: Race, Indigeneity and Gender in the Social Sciences." In *The Equity Myth: Racialization and Indigeneity at Canadian Universities*, edited by Frances Henry, Enakshi Dua, Carl E James, Audrey Kobayashi, Peter Li, Howard Ramos, and Malinda Smith, 239–62. Vancouver: UBC Press.

Smith-Norris, Martha, and Jennifer Hanson. 2018. "Graduate Program Outcomes in History 2000–2015: A Humanities Case Study in Canada." *Journal of Educational Administration* 50 (3): 174–90.

Social Sciences and Humanities Research Council (SSHRC). 2015. *Evaluation of SSHRC Fellowships.* https://www.sshrc-crsh.gc.ca/about-au_sujet/publications/evaluations/2015/fellowships-bourses-eng.aspx.

Social Sciences and Humanities Research Council (SSHRC). 2022a. *Competition Statistics: Interactive Dashboard*. Revised August 11, 2022. https://www.sshrc-crsh.gc.ca/results-resultats/stats-statistiques/index-eng.aspx.

Social Sciences and Humanities Research Council (SSHRC). 2022b. "Government of Canada Launches Pilot Initiative to Further Support Indigenous Master's Students." https://www.canada.ca/en/social-sciences-humanities-research/news/2022/08/government-of-canada-launches-pilot-initiative-to-further-support-indigenous-masters-students.html.

Social Sciences and Humanities Research Council (SSHRC). 2022c. "Imagining Canada's Future: 16 Global Challenges." September 2, 2022. https://www.sshrc-crsh.gc.ca/funding-financement/programs-programmes/challenge_areas-domaines_des_defis/index-eng.aspx.

Statistics Canada. 2020. "Health Reports: Life Expectancy Differs by Education and Income Levels." *The Daily*, January 15, 2020. https://www150.statcan.gc.ca/n1/en/daily-quotidien/200115/dq200115c-eng.pdf?st=a7NUHO_x.

Statistics Canada. 2021. *Table 37-10-0187-01. Work-Integrated Learning Participation of Postsecondary Graduates, by Province of Residence at Interview, Level of Study, Field of Study and Sex*. https://doi.org/10.25318/3710018701-eng.

Statistics Canada. 2022a. "Canada in 2041: A Larger, More Diverse Population with Greater Differences Between Regions." *The Daily*, September 8, 2022. https://www150.statcan.gc.ca/n1/daily-quotidien/220908/dq220908a-eng.htm.

Statistics Canada. 2022b. Table: 37-10-0018-01 (formerly CANSIM 477-0019). Postsecondary Enrolments, by Registration Status, Institution Type, Status of Student in Canada and Gender. Released November 22, 2022. https://www150.statcan.gc.ca/t1/tbl1/en/cv.action?pid=3710001801.

TRaCE McGill. 2019. "Narratives." http://tracemcgill.com/narratives/.

Trotter, Lane D., and Amy Mitchell. 2018. "Academic Drift in Canadian Institutions of Higher Education: Research Mandates, Strategy, and Culture." *Canadian Journal of Higher Education* 48 (2): 92–108. https://doi.org/10.7202/1057105ar.

Truth and Reconciliation Commission of Canada. 2015. *Honouring the Truth, Reconciling for the Future: Summary of the Final Report of the Truth and Reconciliation Commission of Canada.* https://ehprnh2mwo3.exactdn.com/wp-content/uploads/2021/01/Executive_Summary_English_Web.pdf.

Tuck, Eve, and K. Wayne Yang. 2012. "Decolonization Is Not a Metaphor." *Decolonization: Indigeneity, Education & Society* 1 (1): 1–40.

U15 Group of Canadian Research Universities (U15). n.d. "About Us." https://u15.ca/about-us/.

University of British Columbia (UBC). n.d.-a. "Minimum Funding Policy for PhD Students." Accessed October 31, 2022. https://www.grad.ubc.ca/awards/minimum-funding-policy-phd-students.

University of British Columbia (UBC). n.d.-b. "What is a Collaborative PhD?" Accessed October 13, 2022. https://www.grad.ubc.ca/what-collaborative-phd.

University of British Columbia (UBC). n.d.-c. "Public Scholars Initiative." Accessed November 14, 2023. https://www.grad.ubc.ca/psi.

University of British Columbia (UBC). 2022a. "Doctor of Philosophy in English (PhD)." *Graduate and Postdoctoral Studies.* https://www.grad.ubc.ca/prospective-students/graduate-degree-programs/phd-english#:~:text=Completion%20Rates%20%26%20Times,of%206.27%20years%20of%20study.

University of British Columbia (UBC). 2022b. "Doctor of Philosophy in Political Science (PhD)." *Graduate and Postdoctoral Studies.* https://www.grad.ubc.ca/prospective-students/graduate-degree-programs/phd-political-science.

University of British Columbia (UBC). 2022c. "Doctor of Philosophy in Economics (PhD)." *Graduate and Postdoctoral Studies.* https://www.grad.ubc.ca/prospective-students/graduate-degree-programs/phd-economics.

University of British Columbia (UBC), Faculty of Graduate and Postdoctoral Studies. 2017. *UBC PhD Career Outcomes: Graduates from 2005–2013, UBC Vancouver Campus.* https://outcomes.grad.ubc.ca/docs/UBC_PhD_Career_Outcomes_April2017.pdf.

Universities Canada. n.d. "Provincial Quality Assurance Systems." Accessed 5 October 2022. https://www.univcan.ca/universities/quality-assurance/provincial-quality-assurance-systems/.

Universities Canada. 2016. *The Future of the Liberal Arts: A Global Conversation.* https://www.univcan.ca/the-future-of-the-liberal-arts-report/.

University of Toronto. n.d. "PhD Funding Data." Accessed October 31, 2022. https://www.sgs.utoronto.ca/about/explore-our-data/phd-funding-data/.

Usher, Alex. 2020. "Academic Freedom in a Pandemic." *Higher Education Strategy Associates Blog*, May 26, 2020. https://higheredstrategy.com/academic-freedom-in-a-pandemic/.

Usher, Alex. 2022. "Fun with University Enrolment Data." *Higher Education Strategy Associates Blog*, September 21, 2022. https://higheredstrategy.com/fun-with-university-enrolment-data/.

Wayland, Sarah V. 1997. "Immigration, Multiculturalism and National Identity in Canada." *International Journal on Minority and Group Rights* 5 (1): 33–58. http://www.jstor.org/stable/24674516.

Weingarten, Harvey P. 2021. *Nothing Less than Great: Reforming Canada's Universities.* Toronto: University of Toronto Press.

White, Linda A., Sumayya Saleem, Elizabeth Dhuey, and Michal Perlman. 2022. "A Critical Analysis of International Organizations' and Global Management Consulting Firms' Consensus around Twenty-First Century Skills." *Review of International Political Economy*: 1334–59. https://doi.org/10.1080/09692290.2022.2097289.

Winter, Elke. 2005. "Rethinking Multiculturalism After its 'Retreat': Lessons from Canada." *American Behavioral Scientist* 59 (6). https://doi.org/10.1177/0002764214566495.

Young, Lisa. 2019. "We're Missing a Potent Plan to Train the Next Generation of Researchers." *Policy Options*, March 14, 2019. https://policyoptions.irpp.org/magazines/march-2019/were-missing-a-potent-plan-to-train-the-next-generation-of-researchers/.

Index

Page numbers in *italics* refer to figures and tables.

accreditation, 96, 115–116
admissions
    EDID imperative, 196, 216
    efficient, 178, 256, 262
    inclusive, 155, 157, 180, 258, 264
    student focused, 182, 260, 266
Alberta
    arts graduate education (non-degree), 134
    provincial funding, 80, 82
American Historical Association, 112
Anders, George, 10, 35, 36
anti-bias training, 155, 188
anti-racism training, 155, 161, 180
Aoun, Joseph, 33–39
arts, 8–10
arts graduate degrees, typology of
    MA, 110–114
    overview, 107–109, 121–124
    PhD, 116–119
    professional doctorates, 119–121
    professional MA, 114–116
arts graduate education
    attitudes towards, 104–105
    benefits of improving, 13

challenges for, 10, 14, 42
decolonization through, 29
definition of, 10–11
degrees within, 9, 123
EDID imperative, 127–129, 132–133, 141
exclusions from, 9
faculty as affecting, 97–101
federal funding, 84–87
funding within, 49–50
non-degree courses, 134–138
potential of, 13, 42, 141
practices for, 194–198
provincial approvals, 82–83
provincial funding, 78–82
public good and, 11–16, 132–133
quality assurance processes within, 94–97
reimagining, 41, 69–73, 218–220
significance of, 5–6
talent imperative, 130–131, 132–133, 141
wicked problems imperative, 124–127, 132–133, 141
See also EDITS vision, the; graduate degrees, non-HSS; humanities; social sciences
arts graduate education, reimagined
actions for stakeholders, 251–254
audience for, 16–17
claims, 249
MA, 198–205
PhD, 205–213
professional degrees, 213–218
tools for, 250
arts graduate employment rates (Canada), 56
arts graduate stakeholders, actions for, 251–254
arts graduate students
advantages of non-degree credentials for, 135
assistantships for, 143, 165, 181, 237
funding for, 84–87, 149
future steps for, 254
research needs of, 231
supervision of (EDITS), 267–273
talent development of, 164–166
transparency for, 170, 245
various roles of, 91–92
wicked problems imperative, 125–127
work-integrated learning for, 197–198
arts undergraduate education
arts graduate education vs, 92
career outcomes, 57, 58
enrollment in, 14
graduate programs as affecting, 81, 92
income, 61
mental health challenges, 47
assessment of EDITS (hypothetical), 183, 185, 187, 189, 191
assessment of students, 158, 161, 180

Australian Public Service
   Commission, 4

BA (Bachelor of Arts), 56, 57, 58, 61
BHASE, 198
Big Data, 37
BIPOC students, 64, 157
   See also international
      students; non-traditional
      students
Bouchard St-Amant, Pier-André, 81
Business/Higher Education
   Roundtable, 17

calls to action
   across levels, 244–246
   program-level, 223–229
   student, 246–247
   system-level, 238–244
   university-level, 230–238
Cameron, David, 78, 84, 87
Canada Foundation for
   Innovation, 84
Canada Research Chairs, 84
Canada West Foundation, 19
Canada's Fundamental Science
   Review, 85
Canadian Association for
   Graduate Studies (CAGS),
   44, 52, 152, 197
Canadian Association for Social
   Work Education, 116
Canadian arts graduate data, 65, 66
Canadian Association of Programs
   in Public Administration,
   115
Canadian graduate data, 65, 66

Canadian Historical Association
   (CHA), 45, 46, 49–50, 59
Canadian Information Centre
   for International
   Credentials, 134
Canadian Institute of Planners, 116
Canadian Institutes of Health
   Research (CIHR), 84
Canadian universities
   calls to action for, 230–238
   as colonial institutions, 90–91
   competition within, 91–93
   faculty incentive structures
      within, 97–101
   history of, 87–88
   quality assurance processes
      within, 94–97
   rankings, 93–94
career development
   MA, 114
   overview, 122, 123
   PhD, 118–119
   professional doctorate, 120
   professional MA, 115–116
Carlucci, Daniela, 37
Carnegie Foundation for the
   Advancement of
   Teaching, 116–117
Cassuto, Leonard, 112, 117, 195, 196
Centre for Research and
   Intervention on
   Education and Life at
   Work (CRIEVAT), 52,
   53–55, 63
change, barriers to, 101–105
Chen, Hui (Amy), 56,
   57–58, 61

Index **291**

collegial governance, 175, 223
common good. *See* public good
community building
    diverse, 156, 160
    graduate students'
        (hypothetical), 202, 210
    initiatives by universities for,
        195–196
    stakeholder actions for, 253
completion rates (arts degrees),
    44–46
Conference Board of Canada,
    33, 163
coordinated stakeholder actions,
    244–246
Council of Canadian Academies,
    5, 13, 62, 172
Council of Graduate Schools, 70
Council of Ministers of Education,
    Canada (CMEC), 109, 110,
    114, 116, 119
Council of Ontario Universities, 79
coursework
    deliberate, 208
    efficient, 145
    for EDID imperative, 128
    for talent imperative, 130
    for wicked problems
        imperative, 125
credentials, arts graduate. *See*
    arts graduate degrees,
    typology of
curriculum design, 148, 150, 153,
    157, 164–165

data, arts graduate education
    career outcomes, 56–61
    career readiness, 51–55
    completion rates, 44–47
    return on investment, 61–62
    student debt, 51
    student demand, 64–69
    student funding, 49–50
    student satisfaction, 62–64
    student well-being, 47–48
data literacy, 36–38
decolonization, 20, 29, 31–32,
    138, 180
deliberate (EDITS)
    challenges, 153–154
    characteristics, 173
    example (hypothetical),
        184–186
    graduate supervision, 269
    overview, 147–149
    program design, 149–153
    reimagining professional
        degrees (hypothetical),
        214–216, 263
    reimagining the MA
        (hypothetical), 200–202,
        263
    reimagining the PhD
        (hypothetical), 207–210,
        263
    rubric, 179, 257
digital humanities, 37
diversity
    admissions, 157, 180, 196,
        264
    EDID imperative, 127–129,
        133, 138
    implications of SSHRC
        priorities on, 86

inclusive program design
(EDITS), 155–159, 180
in supervisory practice,
270–271
through immigration, 30–31
in universities, 90–91
Diversity Gap Canada, 90
doctorate, arts. *See* PhD; PhD,
professional
domestic students, 31, 63–64, 67,
68, 85
See also international students
Dorn, Charles, 8

EDID imperative
arts graduate education to
address, 27–32, 127–129,
141
dimensions of, 29–32
multiculturalism, 29–30
non-degree arts education
(hypothetical), 138
real-world practices for,
196–197
reconciliation, 28
EDITS (hypothetical
implementation)
reimagining professional
degrees with, 213–218
reimagining the MA with,
199–204
reimagining the PhD with,
205–213
EDITS vision
challenges to, 146–147,
153–154, 159–162, 166–168,
171–172

characteristics, 173
deliberate, 147–154
efficient, 142–147
future potential of, 172–174
graduate supervision using,
267–273
implementation of
(hypothetical), 183–191
inclusive, 154–162
rubric for, 177–182
student focused, 168–172
talent developing, 162–168
education system (Canada)
characteristics of, 77–78
issues within, 1, 71–73
perceived significance of, 1
efficient (EDITS)
challenges, 146–147
characteristics, 173
example (hypothetical),
182–184
graduate supervision,
267–269
overview, 142–143
program design, 144–145
reimagining professional
degrees (hypothetical),
213–214, 262
reimagining the MA
(hypothetical), 199–200,
262
reimagining the PhD
(hypothetical), 205–206,
262
rubric, 178, 256
employment, arts graduate. *See*
student career outcomes

Index **293**

employment rates, national, 56
enrollment trends
    arts graduate programs,
        64–69
    international students, 67, 68
    provincial funding as
        affecting, 79, 103
    STEM, 15
    undergraduate, 14
equity-deserving groups, 48,
    156–159
    See also BIPOC; international
        students
equity, diversity, inclusion, and
    decolonization. See EDID
    imperative
examples (real-world), 195–196, 198
examples, hypothetical, 140,
    183–192
excellent arts graduate programs.
    See EDITS (hypothetical
    implementation)
experiential learning, 151, 179,
    197–198, 242, 272

faculty
    calls to action, 223–229
    deliberate (EDITS), 147–148
    efficiency for (EDITS), 142,
        144, 146, 178, 262
    engagement, 98
    future actions for, 251, 252
    graduate students as,
        58–59
    hiring priorities, 100
    incentives for research,
        98–101, 103
    influencing inclusivity
        (EDITS), 155–157, 180,
        264–265
    student focused (EDITS),
        169–170, 182, 266
    talent developing, 181, 265
    See also supervision, graduate
        (EDITS)
federal funding, 84–87
Federation of Social Sciences and
    Humanities, 17, 240
funding
    arts graduate student, 49–50,
        70
    contributing to growth,
        79–82, 89
    federal, 84–87
    future actions regarding,
        169, 170, 225, 242–243
    inclusivity in, 158
    provincial, 78–82
    time to completion and, 45
    See also Canadian Institutes of
        Health Research, Natural
        Sciences and Engineering
        Research Council, Social
        Sciences and Humanities
        Research Council
funding model, provincial, 78–79

Galarneau, Diane, 51
Gaudry, Adam, 28, 90
gender, 63
Gibson, Laura, 51
goods (as in economics), 7
governmental coordination,
    lack of, 87–89

graduate degrees, non-HSS
  MA career preparedness, 53
  PhD career preparedness, 54, 55
  reasons for pursuing, 52
  student satisfaction, 63
graduate student, data
  career outcomes, 56–61
  career readiness, 51–55
  completion rates within the, 44–46
  debt, 50
  demand, 64–69
  funding, 49–50
  return on investment, 61–62
  satisfaction, 62–64
  time to completion, 44–46
  well-being within, 47–48
graduate student roles, 91–92
granting agencies, 84, 99, 238, 242
  See also Canadian Institutes of Health Research, Natural Sciences and Engineering Research Council, Social Sciences and Humanities Research Council
growth (universities)
  actors involved in, 76, 77
  enrollments, 80, 103
  faculty as affecting, 97–101
  federal funding, 84–87
  governmental coordination affecting, 87–89
  internal competition for, 91–93
  provincial approvals, 82–83
  provincial funding, 78–82
  rankings influencing, 93–94
Guertin, Rebecca, 56, 57–58, 61
Guo, Shibao, 30

Hanlon, Aaron, 14
Hazelkorn, Ellen, 94
Higher Education Quality Council of Ontario (HEQCO), 79
Higher Education Strategy Associates (HESA), 78, 79, 80
highly qualified personnel (HQPs), 87, 242
human capital. See talent imperative
human literacy, 34–36
humanities
  career outcomes, 57, 58
  challenges to the, 14–15
  crisis of the, 15
  descriptions of, 14
  enrollments, 65, 66
  income, 61, 62
  international students, 68
  MA career preparedness, 53
  PhD career preparedness, 54, 55
  reasons for pursuing, 52
  significance of the, 26–27, 32
  student satisfaction, 63
  undergraduate enrollment in the, 14
  use of data within the, 37

immigration, 30–31
imperatives
    arts graduate potential, 141
    challenges to, 24
    EDID, 23, 27–33
    real-world practices for, 194–198
    relation between, 40
    SSHRC as affecting, 86–87
    talent, 23, 24–39
    wicked problems, 23, 24–27
incentives, 78–82, 84–87, 98, 103
inclusive (EDITS)
    challenges, 159–162
    characteristics, 173
    example (hypothetical), 186–188
    graduate supervision, 270–271
    overview, 154–155
    program design, 155–159
    reimagining professional degrees (hypothetical), 216–217, 264–265
    reimagining the MA (hypothetical), 203–204, 264–265
    reimagining the PhD (hypothetical), 210–211, 264–265
    rubric, 180, 258
Indigenous communities
    challenges for, 48, 50
    EDID imperative for, 27–28, 196, 197
    influencing academic practices, 156
    in reimagining arts graduate education, 20
    SSHRC funding for, 86
    Indigenous Undergraduate Summer Research Scholars (IndiNerds), 196
innovation, 97, 102, 176, 197
Institute for the Public Life of Arts and Ideas (IPLAI), 26, 27, 32, 218–219
Intellectual Entrepreneurship Program (University of Texas), 195–196
international students
    enrollment, 67–69, 80
    funding, 49
    inclusivity for, 158
    mental health challenges, 48
    needs of, 166, 169
    tuition, 80
    university rankings and, 94
    See also immigration; BIPOC students; non-traditional students
internships. *See* work-integrated learning
intersectionality, 31

Jay, Paul, 15

Keen, Paul, 166
knowledge keepers, Indigenous, 156–157

Leblanc, Deanne Aline Marie, 29
Lei, Ling, 30
Lorenz, Danielle, 28, 90

MA (Master of Arts)
  career outcomes, 57, 58
  career preparedness
    (evaluation), 53
  completion rates, 44, 45–46
  country-based differences,
    112–113
  EDID imperative, 128, 133
  enrollments, 65, 113
  implications of SSHRC on, 86
  income, 61, 62
  international students, 68
  reasons for pursuing, 52
  reimagining the
    (hypothetical), 199–204
  student debt for, 51
  student satisfaction after, 63
  talent imperative, 130–131, 133
  typology of, 110–114, 123
  wicked problems imperative,
    126, 132
MA, professional
  EDID imperative, 128–129, 133
  talent imperative, 130–131, 133
  typology of, 114–116, 123
  wicked problems imperative,
    126, 132
Maclean's rankings, 93
Mahoney, Kathleen, 29
McMaster University, 8, 196
mental health, 47–48, 159, 170, 180
Mihut, Georgiana, 94
Milligan, Ian, 37, 38
Mitacs, 197, 244, 271
Moreno, Josephine M., 196
multiculturalism, 29–30

Natural Sciences and Engineering
  Research Council
  (NSERC), 84, 86, 152, 243
non-degree, arts graduate
  education
  contribution to imperatives
    (hypothetical), 137–138
  typology, 134–135
non-traditional students, 121, 145,
  158–159, 162

Ontario
  arts graduate education
    (non-degree), 134
  enrollment growth, 81
  provincial funding, 78, 79,
    80, 82
Ontario Ministry of Training,
  Colleges, and
  Universities, 79

parsimonious design (EDITS),
  144–145, 147, 150
path dependency, 101–102
pedagogy, 151–152, 179
PhD (doctorate, arts)
  career outcomes, 56, 57, 58–60
  career preparedness
    (evaluation), 54, 55
  completion rates, 44, 45–46
  concerns for, 45
  country-based differences, 117
  dropouts, 46
  EDID imperative, 129, 133
  enrollments, 65
  funding, 49–50, 84, 86
  income after, 61, 62

international students, 68
mental health, 47–48
reasons for pursuing, 52
reimagining the
   (hypothetical), 205–213
SSHRC success rate, 49
student debt for, 51
student satisfaction after, 63
talent imperative, 130–131, 133
time to completion, 44
typology of, 116–119, 123
wicked problems imperative,
   127, 132
PhD, professional
   EDID imperative, 129, 133
   talent imperative, 130–131, 133
   typology of, 119–121, 123
   wicked problems imperative,
      127, 132
PhD, reimagined, 119
Pierson, Paul, 101–102
Policy Horizons Canada, 86
Porter, Susan, 195
Posselt, Julie R., 157
practices, real-world, 194–198
professional development, 51, 72,
   145, 165–166, 198
program delivery, 178, 197, 256,
   262
program design
   deliberate, 149–153
   efficient, 144–145
   inclusive, 155–159
   student focused, 169–171
   talent developing, 164–166
program-level actions
   culture, 225–228

resources, 228–229
vision, 223–225
provincial approvals, 82–83
provincial funding, 78–82
public good
   arts graduate education and,
      11–16, 132–133
   arts graduate system working
      against, 71
   definition of, 7
   EDID imperative, 27–32
   evolution of, 8
   real-world practices for,
      194–198
   talent imperative, 33–39
   wicked problems imperative,
      24–27
   See also EDITS vision
Public Scholars Initiative
   (University of British
   Columbia), 195

QS World University Rankings, 94
Quebec, 78, 79, 81

Reid, Alana, 56, 57–58, 61
Reithmeier, Reinhart, 58, 59, 60
Reitter, Paul, 15
research assistantships (RAs),
   71, 165, 181, 237
research literacy. *See* research
   training
research products, 152, 179, 197,
   257, 263
research training
   deliberate use of (EDITS), 151
   MA, 113–114

overview, 122, 123
PhD, 118, 119
professional doctorate, 120
professional MA, 115
return on investment (ROI),
    financial, 61–62
Riddell, Jessica, 26
Rittel, Horst W. J., 3, 24–25, 26
Robinson, Carol, 120
Royal Bank of Canada (RBC), 33,
    36, 38–39, 172
Royal Commission on Aboriginal
    Peoples, 29
rubric (EDITS), 177–182

Santarsiero, Francesco, 37
Schiuma, Giovanni, 37
Schmidt, Benjamin, 15
science, technology, engineering,
    and mathematics (STEM),
    12–13, 15, 231, 236
Shah, Hetan, 3
Shanghai Rankings, 94
skill development, 164, 165, 198
    See also talent developing
    (EDITS)
Skolnik, Michael L., 95–96, 97
Smith, Malinda, 157
social sciences
    career outcomes, 57, 58
    career preparedness, 54, 55
    enrollments, 65, 66
    income, 61, 62
    international students, 68
    MA career preparedness, 53
    reasons for pursuing, 52
    student satisfaction, 63

Social Sciences and Humanities
    Research Council
    (SSHRC)
    implications of funding by,
    85–86
    institutional action aimed at,
    238
    as part of Tri-Council, 84
    scholarship success rate, 49
    suggested future actions, 152,
    240, 243, 253
society, Canadian
    challenges for, 1, 3
    needs of, 2
    significance of technology for,
    2, 3, 4
    solutions to challenges of, 3, 6
Statistics Canada
    graduate career outcomes,
    56, 58
    graduate employment
    earnings, 61
    immigration forecast, 30
    student debt, 51
    student demand for arts
    graduate programs, 64,
    65, 66, 68
    suggested future action aimed
    at, 244
    work-integrated learning
    rates, 198
student agency, 246–247
student career outcomes, 56–61
student career readiness, 51–55
student debt, 51
student demand, 64–69
student focused (EDITS)

challenges, 171–172
characteristics, 173
example (hypothetical),
    190–191
graduate supervision, 272–273
overview, 168–169
program design, 169–171
reimagining professional
    degrees (hypothetical),
    217–218, 266
reimagining the MA
    (hypothetical), 205, 266
reimagining the PhD
    (hypothetical), 212–213,
    266
rubric, 182, 260
student funding, 49–50
student research
    for EDID imperative, 128
    for talent imperative, 130–131
    for wicked problems
        imperative, 125–126
student satisfaction, 62–64
student well-being, 47–48
supervision, graduate (EDITS),
    267–273
system-level actions
    culture, 241–242
    overview, 238
    resources, 242–244
    vision, 239–240

talent developing (EDITS)
    challenges, 166–168
    characteristics, 173
    example (hypothetical),
        188–190

    graduate supervision,
        271–272
    overview, 162–163
    program design, 164–166
    reimagining professional
        degrees (hypothetical),
        217, 265
    reimagining the MA
        (hypothetical), 204, 265
    reimagining the PhD
        (hypothetical), 211–212,
        265
    rubric, 181, 259
talent imperative
    arts graduate education to
        address, 33–39, 130–131,
        141
    data literacy, 36–38, 130–131
    human literacy, 34–36, 130
    non-degree arts education
        (hypothetical), 138
    purpose of, 33
    real-world practices for,
        197–198
    technological literacy, 38–39,
        130–131
teaching assistantships (TAs),
    143, 165, 181, 237
technological literacy, 38–39,
    130–131
thesis, graduate, 111, 152, 271
time to completion (arts degrees),
    44–46
Times Higher Educations World
    University Rankings,
    94
TRaCE McGill, 13

Tri-Council, 84
    See also Canadian Institutes of Health Research, Natural Sciences and Engineering Research Council, Social Sciences and Humanities Research Council
Truth and Reconciliation Commission of Canada, 27–28, 216
Tuck, Eve, 20
tuition, graduate, 49, 79–80
tuition, provinces influencing, 79–80

U15 Group of Canadian Research Universities, 52, 93, 238
University of British Columbia
    collaborative PhD at, 196
    completion rates and times to completion, 44–45
    PhD career outcomes, 58–59, 60
    PhD student funding, 49
    Public Scholars Initiative, 195
University of Toronto
    PhD career outcomes, 58, 59
    PhD student funding, 49
university rankings, 93–94
university-level actions
    culture, 233–234
    resources, 234–238
    vision, 230–232
Usher, Alex, 14, 15, 154

vision, lack of, 103–104

Warren, Robert, 37, 38
Wayne Yang, K., 20
Webber, Melvin M., 3, 24–25, 26
Weisbuch, Robert, 112, 117, 195, 196
Wellmon, Chad, 15
wicked problems imperative
    arts graduate education to address, 26–27, 124–127, 141
    definition of, 3, 25
    human relation to, 4–5, 25
    non-degree arts education (hypothetical), 137
    real-world practices for, 195–196
    solutions for, 3
    tame vs, 24–25
work-integrated learning, 151–152, 179, 182, 197–198

www.ingramcontent.com/pod-product-compliance
Ingram Content Group UK Ltd.
Pitfield, Milton Keynes, MK11 3LW, UK
UKHW011604021025
463508UK00002B/123